THE TWELVE CAESARS

THE
TWELVE
CAESARS

MATTHEW
DENNISON

Atlantic Books
London

First published in hardback and export and airside trade paperback
in Great Britain in 2012 by Atlantic Books,
an imprint of Atlantic Books Ltd.

3 4 5 6 7 8 9

A CIP catalogue record for this book is available from the British Library.

Hardback ISBN: 978-1-84887-683-5
Trade Paperback ISBN: 978-1-84887-684-2
E-book ISBN: 978-0-85789-780-0

Designed by carrdesignstudio.com
Printed in Great Britain by the MPG Books Group

Atlantic Books
An imprint of Atlantic Books Ltd
Ormond House
26–27 Boswell Street
London
WC1N 3JZ

www.atlantic-books.co.uk

For my parents, with love

'There is no worse heresy than that the office
sanctifies the holder of it.'

Lord Acton to Mandell Creighton, 5 April 1887

———

'It is a man's pleasures, yes his pleasures, which tell us most
about his true worth, his *gravitas* and his self-control. No one
is so dissolute that his work lacks all semblance of seriousness;
it is our leisure which betrays us… One of the chief features of
good fortune is that it permits us no privacy, no concealment,
and in the case of emperors, it flings open the door not only to
their homes but to their private bedrooms and deepest retreats;
every secret is exposed and revealed to rumour's listening ear.'

Pliny the Younger, *Panegyricus 82*

———

'That old passion for power, which has ever been innate in
man, increased and broke out as the Empire grew in greatness.'

Tacitus, *Histories* II.38

CONTENTS

List of Illustrations

Note on the text

In the interests of readability and accessibility, I have tried wherever possible to restrict footnotes to a minimum. To this end, I have not provided specific notes on quotations from Suetonius' *Lives of the Caesars*: the present account simply contains too many. All unattributed quotations therefore are from Suetonius. In each instance, I have made use of the translation by J.C. Rolfe first published in London by William Heinemann in 1914 – still, almost a century later, distinguished by its combination of accuracy, elegance and charm.

JULIO-CLAUDIAN DYNASTY

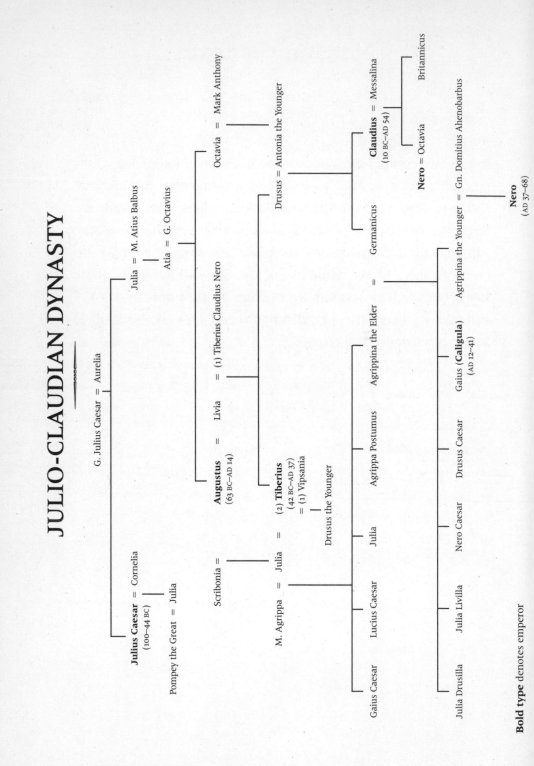

Bold type denotes emperor

FLAVIAN FAMILY TREE

Titus Flavius Petro = Terulla

Flavius Sabinus = Vespasia Polla

Titus Flavius Sabinus

Vespasian = Flavia Domitilla
(9–79 AD)

Titus Flavius Sabinus

Titus = Marcia Furnilla
(79–81 AD)
39

Flavia Domitilla

Domitian = Domitia Longina
(81–96 AD)
51

Flavia Julia

Titus Flavius Sabinus

Titus Flavius Clemens = Flavia Domitilla

Bold type denotes emperor

INTRODUCTION

'Exactitude is not truth,' wrote the painter Henri Matisse in 1947. Readers of the Roman historian Gaius Suetonius Tranquillus must surely agree. In his *De vita Caesarum* – usually called in English *The Lives of the Caesars* or *The Twelve Caesars* – which was probably published in the decade after the accession of the emperor Hadrian in AD 117, Suetonius sought instances of both: not all overlap. Exactitude is apparently one result of much of his careful fact-finding and evidence sifting; many of his truths are verifiable by reference to other surviving primary sources. Equally obviously, there are omissions from the twelve *Lives*; there are also areas where the reader must exercise caution.

In intent Suetonius' approach to biography is comprehensive, embracing both the public and private lives of his subjects, and he essays impartiality, quoting conflicting opinions, demonstrating consistently that arguments have at least two sides, abiding by Virginia Woolf's injunction that the biographer 'be prepared to admit contradictory versions of the same face'.[1] The principal property of his writing is not precision save in the sharpness and bold outline of the many anecdotes he preserves: he adopts (when it suits him) a loose chronology or schematic approach to his material, and his method intermittently suggests a squirrel hoarding nuts, piling and compiling details. He is not writing history as the ancients understood it – an account of the public and political life of the state in war and in peace: chronological, annalistic, thematic, interpretative. His work is life-writing, then as now accorded lowlier status, susceptible to intrusions of the subjective and admitting the possibility of alternative truths: a bravura unmasking of the office-holder behind the office. Given the open-handedness of his approach, his refusal either to endorse or to condemn, the cumulative effect of Suetonius' research retains an exhilarating, mobile quality reminiscent of Impressionist and Pointillist paintings: an emphasis on looking and seeing; a manipulation of light and shadow; passages of bold colour; a vigorous quest for truth; a certain deliberate liveliness unconstrained by academic convention.

In a survey of female biography written at the turn of the nineteenth century, Mary Hays wrote: 'The characteristic of the Roman nation was grandeur: its virtues, its vices, its prosperity, its misfortunes, its glory, its infamy, its rise and fall were alike great.'[2] It was a statement of its time, a reiteration of that grandiloquence which history painters of the later eighteenth century had sought to extract from Roman subjects. But successive generations of readers have agreed with Hays' vision of Rome, and it is possible to enjoy Suetonius' biographies as the expression of this 'grandeur' coloured by a dozen different prisms, a compendium of glory and infamy, virtue and (notably) vice.

No account of Rome's twelve rulers from Julius Caesar to Domitian can escape the long shadow of Suetonius. To attempt to do so would be contrary: that has not been my intention. The present work revisits Suetonius' 1,900-year-old survey in acknowledgement of the immense riches both of its subject matter and of the author's treatment. I have not attempted to imitate my starting point, which would not be possible, nor to offer a commentary on it, an academic appreciation or a riposte. Rather the present work, like Suetonius', looks at the breadth of its subjects' lives in an effort to uncover the human face of eminence and snapshots of vanished moments which are utterly remote from our own experience but intermittently familiar. Only implicitly does it address Lord Acton's famous assessment of the connections between access to power and personal corruption which are all too evident in several Caesars' spectacular failings.

Instead, the present *Twelve Caesars*, informed by additional primary sources and associated secondary material including paintings, revisits aspects of that earlier magnum opus in an effort to create for the generalist reader portraits which recall telling facets of twelve remarkable men: the political seen through the personal, the private impulse exposed to public scrutiny, even the history of their histories, which expresses another kind of truth. None of these portraits is exhaustive; none is encyclopedic. None aims primarily to titillate, none to instruct or offer moral exempla. Material is arranged by turns thematically and chronologically, a loosely knit garment, the intention to cast light on the origins, nature and impact of lives and careers which cannot otherwise be satisfactorily confined within a book of this length. Each of these vignettes, I hope, explores 'the creative fact; the fertile fact; the fact that suggests and engenders'.[3] The present work is an entertainment, and will have succeeded in its aim if a single reader is inspired to return to that earlier, justly celebrated *Twelve Caesars*.

JULIUS CAESAR

(100–44 BC)

———

'Too great for mortal man'

Isolated by eminence, 'the bald whoremonger' Gaius Julius Caesar conceals from us the innermost workings of heart and mind. 'Twas ever thus. Repeatedly he came, saw, conquered; he wrote too, and with impassioned gestures and in a high-pitched voice he importuned his contemporaries if not for love, then for acquiescence, assistance, acknowledgement, awe, acclaim, an approximation of ardour and, above all, admiration and action. He did not stoop to explanations, but asserted unblushingly that dearer to him than life itself was that public renown the Romans called *dignitas* (a quality he rated higher than moral decency, according to Cicero).[1]

The scale of his achievements dazzled and repelled his contemporaries. (So too a habit of playing fast and loose with the strict legalities of those offices of state he won by bribery, force of will and sheer charisma.) Ancient sources, including Cicero's letters, betray this ambivalence: they omit to unravel any motive bar vaunting self-belief. Openly Caesar regarded himself as the leading man of the state. He could tolerate no superior and once announced that he preferred the prospect of pre-eminence in a mountain backwater to second place in Rome. Suetonius claims that he 'allowed honours to be bestowed on him which were too great for mortal man… There were no honours which he did not receive with pleasure.' We know too well the outcome.

Intermittently his character was cold, the white heat of ambition his defence against the loneliness of epic hubris. We learn as much of the man himself from the handful of portraits which survive from his own lifetime: long-nosed and broad-browed, with strong cheekbones, a resolute, direct gaze and the receding hairline which caused him such anguish. Their style has yet to evolve that bland idealization which will transform the public face of his successor Augustus from autocratic wunderkind to ageless marble dreamboat. As the written sources confirm, Caesar's was not the appearance of a hero (nor was blandness among his characteristics). He dressed with eccentric flamboyance, customizing the purple-striped tunic that was the senator's alternative to the toga with full-length fringed sleeves and a belt slung loosely about his waist; later he affected scarlet leather boots. Fastidiousness bordering on vanity reputedly extended to depilation of his pubic hair. It is the sort of detail by which the Romans habitually found out their heroes' feet of clay and we may choose to disregard it if we will.

Of the twenty-three dagger wounds inflicted on Caesar on the Ides of March 44 BC by that conspiracy of friends, Romans and countrymen – not to mention cuckolded husbands and former colleagues – only one was fatal, poetically a wound to the heart (or near enough). It was not a poet's death, although Caesar had written poetry – one composition, appropriately called 'The Journey', undertaken on the twenty-four-day march from Rome to Further Spain. Rather it was the death of a man who had sown and reaped mightily. As he announced at Marcus Lepidus' dinner party while dissent fomented, his choice had always been for a speedy death. Conspiracy did not thwart that final ambition. Given his apparent disregard for the good opinion of Rome's governing class, his destiny, as Plutarch concluded, was 'not so much unexpected as... unavoidable'.[2]

Compulsively adulterous, subject to the aphrodisiac of power as he resisted submission in every other aspect of his life, he cultivated a legend of personal distinction and vaulting audacity in which none believed more fully than he. At a time when unbridled self-esteem was inculcated in the majority of senators' sons, Caesar succumbed in splendid fashion.[3] He dreamed, a soothsayer explained to him, that he was destined to rule the world: a restless spirit, unchecked energy and an irrational need for paramountcy drove him towards that preposterous goal. 'Caesar's many successes,' Plutarch wrote, 'did not divert his natural spirit of enterprise and ambition to the enjoyment of what he had laboriously achieved, but served as fuel and incentive for future achievements, and begat in him plans for future deeds, and a passion for fresh glory, as though he had used up what he already had.'[4] Those achievements were to change the political map of Europe and divert the course of Western history, connecting the untamed lands of the north with the culture and, in time, belief systems of the south; against that, reorganization of the calendar and a month named in his honour appear small beer. What Suetonius describes as 'incredible powers of endurance' facilitated feats of comic-book daring and derring-do, and doggedness in the face of opposition which, in different forms, proved unrelenting.

For seven days following Caesar's murder, the sun was dark as if eclipsed; skies above Rome thrilled to the nightly appearance of a comet of surpassing splendour universally acknowledged by the credulous as the dead man's soul. In death he was deified; his legend had begun in life. If some of the evil that he did lives after him, as Shakespeare has Mark Antony assert in his funeral oration for Caesar, not all of the good lies interred with his bones.[5] Revisionism began with the last of those dagger wounds. Even Cicero, whose relationship with

Caesar was notoriously troubled, admitted that 'his character was an amalgamation of genius, method, memory, culture, thoroughness, intellect and industry'.[6]

———

On every level Caesar was himself the architect of his own mythology: we shall discover that it is a trait of those who aspire to pre-eminence. His seven books of *Commentaries on the Gallic War*, covering the period of his proconsulship of Gaul from 58 to 52 BC, present his self-appointed task of subduing Gaul for the empire (and himself) in the light of military manoeuvres necessitated in the interests of national security. The truth is both different and less clean-cut. Those who contributed to his successes, notably his second-in-command Quintus Atius Labienus, scarcely check the progress of this narrative of military apotheosis; nor are rare setbacks acknowledged as failure or wrong calls on Caesar's part.[7] (Not surprisingly, Labienus later transferred allegiance away from Caesar.) It would be easy to dismiss him as a fraudster or a confidence trickster, but none was convinced more fully than he. In Suetonius' account, belief in his own superhuman destiny shapes Caesar's thoughts throughout his mature career, attested in the unusually large number of direct quotations the biographer preserves. This for Suetonius was central to any understanding of Caesar, as well as his interest as a biographical subject. It probably explains why Suetonius felt able to dismiss the conquest of Gaul in a single paragraph, focusing instead on those qualities which permitted Caesar to pull off such a grandiose scam by inspiring and sustaining a relationship of lover-like devotion between himself and the soldiers who followed him year after eventful year, and who even offered to fight for him without pay.[8] For Suetonius'

Caesar, dogged by debt, the attraction of proconsulship of Gaul was that, of all provinces, Gaul was 'the most likely to enrich him and furnish suitable material for triumphs'. By dint of iron will, and relentless exploitation of blood and iron, his guess came good. This was not heroism in the cause of the senate and the people of Rome. In placing self before service, Caesar acted in the spirit of the times. An ailing republic failed to enforce – or to generate – those mechanisms needed to contain the ambitions of dangerous men. In his *Parallel Lives*, written in the century after his death, Plutarch twinned Caesar with Alexander the Great. No shrinking violet, Caesar made the same comparison himself, regretting his own tardiness in the face of Alexander's prodigiously well-spent youth. Like his all-conquering predecessor, in time he bestrode the earth like a Colossus. In the final call, such might could not be reconciled with a republic dedicated through five centuries to curbing individual eminence.

Gaius Julius Caesar was an aristocrat when noble birth was still at a premium in Rome. The family into which he was born on 13 July 100 BC was ancient, obscure and of slender means: patricians, members of the city's oldest aristocratic class. In his veins, he claimed, flowed the blood of kings, heroes and a goddess: invincibility was coded into the physical chemistry of his being like lesser men's predisposition to freckles or thick ankles. Among descendants of the Julii were Venus, her son Aeneas (Trojan hero and progenitor of the Roman race) and those kings of Alba Longa who counted among their offspring Rhea Silvia, the mother of Romulus and Remus. It was as hard to disprove as to prove, although Velleius Paterculus, that enthusiastic chronicler of the Julio-Claudians, described it as 'a claim acknowledged by all those who study the ancient past'.[9] Perhaps. Such lofty assertions overrode the curiously unelevated etymology of the 'Caesar' cognomen, which may have referred to Punic elephants or blue-grey eyes or the family trait of a luxuriant thatch of hair (the last singularly inappropriate in Caesar's case) or, more graphically, to birth by caesarean section. Years later, triumphant in Spain, Caesar would commend his troops for storming the heavens; from the outset he claimed for himself by dint of birth something approaching direct heavenly access. 'Our stock... has at once the sanctity of kings, whose power is supreme among mortal men, and the claim to reverence which attaches to the Gods, who hold sway over kings themselves,' Caesar told mourners in a funeral oration for his father's sister in 69 BC. Of such is the discourse of omnipotence. It was a language with which he kept faith lifelong.

Despite holding a priesthood of Jupiter and the prestigious office of *pontifex maximus*, nothing survives to illuminate Caesar's religious outlook bar his unshakeable belief in a goddess Fortuna directly concerned with his own destiny and his hunch concerning the benefits of heavenly paternity, however remote. Later, in a gesture that combined family piety and caste complacency, he built a temple to Venus Genetrix. He also made use of his aedileship in 65 BC to challenge convention by hosting, after a delay of twenty years, funeral games in honour of his father, another Gaius Julius Caesar. The 320 pairs of gladiators who appeared in front of Rome's crowd that year dressed in elaborate silver armour testified not only to Caesar's lavish generosity but to the distinction of the older Caesar and, by implication, the whole Julian *gens*, including of course Caesar himself.

Patricians the Caesars may have been: in recent generations they were mostly strangers to prominence or effective power.

Caesar's father died when his son was sixteen. He collapsed putting on his shoes. It was symptomatic of decline and fall, as was the marriage Caesar *père* had organized for his son to the daughter of a wealthy equestrian. (The teenage Caesar subsequently broke off the engagement – or terminated the marriage if indeed the young couple were actually married – choosing instead Cornelia, daughter of Lucius Cornelius Cinna, four times consul, fellow patrician and, at the time, the most powerful man in Rome. It ought not to surprise us.) A recent history of family mediocrity, added to his marriage to Cornelia, would play a pivotal role in determining the course of Caesar's life.

Caesar's legacy has been debated since the moment of his slaughter. His great-nephew Octavian, the future emperor Augustus, exploited the memory of his murdered forebear to destroy for ever the Republic which in its turn had destroyed him. It was Octavian who had the sarcophagus and body of Alexander the Great removed from its shrine so that he could honour Alexander in death with flowers and a golden crown. The great-nephew discerned the same parallels which afterwards inspired Plutarch and had inspired Caesar himself. Alexander, of course, was not the only recipient of a golden crown in Octavian's lifetime. It was symbolically his own reward for realizing through conquest, mass-manipulation and deft political sleight of hand what Caesar's less compromising self-promotion had foretold but flunked: an autocracy – monarchy by another name – in place of that 'democratic' oligarchy which was the proud boast of the Republic. The conquest of an empire, including Caesar's own contributions of Gaul and Lusitania, made Rome rich: Gaul alone yielded an annual tribute of forty million sesterces (and incidentally cleared Caesar's chronic debt). Caesar's heirs enjoyed riches and empire. Provincial legions and provincial governors, both products of empire, would ultimately destabilize the settlement created by Caesar's heirs – witness the turbulent 'king-making' of the Year of the Four Emperors – just as Caesar had exploited legionary loyalty and the fruits of provincial governorship to provoke, and in time prevail in, civil war.

Covetousness killed him: the longing for absolute power. 'The animal known as king is by nature carnivorous,' Cato the Elder had said in the century before Caesar's birth;[10] in Rome, kingship remained an impermissible aspiration. That Caesar himself betrayed aspects of 'carnivorousness' is undeniable: Plutarch estimates that a million Gauls were killed in the Gallic campaign, with another million taken into slavery. Too late in the wake of conquest to repudiate Mark Antony's gift of a crown at the festival of the Lupercalia or to spurn the crowd's acclaim with the statement 'I am Caesar and no king.' Too late in 46 to demand the erasing of a statue inscription which labelled him a demi-god. His face appeared on coins – a first for a living Roman; like the monarchs of the East he had humoured divinity to the extent of permitting his own statue to be set up in Rome's Temple of Quirinus. His cult was integrated within state worship: his lieutenant Mark Antony was nominated its priest. In February 44, Caesar was appointed *dictator in perpetuum*, king in all but name. He had held the dictatorship before, as early as December 49: opportunities for repudiation had surely not been lacking. Plutarch asserts without equivocation that 'the most open and deadly hatred towards him was produced by his passion for the royal power'.[11] Like Gaius and Domitian after him, he paid for the tyrannous impulse with his life.

In the last years of the family's aristocratic obscurity, a daughter of the Julii married a man considered by Romans a *novus homo* or 'new man' (one whose family had not previously entered the senate and held the consulship): Gaius Marius. Among the outstanding generals of Roman history and elected seven times a consul, Marius was rich, famous and prominent. He was also closely associated with one of late-Republican Rome's two loose political groupings which, while not equivalent to the political parties of modern democracies, represent a roughly similar bifurcation of opinion. Neither group was motivated by altruism; both targeted power. The Populares apparently embraced the aspirations of the mob, setting popularism against the dominance of Roman politics by the senate. The Optimates championed the interests of 'the best', where 'the best' were drawn for the most part from the city's oldest and grandest families. Theirs was a defence of the status quo, but since many of the Populares were themselves aristocrats, it was clearly an evolving status quo on the brink of transformation. In answer to his own question, 'And who are the best?', Cicero scorned impartiality and hazarded an increase in the Optimates' power base. 'They are of all ranks and infinite in number – senators, municipal citizens, farmers, men of business, even freedmen... They are the well-to-do, the sound, the honest who do no wrong to any man. The object at which they aim is quiet with honour. They are the conservatives of the State.'[12] Marius led the Populares. After his death, he was succeeded by Caesar's father-in-law Cinna – strong ties twice over on Caesar's part.

At the outset of his career, Popularist sympathies unexpectedly placed Caesar on the back foot. 'Quiet with honour' held no interest for the tall but slight young man already nurturing vigorous ambitions (though almost certainly not at this stage the settlement he ultimately achieved in the months preceding his assassination). Like many men in Rome, he found himself opposed to Sulla, who in 82 BC, in pursuit of a long-term, self-appointed purpose of preventing the city from being overwhelmed by a single faction – Marius' Populares – seized control by military force. Sulla revived the role of *dictator* which Caesar would later annex. This granted him a temporary award of supreme power and allowed him to outlaw any whom he considered enemies of the state. It was a process known as proscription which placed prices on heads while stripping its victims of their estates, citizenship, legal protection and ultimately their lives. At eighteen, in possession of a single priesthood and no fortune, well born but not well known, Caesar lacked the public profile to provoke proscription. Instead, Sulla ordered him to divorce his wife (Cinna's daughter) and forfeit her dowry to the state's depleted coffers. Invariably cash-strapped, Caesar yielded the money. His refusal to divorce Cornelia left him no alternative but to flee. He escaped from the *dictator*'s agents only once his mother Aurelia had used her influence with the Vestal Virgins and a number of prominent kinsmen to obtain from Sulla a grudging and prophetic pardon: 'Bear in mind that the man you are so eager to save will one day deal the death blow to the cause of the aristocracy.' Rightly Sulla discerned in Caesar many Mariuses. Like his deceased uncle, Caesar would retain ever after Popularist sympathies and the mistrust of the Optimates. He learned early to exploit the support of the Roman masses to advance his personal agenda. Eschewing, and often prevented from, cooperation with the senate, his behaviour instead demonstrates a repeating pattern of crowd-pleasing spectaculars in public and illicit political manoeuvring behind closed doors.

Before then, scandal swiftly followed success. It is a com- bination which recurs throughout Suetonius' *Lives*: oscillating good and bad – leavened with scurrilous details, tittle-tattle and superstition – alternately humanize and demonize the author's portraits of Rome's rulers. In Caesar's case, both success and scandal arose during his first overseas military posting. In the province of Asia, alongside its governor Marcus Minucius Thermus, the nineteen-year-old Caesar took part in the siege of Mytilene. There he acquitted himself with such conspicuous and outstanding valour – although the sources do not divulge details – that he won the civic crown, Rome's highest award for bravery and one traditionally reserved for exceptional gallantry in the protection or preservation of another man's life.

Perhaps the oak-leaf chaplet which marked the award turned his head. On his subsequent dispatch to Bithynia, entrusted with a diplomatic mission of persuading King Nicomedes IV to send a fleet to Asia at Thermus' request, Caesar forgot himself. He indulged in a dalliance with the ageing Eastern monarch. Short in duration, nevertheless it dogged him for the remainder of his life. That the teenage war hero should have consented to be buggered by a geriatric royal pederast – one version has Caesar arrayed in purple robes, recumbent and alluring on a golden couch, an image better suited to his future mistress Cleopatra – would continue to titillate Caesar's enemies for the next four decades. For there was a subversive quality to such submission: an instance of Roman vigour in thrall to the degeneracy of the East; a client king dominant over Rome's representative; decrepitude corrupting and overwhelming youth; a suggestion that Caesar was open to influences Rome would not condone. Heedless or unaware of the rumours he generated, Caesar tarried at Nicomedes' court. Afterwards he compounded that initial indiscretion by returning to Bithynia on unnamed business which Roman gossips derided with undisguised scepticism.

Suetonius describes Caesar as seducing 'many illustrious women'. His paramours included queens and consorts, notably Eunoe the Moor and Cleopatra. Closer to home, his 'unbridled and extravagant' intrigues did not baulk at the wives of political associates. On Servilia, mother of his best-known assassin Brutus, he lavished a magnificent pearl valued at six million sesterces: it was Servilia he loved best. In 81 BC, in Bithynia, his surrender to Nicomedes is a lone instance both of sexual passivity and of homosexuality. Caesar's enemies clung to it with relish. His wholesale cuckolding made him fair game. Nicomedes' seduction was the only recompense for small fry blistered by the trail of this dazzling comet. Their taunts retained a bitter tang absent from the baser ribaldry of Caesar's troops, for whom an old man's cock was laughing matter. Suetonius claims the soldiers' ditty became proverbial: 'All the Gauls did Caesar vanquish, Nicomedes vanquished him.' In the long term, damage (save to the pride of a libidinous Lothario) was limited. Nero, the last of Julius' line, would pay more heavily for playing the woman's part and subverting Roman expectations of male and female, active and passive, dominant and submissive.

In Rome, Sulla surrendered the dictatorship. (That action would afterwards earn him Caesar's contempt, a statement in itself of the value the younger man attached to power.) He retired and shortly died. He had declared war on his fellow Romans and been rewarded with sole rule. In the process Caesar was one of many men forced into exile. Undoubtedly, personal animosity aside, Sulla's record impressed him. When he returned to Rome in 78 BC, Caesar did not accept the invitation of the new leader of the Populares, Marcus Aemilius Lepidus, to join him against the Optimates, proof that ambition was balanced by a degree of political acumen. He turned his hand to law instead, prosecuting the former governor of Macedonia, the prominent Sullan Gnaeus Cornelius Dolabella, for irregularities in his governorship. Although Caesar lost the case, he won friends and reputation. He also made powerful enemies. Fleeing voluntarily on this occasion, he headed for Rhodes and lessons in rhetoric from a leading teacher of oratory, Apollonius Molo. But he was stopped halfway. The hiatus was caused not by politics but money. Pirates took Caesar prisoner. For their bumptious cargo they demanded the large ransom of twenty talents of silver. Caesar set his own value at more than double that amount, the enormous sum of fifty talents.

In total, Caesar spent thirty-eight days as the pirates' prisoner. In Plutarch's version, the experience singularly failed to unnerve him. Rather, he treated the men, whom he openly dismissed as barbarians, as shipmates-cum-bodyguards, a captive audience for the speeches and poems with which he diverted the tedium. The fifty-talent ransom was probably provided by the city of Miletus, to which Caesar hastened once the pirates had set him free. There he commandeered a clutch of vessels and returned to the pirates' ship, where former captive turned captor. He took the same pirates prisoner and requested the governor of Asia to order their execution at Pergamum. That last functionary delaying, Caesar himself organized their death by crucifixion. It was no more than the promise he had made the pirates when first they captured him. Their mistake had been to '[attribute] his boldness of speech to a certain simplicity and boyish mirth'.[13] Suetonius reports the same incident to illustrate Caesar's 'mercy': 'When he had got hold of the pirates who had captured him, he had them crucified since he had sworn beforehand that he would do so, but ordered that their throats be cut first.' In its way it was a variant on Caesar's theme of *veni, vidi, vici,* 'I came, I saw, I conquered.' Dispassionately he had fulfilled his threats; justice (as Caesar saw it) had been done and seen to be done, even if numerous legal irregularities were suggested by the rapid process of its accomplishment – a man with no official standing demanding the payment of his ransom by a provincial city, then bypassing the procedures for justice ordinarily administered by the governor. For the next four decades, Caesar would pursue just such a course. He himself supplied courage, bravado, energy, an inflated sense of personal worth, and impatience with the minutiae that clogged the political process. In return, resistant to scrutiny, he expected compliance and enhancement of his *dignitas*.

Caesar was elected to a vacancy in the College of Pontiffs in 73 BC; three years later, he served as military tribune, an undertaking in his life of which virtually nothing is known. After adventures, acclaim and a degree of notoriety, it represented a point of embarkation, first steps on that ladder of magistracies which constituted the senatorial career of many of Rome's aristocratic young men, the *cursus honorum*, or course of honours. These first appointments reveal neither novelty nor distinction: the path was preordained. Earlier, probably in 76 BC, Cornelia had given birth to the couple's only child, a daughter called Julia. Cornelia herself died around 69 BC. Her death, like her life, aside from cementing first loyalties to the Popularist cause, apparently made only limited impact on the direction of Caesar's fate. His decision to hold a large public funeral for Cornelia, the first of its sort in Rome for such a young woman, increased his popularity with the mob, who interpreted the gesture sentimentally as proof of affection between husband and wife (Nicomedes and numerous affairs on Caesar's part notwithstanding). Later he would hold a similar funeral for Cornelia's daughter.

In the wake of bereavement came a departure. In this instance, Caesar's destination was Further Spain, at that stage a province of limited attractiveness to a sophisticated, cosmopolitan Roman still not thirty. He could not have chosen to serve out his quaestorship so far from the capital; he remained no longer than he had to, returning to Rome after a year. In Spain, however, in the city of Gades (modern Cadiz), Caesar came face to face with a statue of Alexander the Great and the certain knowledge of the magnitude of the task that lay ahead of him. Perhaps that encounter shaped his response to those offices which he assumed on his return to Rome. Caesar served as aedile in 65 (two years ahead of the minimum age qualification of thirty-seven) and praetor in 62. On both occasions he found himself coupled in office with Marcus Bibulus, inimical and Optimate, a staid conservative. In the case of the aedileship, Caesar exploited the appointment for maximum political capital. Rigorously he curried the favour of the masses and consistently overshadowed his less dynamic partner in a dazzling and extravagant programme of public games and spectacles which included those belated gladiatorial funeral games held in honour of his father; he also restored to positions of prominence trophies of victories against the Germans won by Marius, his uncle by marriage (previously Sulla had destroyed these).

In 64 BC, proof that the direction of Rome's political winds was changing, Caesar presided as a magistrate over the trials of those who had accepted payments from Sulla in return for killing proscribed men. Generous to the defeated as he would remain in every important contest in his life bar his treatment of

Germans and Gauls, he did not approach the task in a spirit of vindictiveness. Instead the undertaking provided him with further opportunities to lay claim to Marius' legacy, a rich 'inheritance' of populist distinction and martial prowess. At the end of 63, as a result of further large-scale spending, Caesar won the position of *pontifex maximus*, head of the College of Pontiffs to which he already belonged and chief priest of the state cult. This prestigious appointment provided him with a house in the Forum. It was a foothold in the very centre of Rome which the cash-strapped Caesar, modestly housed in the Subura, had previously lacked.

As it turned out, Spain bookended Caesar's ascent of the *cursus honorum*. He returned to the province in 61 BC as proconsul, his first overseas command. Spanish proconsulship earned him a triumph in Rome. Caesar forfeited public adulation in order to stand as a candidate for the consulship of 59 (an example of close observance of legal niceties on Caesar's part, necessitated by the vocal hostility of arch-Republican and drunkard Cato). His candidacy was successful. As with the aedileship and praetorship, Caesar's colleague was Bibulus.

Spain had served as the location for Caesar's quaestorship, his first proconsulship and the award of an (albeit uncelebrated) triumph. More than this, in time it was the site of his first epileptic fit and, in the wake of war waged against fellow Romans, that dream which an unidentified soothsayer interpreted as foretelling world dominion. The dream itself left Caesar shaken – understandably, since its substance was his rape of his mother Aurelia. On his return to Rome, he remarried. His choice fell on a granddaughter of Sulla and distant kinswoman of Pompey the Great. Her name was Pompeia and he would divorce her in time on suspicion of an affair with an audacious rabble-rouser who donned women's clothes to make good a secret assignation. Justification for that divorce inspired Caesar's well-known assertion that, guilty or otherwise – taking no account of double standards – his wife must be above suspicion.

―――――✦―――――

In the long term, Caesar's achievement was not to be a programmatic ascent of the offices of state as prescribed by Republican precedent, culminating in a benign term as consul. Nor perhaps should it have been, given those extraordinary capabilities to which even hostile sources attest. Such was Caesar's mental agility and the acuteness of his concentration that he merited inclusion in the thirty-seven-volume encyclopedia of natural history compiled by Pliny the Elder. 'I have heard,' Pliny wrote, 'that Caesar was accustomed to write or dictate and read at the same time, simultaneously dictating to his secretaries four letters on the most important subjects or, if he had nothing else to do, as many as seven.'[14] (As *dictator*, Caesar later courted popular disfavour by dictating and reading letters while watching gladiatorial fights.) As with his mind, so too his body. It was as if his pulse beat to a tempo of its own and his limbs were endowed with more than human strength and facility. Suetonius commends his horsemanship, his skill in arms, that vitality which never flagged:

> On the march he headed his army, sometimes on horseback but oftener on foot, bareheaded both in the heat of the sun and in rain. He covered great distances with incredible speed, making a hundred miles a day in a hired carriage and with little baggage, swimming the rivers which barred his path or crossing them on inflated skins and very often arriving before the messengers sent to announce his coming.

The biographer records an occasion when, harried by the enemy in the waters off Alexandria, Caesar left the one safe small skiff to his men and himself plunged into the sea. He swam using a single arm, his left arm holding important papers clear of the water. For good measure he dragged his cloak behind him, clenching it between his teeth in order to prevent the enemy from snatching it as a trophy. Less hair-raising journeys he beguiled, as we have seen, in writing or poetry. He was a stranger to idleness and the greater part of reasonable fear. Little wonder that he inspired in the men with whom he fought such fervent devotion. His standards of discipline were high without approaching that martinet cruelty which afterwards proved Galba's undoing: he closed his eyes to minor misdemeanours. He led by inspiration, without undue recourse to the mumbo-jumbo of omens and portents, trusting in that lodestar which seldom deserted him on the battlefield, his generalship as much a matter of speed and novelty as of tactical finesse; and he treated his soldiers, whom he addressed as 'comrades', with something approaching love.

Such capabilities, married to Caesar's overweening confidence, could not easily be confined within the orderliness of year-long magistracies. That power which Caesar eventually exercised in Rome arose in part from an accumulation of *dignitas*, *auctoritas* and military glory, from full-throttle cultivation of popular support and from his ability to judge whose coat-tails afforded the best ride at any given moment. Caesar's loyalties lay consistently with himself: throughout the decade of the sixties, which he began as a virtual unknown, he sought to create a network of personal alliances which would serve as a springboard to mastery. If Suetonius' Caesar does not breathe the word 'revolution', it is implicit in the many twists and turns of the second half of his career. With the consulship attained, Caesar aimed at some larger channel of power, an aspiration in which he was not alone in this period of flux anticipating meltdown. His thirst could be slaked only by creating alternatives to the Republican mechanisms of government which had served the city through five centuries. Others thought the same, and had done for years now. 'Soon Gaius Marius, from the lowest class, and Lucius Sulla, the most savage of the nobles, turned free government, conquered by arms, into tyranny,' Tacitus wrote. 'Gnaeus Pompey came next, less obvious but no better, and now nothing was sought except dominion of the state.'[15] Marius, Sulla, Pompey... Caesar... Given the nature of the contest, only one man could prevail.

In advance of his consulship in 59 BC, Caesar brokered what Suetonius calls a 'compact'. His partners were that same Gnaeus Pompey, pre-eminent among the current generation of Roman generals and the son of a Sullan loyalist, and Marcus Licinius Crassus, the richest man in Roman history and vanquisher of Spartacus to boot. At the heart of the arrangement was an agreement 'that no step should be taken in public affairs which did not suit any one of the three'. A secret, if informal, alliance between Rome's leading militarist and that magnate whose vast riches had bankrolled several of Caesar's election bids, it demonstrated a recognition on Caesar's part that, in 60 BC, power in Rome rested on twin foundations of money and might.

Prior to Caesar's intervention, the relationship of Pompey and Crassus was discordant. Cassius Dio describes them as 'at enmity with each other':[16] Crassus' jealousy supplies an explanation. In the short term, the certainty of mutual advantage overrode the larger misgivings of all three members of what historians have called the 'First Triumvirate'. Caesar undertook as consul to expedite measures of Pompey and Crassus previously blocked by the senate; in return, their influence would secure for him a province sufficient to clear his enormous debts.* And this is what happened. But in riding roughshod over the inevitable objections of his fellow consul and old sparring partner Bibulus, Caesar came close to acting illegally. Such was Bibulus' determination not to cooperate with Caesar that he sought to derail the latter's programme entirely by declaring every day inauspicious for senatorial business and all transactions suspended accordingly. Caesar, inevitably, discovered an alternative methodology: he published daily accounts of government business and moved to check bureaucratic rapacity in the provinces. Neither Bibulus, unmellowed by long familiarity, nor his supporters would quickly forget the chamber pot emptied over his head. Irregularities in his consulship – in his own mind forced upon him – made doubly pressing Caesar's need to escape from Roman justice (or revenge) into a lucrative province at the end of 59. He did not entertain the senate's derisory offer of stewardship within Italy, a custodianship of forests and woods. Instead, thanks to the triple inducement of that money (Crassus), armed force (Pompey) and mob support (Caesar) which the triumvirate commanded, Caesar was awarded Cisalpine Gaul (north Italy) and Illyricum for a five-year period. Against the advice of Cato, who regarded the step as akin to 'placing the tyrant in the citadel',[17] the senate subsequently added Transalpine Gaul on

---

* Despite a cultivated abstemiousness in his private life, Caesar spent hugely on elections, invariably other people's money, with predictable results. Suetonius suggests, for example, that such were his debts by the end of 62 that he was forced to leave Rome under cover of darkness to escape his creditors.

the Mediterranean coast. In military terms it represented a total of four legions at Caesar's disposal. The stage was set. Following his divorce from Pompeia, Caesar married for the fourth and last time – Calpurnia, daughter of Lucius Piso – and departed Rome for immortality.

For the next eight years, acting upon his own initiative, Caesar divided each year into two seasons. He spent the summer campaigning season north of the Alps: in addition to the conquest of Gaul, an achievement unrivalled by the greatest of his contemporaries, he crossed the Rhine and twice journeyed to Britain. The winter season he devoted less showily to civil administration in the peaceful provinces of Cisalpine Gaul and Illyricum on the Balkan coast. (Subsequently, in 49, he bestowed citizenship on the inhabitants of Cisalpine Gaul north of the River Po, thereby completing the unification of Italy.)

There were setbacks: Lucius Domitius Ahenobarbus' threat that, if elected consul for 55, he would demand Caesar's recall to Rome to answer charges about his behaviour in 59, a curtailment and an indictment the latter dare not countenance; and the revolt of the Gaulish chieftain Vercingetorix, king of the Arverni, in 52, backed by a large coalition of the tribes of central Gaul. But nothing seriously challenged Caesar's overwhelming, passionate and entirely self-serving desire for what Sallust described as 'an unprecedented war' which gave his ability the chance to display itself.[18] Lavishly Plutarch enumerates the magnitude of his achievement: 'He took by storm more than eight hundred cities, subdued three hundred nations, and fought pitched battles at different times with three million men, of whom he slew one million in hand-to-hand fighting and took as many more prisoners.'[19] As he had always intended, as we know he had to, Caesar exploited the killing fields of Gaul for that glory an intractable senate stubbornly withheld from him. The cost of so personal a victory included wholesale destruction of two tribes: the men, women and children of the Tencteri and Usipetes, mown down by Roman cavalry in a day of fighting which yielded a death toll estimated by Caesar at 430,000.[20] It was genocide in the service of self-promotion; at best the killings were political. Although Romans thrilled to the grandeur of Caesar's victories, awarding him extended celebrations of thanksgiving, when the smoke of sacrifice darkened the city's altars and the gods themselves were besought to witness the empire's growing magnificence, such unambiguous brutality directed against a civilian population provoked mixed reactions even in Rome. Such ruthlessness, even if we dismiss it as blinkeredness, must colour our assessment; certainly it stimulated reflection among Rome's senators. 'All that part of Gaul which is bounded by the Pyrenees, the Alps and the Cervennes, and by the Rhine and Rhône rivers,' Suetonius wrote, 'a circuit of some 3,200 square miles… he reduced to the form of province.' Secure as long as he remained in that province (in which he now had at his disposal no fewer than ten legions), Caesar was at last rich and great. He was not yet fifty.

In 55 BC, in response to Ahenobarbus' threat, the members of the triumvirate had met at Luca (modern Lucca). On that occasion, fissures were more evident than goodwill in this flimsiest of opportunist coalitions. Caesar's diplomacy, spiced by charm, won the day. Crassus and Pompey held the consulship in 55 in Ahenobarbus' place, electoral victory theirs through purchase and intimidation. They extended Caesar's proconsulship of Gaul for a further five years and devised on their own behalf a bill that was passed by the tribune Trebonius. This granted each of them a similar five-year proconsulship – Syria for Crassus and two provinces of Spain for Pompey. (In the event, permitted to remain in Italy through an additional commission which placed him in charge of Rome's grain supply, Pompey governed the latter through legates, preferring to remain on his country estates with his young wife, Caesar's daughter Julia.[21]) Afterwards Caesar planned a second consulship, for 48, beginning, as Roman law dictated, a decade after completion of his previous term. Despite his victories and that inordinately enhanced *dignitas* by which he set such store, the misdeeds of his first consulship could not be erased. Caesar remained a man on the run.*

Only as consul invested with *imperium,* that power of military command possessed by magistrates and pro-magistrates for their term of office, could Caesar survive in Rome unscathed: any other return risked legal proceedings. At that point, all the achievements of the last two decades became forfeit to technical niceties maliciously exploited by enemies who, quite correctly, saw in Caesar a threat not only to their own positions but to the very continuance of the Republic as they knew it. It may be true that even now Caesar's principal aim was not supreme power for himself per se. But a man so lavishly endowed with dynamism could scarcely embrace the treading-water prevarication of a system whose impotence he had explicitly recognized in the triumvirate. That alliance had attained its ends outside the ordinary sphere of senatorial action: its was the new reality of Roman politics. Where even the qualified democracy of the senate

---

* Ahenobarbus had first attempted to initiate an inquiry into Caesar's conduct as consul as long ago as the end of 59, in company with his fellow praetor Gaius Memmius: as we see, neither the implication nor the impulse behind that motion had disappeared.

was powerless, iron-fisted authoritarianism promised to break through every impasse. For its protagonists it offered action and progress. Impossible that Caesar should forsake either. Authoritarianism then it must be, a policy which precluded the senate's self-regarding inertia. A second consulship for Caesar would avert for another year indictment and crisis. It also promised to place him once again nearer to that position from which he could bypass senatorial constitutionalism in pursuit of his own goals.

But Caesar had failed to consider the omnipresence of death. In the event, not one but three deaths served to unravel his best-laid plans. A year after the triumvirate's meeting at Luca, in August 54, Pompey's wife and Caesar's daughter, Julia, died in childbirth. Briefly, mismatched father- and son-in-law were united in grief. That the bond between them was weakened, both surely acknowledged. 'Their friends were greatly troubled too,' according to Plutarch: 'they felt that the relationship which alone kept the distempered state in harmony and concord was now dissolved.'[22] Pompey declined Caesar's suggestion that the older man marry Caesar's great-niece Octavia, while he marry Pompey's daughter Pompeia (an instance of politic bed-hopping which would have required three of the four participants to divorce existing spouses). In 53, Crassus was roundly defeated by the Parthians at Carrhae, his body decapitated, his troops butchered, Roman standards seized by the enemy. A crucial intermediary between Caesar and Pompey had vanished at a stroke. In the aftermath of Rome's humiliation, which Caesar later vowed to avenge, on 6 December Publius Clodius Pulcher, patrician-born rabble-rousing tribune of the plebs and one-time rumoured lover of Caesar's third wife Pompeia, was killed. Assassinated in Suetonius' account, he may have died in an outbreak of

politically motivated gang violence on the Appian Way outside
Rome. Certainly Clodius' funeral gave rise to rioting, which
in turn engendered panic on the part of the senate; in the air
a sense of escalating lawlessness, of the state inadequate to
address new challenges. 'There were many,' Plutarch reports,
'who actually dared to say in public that nothing but monarchy
could now cure the diseases of the state.'[23] Attention turned
to Pompey. At Cato's suggestion Caesar's remaining fellow
triumvir was appointed sole consul without an election but
with enhanced powers, which he in turn used to legitimize
Caesar's desire to stand for the consulship in his absence.
He also obtained a five-year extension to his own command
in Spain. Shortly afterwards, in an unexpected change of
heart, Pompey passed a law preventing absenteeism among
candidates for the consulship. Late in 52 he sugared the pill
by sanctioning a second public thanksgiving – on this occasion
twenty days long – for Caesar's defeat of Vercingetorix. In
Plutarch's version, Pompey's former contempt for Caesar as
his junior in age, achievement and distinction had belatedly
turned to fear.

For Caesar, thanksgiving in Rome was a sideshow. What
mattered was his election to the consulship for a second time
and, equally importantly, the management of that election in
such a manner that his enemies were denied any opportunity
of placing him on trial for previous misdemeanours. This
was possible only if he retained proconsular *imperium*, which
obtained only so long as he remained outside Rome. Electoral
victory *in absentia* had become a point of honour, more
important to Caesar than the evident loss of Pompey's former
amity. In the service of the Republic he had won victories
unrivalled in its history: he refused to countenance the
possibility of arraignment for transgressions of the previous

decade. While the senate's line hardened, Caesar issued an ultimatum: either he be allowed to stand for election as proconsul of Gaul or, in the event that he was forced to give up his province, other holders of military commands (a reference to Pompey) behave in like manner. They were, in his own words, 'very mild demands'. Cicero described it as a 'fierce and threatening letter'[24]. Either way, the import was clear. Caesar would not compromise. Nor in the event would a hostile senate. On 7 January 49 BC, the senate approved the *senatus consultum ultimum* which made Caesar a public enemy of Rome. Plutarch claims Pompey's new father-in-law Scipio as instigator of the decree. Caesar's response determined the future of his life. It also changed history, and not only that of Rome.

Early in the morning, on 11 January, in company with a single legion, Caesar crossed the Rubicon. In crossing the narrow stream which separated Cisalpine Gaul from Italy, he crossed from legality to illegality, from the status of heroic outlaw to traitor. It was a step not lightly made in Suetonius' account, in which, at this critical juncture, an intervention of the supernatural strengthened Caesar's resolve. 'There appeared hard by a being of wondrous stature and beauty, who sat and played upon a reed... [T]he apparition snatched a trumpet... rushed to the river, and sounding the war-note with mighty blast, strode to the opposite bank.' The ancient sources vie with one another in their presentation of Caesar's historic transgression. 'The die is cast,' cries Suetonius' hero, admitting the possibility of fatalism, then tearfully he implores his troops, tearing the clothes from his breast. Plutarch offers instead a quotation from the Greek dramatist Menander: 'Let the die be thrown!' It is a challenge, a compact with destiny, the stuff of legends: impossible to remain unmoved. Except that Caesar is not a victim unfairly penalized.

Defence of his *dignitas* is the only justification he offers for a war in which his own countrymen will suffer and die – that self-seeking cause is victorious, of course. It is a conflagration with no foundation in ideology, principle or hope. As with so much in our story, its focus is power.

In the aftermath of victory, gifts and games. Suetonius records 'a combat of gladiators and stage plays in every ward all over the city… as well as races in the circus, athletic contests and a sham sea-fight'. So great were the crowds of spectators that many were killed in the crush. There were public banquets, gifts of grain and oil; a payment of 300 sesterces to members of the public, booty to Caesar's foot-soldiers and land for their retirement.

Pompey had led the army of the Republic, pursued by Caesar, to Thessaly. There, at Pharsalus, Caesar won a decisive victory; Pompey escaped only to be murdered by the king of Egypt. Ignorant of his fate, Caesar arrived in Egypt to find Pompey already dead. He consoled himself with Cleopatra, whom he put on the throne in place of her brother Ptolemy XIII and took as his mistress. There were hostile legions in Spain and at Massilia, in Pontus and in Africa. At Thapsus, on the African coast, Caesar's men overwhelmed fourteen legions of the Republican army. On that April day in 46, if we choose to believe the sources, 10,000 Pompeians died; Caesar's side sustained little more than fifty casualties. Three months later, Caesar was back in Rome. His victory had taken three-and-a-half years. In a gesture redolent of past glories, the senate voted him forty days of thanksgiving. He celebrated four triumphs. At the end of the Gallic triumph, Vercingetorix was killed by strangulation: a prisoner, he

35

had waited six years for his humiliation on the streets of Rome. Exhibits in the Pontic triumph included a bronze tablet inscribed with the legend *'veni, vidi, vici'* in celebration of that speediest victory. For his part, Caesar received the right to be preceded through the streets of Rome by seventy-two lictors.[25] It constituted an unprecedented distinction. That same year also witnessed his third consulship, an appointment to the dictatorship for ten years, and an award which encompassed aspects of the censorship including controlling membership of the senate.* The consulship was renewed in the following year and the year after. In February 44 Caesar was named *dictator* for life – as Plutarch describes it, 'confessedly a tyranny, since the monarchy, beside the element of irresponsibility, now took on that of permanence'.[26] It was an accumulation of honours akin to Banquo's commendation of Macbeth: 'Thou hast it now: King, Cawdor, Glamis, all…' For Caesar, as for Rome, endgame had been reached.

—∞—

Once Cato had claimed that Caesar was the only man who undertook to overthrow the state when sober. Unrivalled power – corrupting or intoxifying, as we will – overrode that sobriety, muddied his responses to those around him, occluded his vision, blurred the boundaries of possibility. Arrogant in eminence, he offended senate and commons alike. 'So far did he go in his

---

* Given persistent pockets of disaffection among the now largely disenfranchised senate, Caesar would have recourse to these powers in order to advance his wide-ranging, essentially benevolent legislative programme. He increased senate membership from 600 to 900, including non-patricians and provincial representatives sympathetic to his cause.

presumption,' Suetonius reports, 'that when a soothsayer once reported direful inwards without a heart, he said, "They will be more favourable when I wish it; it should not be regarded as a portent, if a beast has no heart."'

In the Rome of the sources, portents are never superfluous (Tacitus described it as 'a city which found a meaning in everything').[27] They punctuate the rise and fall of human existence as surely as life and death. To overlook – or worse, disdain – the asomatous was just another instance of Caesar's failing judgement. Overworked and tired, increasingly plagued by epilepsy, he made plans nevertheless for a three-year absence from Italy, beginning on 18 March, to avenge Crassus' defeat in Parthia. His plan finally ended the procrastination of that conspiracy of sixty senators under Marcus Junius Brutus, which, on the Ides of March, forcibly prevented his departure, almost on its very eve. Anticipating tragedy, horses left by Caesar to graze the banks of the Rubicon wept copiously; a bird called a king-bird, flying into the Hall of Pompey with a sprig of laurel in its beak, was pursued and killed by larger birds; a burning slave, cloaked in flames, survived uninjured; and Caesar's wife Calpurnia dreamed that the pediment of their house collapsed and that Caesar was stabbed in the arm. On more than one occasion, a soothsayer called Spurinna warned Caesar to beware of danger that would come to him no later than the Ides of March. In response he disbanded his Spanish bodyguard.

And so it came to pass that Gaius Julius Caesar, described by Suetonius as invariably kind and considerate to his friends, died at the hands of a conspiracy whose members were all known to him. Many centuries later, the scene was painted by the Italian Neoclassicist Vincenzo Camuccini. Camuccini's re-creation depicts a frieze-like orchestration of balletic fury, its focus a crimson-clad Caesar languid in fearless profile. The truth cannot have been so orderly. Under the rain of dagger blows, a single groan escaped Caesar's lips; also, in some accounts, the words 'You, too, my child?', uttered in Greek to Brutus. Thanks to Shakespeare, who rendered that dying cadence 'Et tu, Brute?', the murdered tyrant became a tragic hero. Our story is rich in such apparent contradictions and ambiguities.

AUGUSTUS

(63 BC–AD 14)

'All clap your hands'

Augustus described himself as a player in the comedy of life. Undoubtedly the man who appended to his dispatches the seal of Alexander the Great and who responded with pique to the inclusion of his name in the writings of any but the most eminent authors treated that comedy and his own role in it with seriousness. 'He had clear, bright eyes in which he liked to have it thought that there was a kind of divine power, and it greatly pleased him, whenever he looked keenly at anyone, if he let his face fall as if before the radiance of the sun.' Quasi-divinity became Augustus' lot in life long before Numerius Atticus, kneeling at his funeral pyre, earned a million sesterces by witnessing the ascent of his spirit to heaven 'in the same way, as tradition has it, as occurred in the case of Proculus and Romulus'.[1] Adoption by Julius Caesar had made him the son of a god at eighteen; the very name 'Augustus' ('the increased one') embraces in its etymology associations of the sublime and ordinary human abilities extraordinarily magnified.

He boasted of transforming brick-built Rome into a city of marble, 'adorned as the dignity of the empire demanded': his boastfulness, though on occasion disingenuous, seldom encompassed levity. (The habit of propaganda, once entrusted to Virgil and Horace, was too strong. The *Res gestae divi Augusti* ('Acts of the Divine Augustus'), his valedictory inventory of his achievements inscribed in bronze outside his mausoleum, asserted unblushingly and without elaboration achievements history has yet to surpass.) As his contemporaries acknowledged – as we continue to acknowledge – the talents of this divine comedian extended beyond rebuilding Rome. He was the architect of a revolutionary settlement which hoodwinked the majority and held in check for his lifetime the disaffected few. In the turbulent aftermath of Caesar's murder, it carved peace from chaos and conjured prosperity from civil strife and bloody factionalism; relief at the advent of that peace facilitated Augustus' 'revolution'. In time it directed the lives of all ten successive Caesars and shaped the experience of countless millions across Rome's empire. In its way it was every bit as influential as 'the radiance of the sun' glimpsed in those eyes which Pliny the Elder described as being as widely spaced as a horse's. Impossible that its creator should avoid assertions of divinity: on the face of it his actions amounted to more than one man's portion.

Asking whether he had played the comedy of life fitly, the dying Augustus answered his own question and begged our recognition:

> Since well I've played my part, all clap your hands
> And from the stage dismiss me with applause.

Augustus understood the theatre of politics. He was not, like Julius Caesar, impatient of those pragmatic deceits by which personal ambition was reconciled to convention. He understood that, in espousing Caesar's legacy, all his world became a stage: when the time was ripe, his own role was that of Rome's principal strutting player. Perpetual dictatorship had cost Caesar his life. When the people did their best to force the dictatorship upon Augustus, like an actor in the theatre 'he knelt down, threw off his toga from his shoulders and with bare breasts begged them not to insist'. His career was one of manipulation, his sleight of hand worthy of a conjurer: his 'restoration of the Republic' became a suit of new clothes for an emperor. His ascent to a position approaching majesty, described by his contemporaries as *princeps* ('leader'), took him a dozen years; his 'reign' lasted four decades. 'He thought nothing less becoming in a well-trained leader than haste and rashness,' Suetonius records. His favourite sayings included 'More haste, less speed' and 'That is done quickly enough which is done well enough'. After the all-consuming whirlwind of Caesar's fiery glory, the victory of his great-nephew offered Romans drama of a different kind. The ruler who displayed to curious crowds a rhinoceros, a tiger and a snake measuring fifty cubits, and 'who surpassed all his predecessors in the frequency, variety and magnificence of his public shows', insisted on his own place centre-stage. For the first time in Roman history, this canny impresario enrolled his family as supporting actors and politicized every intimate domestic impulse from weaning to weaving, carefully displayed for public consumption. His greatest monument, the Ara Pacis Augustae, dedicated in 13 BC and celebrating that settlement he imposed empire-wide, is decorated with friezes carved with images of his extended family. They preserve in marble the *dramatis personae* of the Augustan spectacular.

In the drama of his life, the comic impulse was balanced by something darker (intimations of tragedy); offenders included his daughter and his granddaughter, both Julias. For his part Augustus donned the mantle of epic heroism crafted in his service by unrivalled poets, patrons and scribblers united in their vision of a new Golden Age. His own happy ending, which bestowed on Rome and her empire the singular glory of the *pax Augusta*, was seldom rivalled in the reigns of his successors, though the strength of that peace was such that it survived through generations. In Augustus' life, statecraft and stagecraft combined. Even the decoration of his houses included an element of theatrical fantasy. In preference to costly paintings or statues, rooms were full of 'the monstrous bones of huge sea monsters and wild beasts, called "the bones of the giants" and the "weapons of the heroes"', a topsy-turvy visual idiom which challenged distinctions between appearance and reality and created an environment of super-scaled make-believe in which Augustus reigned supreme as a mythic conqueror at home with heroes and giants. The creation of the principate was a magnificent piece of improvisation. As with any theatre, it depended for its success on a suspension of disbelief among its audience, the challenge not only for Augustus but for each of his successors.

Augustus' story reverses the pattern that will emerge in the course of our survey. For the record of those Caesars who follow him is one of decline over the passage of time; reigns which, joyful at the outset, end in personal disillusionment, the evaporation of early hopefulness succeeded by bloodshed, brutality and the unthinking pursuit of self (Vespasian and Titus are exceptions). Augustus, by contrast, who first contemplated world domination in his teens, embarked on that unthinkable course with a ruthless single-mindedness which made few concessions to finer scruples; benevolence came later. This giant of world history is described by Suetonius prior to his emergence as *princeps* as having 'incurred general detestation by many of his acts'. If we believe Suetonius' account, that loathing is well founded. One day the praetor Quintus Gallius approached Augustus with folded tablets concealed among his clothes. Augustus' suspicions immediately descried a hidden sword.

44

Gallius was removed from the gathering and tortured: of course no confession of intended wrongdoing emerged. Still Augustus ordered his execution. For good measure, first he '[tore] out the man's eyes with his own hand'. It is a vigorous contradiction of the author's subsequent assertion that 'the evidences of his clemency and moderation are numerous and strong'. We will discover that clemency is the luxury of the autocrat, a benignity available to those whose position of superiority is unassailable. At the end of his life, Augustus was able to bequeath just such a position to his heirs. Behind that legacy lay a scramble for supremacy which concealed ugly and discreditable truths. There were good reasons why the future emperor Claudius was persuaded to exclude from his history of Rome an account of Augustus' rise to power. Unlike those of Julius Caesar, Augustus' illegalities never seriously threatened to find him out. Among his manifold achievements that were denied Julius was longevity: he survived long enough to outlive the memory span of many of his contemporaries.

Suetonius endows Augustus with a supernatural endorsement of unparalleled richness, beginning with the 'warning that nature was pregnant with a king for the Roman people' which presaged his birth in a small house on the Palatine on 23 September 63 BC. At the turning points in his life omens and portents abound. For the early biographer, this sanction of the numinous serves the essential purpose of exempting Augustus from culpability: the fates have decreed the course of his life – the completion of the transition from Republic to Empire. It is a dialectic which seeks to erase ambition and which Augustus himself contradicted in those actions and edicts which asserted his dynastic intent and his craving for long continuance of his settlement: 'bear with me the hope when I die that the foundations which I have laid for the State will remain unshaken.' Unrivalled in life in authority and renown, after his death he received from a grateful state the sanction of divinity. Suetonius subscribes to the irresistibility of that impulse, discounting the political expediency to Augustus' successors of his own status as a god.

His first and best-known opponent, Mark Antony, insisted that Augustus owed everything to a name, the name of Julius Caesar bestowed on him by testamentary adoption following Caesar's bloody death. Caesar was Augustus' great-uncle, though in Rome, inevitably, rumour construed the young Augustus, then called Octavian and described as 'unusually handsome and exceedingly graceful', as the older man's catamite. (A habit of softening the hairs of his thighs by singeing them with hot walnut shells cannot have helped in the emergence of such a tradition; Lucius Antonius also claimed that Octavian had offered himself to Aulus Hirtius for 3,000 gold pieces.) But the connection of great-uncle and nephew transcended heredity (or lust): their affinity was one of character and spirit. Augustus' mother and stepfather vigorously opposed Octavian's assumption of Caesar's name. Atia's admonishments fell on stony ground. 'His divine soul... spurned the counsels of human wisdom,' Velleius Paterculus records, 'and he determined to pursue the highest goal with danger rather than a lowly estate and safety.'[2] It was indeed the avowal of a 'Caesar'.

Cato, we have seen, claimed that Caesar was the only man who undertook to overthrow the Roman state when sober. It was an accusation better levelled at Augustus. For while Caesar, punch-drunk with ambition, lost sight of political realities, Augustus' focus never wavered: his sobriety was central to that cult of personality which underpinned his rule. Amassing unprecedented power and riches – in his final two decades he received 1,400 million sesterces in bequests from friends – he offered Romans a display of considered modesty as accomplished in its dramatic mendacity as anything presented on the classical stage by those pantomime actors whom he so admired. 'You must take great care not to write and talk affectedly,' he cautioned his granddaughter Agrippina: his instincts recoiled from ostentation even in speech, 'the noisomeness of far-fetched words', or the florid style of his friend Maecenas, sponsor of Virgil, Horace and Propertius, which he dismissed as 'unguent-dripping curls'. Only Augustus' ease and affability mitigated a deliberate austerity inspired by the customs of the Republic, with its emphasis on communal wellbeing. Suetonius pulls no punches: 'In the... details of his life it is generally agreed that he was most temperate and without even the suspicion of any fault.'

He lived in the same small house on the Palatine for forty years. His furniture was such as would stifle pride in a middling citizen of Hadrian's reign, the time of Suetonius' writing. There was a cultivated ordinariness to his clothes, which he claimed his sister Octavia, his wife Livia or his daughter Julia made for him (incredible claims in relation to Livia and Julia). He ate simple food sparingly: green figs, coarse bread, small fishes, handmade moist cheese, a handful of dates or firm grapes, sharp apples, cucumber and young lettuce, that diet Tityrus offers Meliboeus in Virgil's first *Eclogue*; occasionally he soaked his bread in cold water. He drank with similar restraint. Assiduous in the service of the state, he worked late into the night free from the befuddlement of gluttony or hard drinking. His study was small, squirrelled out of sight at the top of the house and called 'Syracuse' in reference to the mathematician and philosopher Archimedes. Physical discomfort was a badge of honour, proof of the wholeheartedness of his dedication to Rome's custodianship. When his granddaughter Julia built a particularly sumptuous country retreat, Augustus pulled it down. So easily was luxury sacrificed to a political manifesto.

Cynical sources may doubt the sincerity of this affectation of the mundane: none can deny the rigour of Augustus' stance.

His legacy is fecund, the cultural and economic efflorescence of his reign symptomatic of fertility at a moment when Roman strength burgeoned at home and abroad. But Augustus himself, although a dedicated philanderer whose interest in sex never faltered, had only a single child. Julia was his daughter by his first wife, Scribonia, a stern-faced matron of the old school whom he divorced on the day of Julia's birth on the flimsy pretext that he was 'unable to put up with her shrewish disposition'. (In fact he was consumed with lust for Livia and, conspicuously parvenu in a political environment of entrenched snobbery, equally desperate for the unique political legitimacy of Livia's aristocratic Claudian heritage.) The story of Augustus' reign is one of consistent political realignment, of the transference of powers associated with formerly elected offices to an unelected head of state. The human drama, first played out behind closed doors on the Palatine and afterwards in the more public arena of coinage and consulships, focuses on Augustus' quest, in the absence of a son of his own, for an heir for these greedily hoarded powers. In itself it indicates the success of the *princeps'* process of encroachment and monopoly. It was a search which would consume significant energies on Augustus' part. His eventual choice of successor shaped the course of the principate as surely as any of his actions.

———∘∘∘———

In 44 BC, Gaius Octavianus, a sickly and catarrhal young man of equestrian stock, described by Suetonius as well endowed with birthmarks but inclining to shortness and even limping on occasion, recognized a challenge: 'he considered nothing more incumbent on him than to avenge his uncle's death.' The uncle in question was a great-uncle, the brother of his maternal grandfather's wife Julia. Julius Caesar's death on the Ides of March elevated him to the position of most famous man in the Roman world. He would afterwards become a god; in the meantime he was the first of many casualties of the death-throes of the Roman Republic. Without a son of his own, he had divided his immense fortune between the people of Rome, bequeathing to every man 300 sesterces and gardens beyond the Tiber, and the studious youth in whom we assume he glimpsed something of himself. He also offered to Gaius Octavianus that lustrous name whose incalculable value his fellow consul Mark Antony correctly estimated, and the combined loyalty of troops and clients across the Roman world. Under the Republic, no man could leave more. The unprecedented position occupied by Caesar was his by gift of the senate and the people of Rome, an amalgam of constitutional empowerments invested in him personally, not his to bestow. For a puny stripling studying rhetoric in Illyricum, its august resonance represented nevertheless a sonorous wake-up call.

To the friends who greeted Octavian on his return to Rome in early May 44 BC, the exact nature of his inheritance from Caesar was clear: 'at the moment of his entering the city, men saw above his head the orb of the sun with a circle above it, coloured like a rainbow, seeming thereby to place a crown upon the head of one destined soon to greatness.'[3] This useful fiction reassured those of Caesar's veterans who had pledged their loyalty to their lost leader's heir, endowing the young man who arrived in Rome not only with meteorological endorsements but effectively a private army. In that springtime confusion, as Roman politicians struggled in pursuit of elusive consensus, dissent was powerful and far-reaching. Chief among the ranks of the unbelievers was Mark Antony himself, Caesar's Master of the Horse (his second-in-command), extravagant, genial, feckless and sensuous, a patrician rapscallion. Antony regarded himself as Caesar's true heir. Unwilling to humour a young man whose equestrian origins and rumoured effeminacy he dismissed with determined contempt, he made clear to Octavian his plan of withholding from him for as long as possible payment of Caesar's will. He also asserted his intention of maintaining that mastery of Rome which he had won in the disarray consequent on the tyrannicides' failure to decide on any plan of action bar Caesar's murder. Octavian adopted the line that intermittently would characterize his political behaviour for the next half-century. Borrowing enormous sums of money, he himself paid Caesar's bequest to the people of Rome. He took pains that the nature of his action was widely disseminated and understood. He also staged lavish games in Caesar's honour. In private he discussed with Cicero the restoration of the Republic. Perhaps no one but Octavian apprehended the full irreconcilability of these impulses. His career as juggler began early.

In allying himself with Crassus and Pompey, Caesar had enlisted money (Crassus) and military support (Pompey) to promote his political aspirations. Thanks to Caesar, Octavian possessed both already. It was not enough to invest his cause with either legality or legitimacy. This man too young for senatorial office required both. They came in 43, when the senate awarded him the rank of propraetor with *imperium* and dispatched him to Gaul. He accompanied the consuls Hirtius and Pansa, their joint purpose to oppose Mark Antony in his attempt to seize control of the province for himself. At the battle of Mutina, Caesarean forces defeated Antony, who fled. Hirtius and Pansa both died. Only Octavian could return to Rome. But in Rome the senate was laggardly in rewarding his victory.

It denied him one of the consulships made vacant by Hirtius and Pansa's deaths. Incensed, Octavian marched on the city at the head of eight legions of cavalry and auxiliaries. It was *force majeure*, but consulship was the prize. As in his 'father's' career, military menace had won those concessions dialogue denied. It was to become a feature of the principate that Augustus bequeathed to his heirs – the iron fist within the velvet glove, the omnipresence of militarism in a regime ostensibly based on charisma and civic-mindedness.

They chose an island to meet on, the consul Octavian, Mark Antony and Lepidus. It was November 43 and the three men – Caesar's heir, his former second-in-command, and the *pontifex maximus* who the previous year had become Mark Antony's Master of the Horse – had decided on an alliance. Like a previous triumvirate, collaboration masked deep fissures: mutual mistrust, personal enmities. In this case its duration spanned a decade. Opposed to the gathering strength of the tyrannicides, these second triumvirs united in the name of Caesar. It was a contentious legacy, which provided nevertheless the ideological basis for their overthrow of constitutional government in Rome. Their intention was mastery of the Roman world, an unwieldy aim which demanded defeat of the armies of the East, rallied now under Brutus and Cassius, and the removal of Pompey's son Sextus Pompey, currently encamped on Sicily in charge of the Roman navy. Dominance could be achieved by the sole means of war.

Death and suffering are not the only costs of war: there is a fiscal price too. Although the trio awarded themselves consular power for five years each, their overwhelming need was money.

Velleius Paterculus attributes their solution to Antony and Lepidus: Octavian 'protested, but without avail, being but one against two'.[4] For a second time, a triumvirate of self-seeking opportunists imposed proscriptions on Rome. First reservations banished, Octavian responded with ruthlessness. In Suetonius' account, there is nothing half-hearted in his dedication to this policy of killing and plunder, in which up to 300 senators and 2,000 equestrians lost their lives; without compunction he added to the list his own guardian, Gaius Torianus, a former colleague of his father. Octavian paid in the blackening of his reputation – among other claims, he was accused of covetousness in the matter of Corinthian bronzes belonging to those proscribed; perhaps his later wariness of luxurious decoration can be traced to this early poor judgement. His reputation also suffered at the battle of Philippi, at which, fighting alongside Mark Antony, he helped inflict decisive defeat on the forces of Brutus and Cassius. The lion's share of victory belonging to Antony on that occasion, it was Octavian who behaved with greatest brutality. His behaviour contrasted with Caesar's much-vaunted clemency towards the vanquished. Under such circumstances, Octavian's boast, valid from 1 January 42, to be the son of a god, following divine honours voted to Caesar by both senate and triumvirate, surely rang hollow.

The division of spoils following Philippi that October was concerned with nothing less than the entirety of the Roman world. The bulk fell to Octavian (the west of the empire including Italy) and Mark Antony (the east of the empire and that area of Gaul to the north of the Alps). Suspected of disloyalty with Sextus Pompey, Lepidus received shorter shrift: the province of Africa, a clear demotion. At Philippi had died an idea of Rome's Republic as hitherto understood; with it fell many of its leading families. The way lay clear for innovation in Rome. The ultimate victor was that man who, dedicated to personal ambition with bloody single-mindedness, disguised self-fulfilment as the restoration of age-old ideals of mutuality and power-sharing. Little wonder they called him Augustus. His 'increase' consisted of those powers which, destroyed on the battlefields of Philippi, he appropriated from the wreckage in the service of his own ends. It was a splendid hypocrisy, which nevertheless imposed on Rome stable government and consistency of policy-making. To obtain power, Octavian needed to defeat the Republic; to sustain his power, he feigned its resuscitation.

His inheritance lacked ballast. Caesar gave Octavian his reputation; its ideological foundations were flimsy. It was a cult of personality, as Augustus' rule would be. By exploiting personality, Octavian in time defeated Mark Antony. His target, when after almost a decade of more or less inimical jockeying for position, open hostility was at last acknowledged between Octavian and Antony, was not his fellow triumvir. He chose instead a woman, Cleopatra VII, last queen of Egypt.

Following a long and highly public affair, Cleopatra had replaced Octavian's sister Octavia as Antony's wife. That in itself was offence enough, since Octavian had bestowed on Octavia a grant of sacrosanctity which meant that any slight against his sister challenged Rome itself: at a stroke Antony's infidelity became essentially treasonable. It was just the beginning. Octavian reimagined their contest as a battle between East and West. He enlisted in support of this specious ideological debate the fixed xenophobia of the Republican mindset, alongside that mistrust of luxury which traditionally had formed a feature of Rome's lexicon at moments of national unease. Octavian's

Cleopatra is a quintessence of otherness, an amalgam of those characteristics Rome regarded as backslidings: extravagant, indolent, sexually predatory, politically tyrannous. Her female failings, it was asserted, had corrupted Antony's martial vigour. Octavian demonized Cleopatra and invested his own cause – the only purpose of which was to strip Antony of power – with the nimbus of a moral crusade. As the triumvirate drew to its close late in 33, he pitted the old-fashioned virtues of his own wife Livia against the painted harlotry of his enemy's squeeze, and then, 'when Caesar had made sufficient preparations, a vote was passed to wage war against Cleopatra, and to take away from Antony the authority which he had surrendered to a woman'.[5] For good measure beforehand, Octavian insisted on an oath of allegiance from all those in the western empire: 'all Italy swore my name of its own free will and chose me as leader in the war in which I conquered at Actium.'[6]

We know the outcome. Defeat at Actium. The siege of Alexandria. Antony's suicide in age-old fashion falling on his sword. Cleopatra's eroticized demise thanks to a serpent clasped to her breast, symbolically a victory for maleness (Octavian and Rome, represented by the snake) over the weaker flesh of female Egypt. An outpouring of Augustan poetry, in which the victory of Octavian's commander Marcus Agrippa appears inevitable, preordained. Octavian a sole survivor, Egypt annexed as a province administered not in the name of Rome but in that of Octavian. All the riches of the East available to the victor: the windfall which funded Octavian's settlement of army veterans threatening mutiny. A telling detail recorded by Suetonius: 'He greatly desired to save Cleopatra alive for his triumph, and even had Psylli brought to her, to suck the poison from her wound, since it was thought that she died from the bite of an asp.' This looks like gloating, vindictiveness – in love and war the victor's part. 'I spared all citizens who sued for pardon,' Octavian recorded. Cleopatra had not implored his forgiveness and chose to remain unto death mistress of her own destiny. The short-term outcome for Octavian was that, in the triumph of Actium, celebrated in Rome in the late summer of 29, Cleopatra appeared not in person but in effigy. She vied for the attention of the crowds with Octavian's nephew Marcellus, the son of his sister Octavia, and his stepson Tiberius, elder son of his second wife Livia, who accompanied Octavian's progress. Among the 'prizes' of victory in the East were the first stirrings of dynasticism.

For Octavian the challenge of peace was one of clarification. Latterly his power had derived from a series of consulships held continuously since Actium. To that office he added significant military support, even after his rationalization of the army following his retirement of veterans. It was a hazardous position, this approximation to military dictatorship, too close for comfort to that once occupied by Caesar. Fifteen years after the latter's murder, Octavian had no intention of featuring in his own Ides of March.

His response was to do nothing while appearing to change everything. In a speech to the senate on 13 January 27, Octavian gave back those powers he had been granted for the defeat of Antony. Dio's version of that speech combines Caesarean high-handedness and that bald swank typical of the *Res gestae* with a degree of humility which was the leaven of charm by which Octavian consistently achieved consensus:

> The fact that it is in my power to rule over you for life is evident to you all. Every one of the rival factions has been

justly tried and extinguished... the disposition both of yourselves and of the people leaves no doubt that you wish to have me at your head. Yet for all that I shall lead you no longer, and nobody will be able to say that all the actions of my career to date have been undertaken for the sake of winning supreme power. On the contrary, I lay down my office in its entirety and return to you all authority absolutely.[7]

This crafty *coup de théâtre* achieved the desired result. Octavian was created 'Augustus', his consulship (shared with Agrippa) confirmed for the year. Far from surrendering power, the new Augustus received for ten years a large overseas province, which consisted of Gaul, Spain, Syria, Egypt, Cilicia and Cyprus (and hence a significant number of Roman legions); he combined consular and proconsular powers. 'Imperator Caesar divi filius Augustus' chose to be addressed as *princeps*, a title eminent Romans had held before him: it suggested leadership without associations of monarchy. To highlight the magnitude of his achievement in Rome's service, he closed the gates of the Temple of Janus. It was a symbolic act, which indicated peace across the Empire. For more than two centuries, since the end of the First Punic War, the gates had stood open. For those in Rome assailed by doubts, their closure represented the real justification for Augustus' special treatment. No sleight of hand is wholly invisible, but the gift of peace after long years of war excused empty words and casuistry. In the same year, Augustus departed Rome for Spain.

His return, after an interval of three years, was postponed by illness, a protracted interlude in which, perhaps prey to intimations of mortality, he embarked on a heavyweight autobiography extending to thirteen volumes. Back in Rome, he fell ill again. He entrusted his signet ring to Agrippa. For reasons of lessening his workload or in response to senatorial disaffection, he marked this second recovery by resigning the consulship for the first time in a decade. Since this left him no constitutional basis for power in Rome, a refinement of the settlement of 27 became necessary. To this end, Augustus received from the senate a grant of *maius imperium*, power superior to that held by any other magistrate or proconsul, and tribunician power. Together they invested him with supremacy at home and abroad, both within and outside Rome. These were the wide-ranging powers which would afterwards comprise Rome's 'throne'. Enhanced by Augustus' personal authority and the degree of influence he exercised over the senate (an influence he had increased after revising senatorial membership in 28 BC), they granted Augustus a high degree of independence. Truthfully he could claim, 'After this I excelled all in authority':[8] now the claim was safe. Only the most beady-eyed were mindful that in exercising the powers of office without holding those offices or even standing for election, Augustus' claim of a republic restored was that of a republic exposed to fundamental change.

In 23 BC the elegist Propertius was in commemorative mode. 'What profit did he get from birth, courage or the best of mothers, from being embraced at Caesar's hearth?' he asked rhetorically. 'He is dead, and his twentieth year left ruined: so bright a day confined in so small a circle.'[9] The poet's subject was Augustus' nephew Marcellus, one of those two youths who had accompanied the *princeps* in his triumph of Actium. His death was more than a cause of sadness for Augustus.

Seneca claimed that Marcellus had possessed 'the certain hope of becoming emperor':[10] he was the first of a number of choices Augustus would make in his efforts to perpetuate beyond his own lifetime the settlement of 23. In time those efforts inflicted unhappiness on both Augustus and his large extended family; they established a leitmotiv of this history of the twelve Caesars. Only Claudius, Vitellius and Vespasian had sons of their own: Claudius frittered away his son's patrimony through uxoriousness, while Vitellius' reign was too brief for inheritance. Vespasian by contrast was succeeded by not one but two adult sons. In his unique case, the possession of viable male heirs precluded that destabilization from inside and outside the emperor's family that was brought about by speculation and place-seeking. In the case of the emperor Galba, as we will see, the choice of the 'wrong' heir became a major contributory factor in the regime's collapse.

Two years before his death, Marcellus had been married to his cousin, Augustus' daughter Julia. A youthful widow, Julia was shortly remarried by her father to his leading militarist, Marcus Agrippa. The first of the couple's five children, a son Gaius Caesar, was born in 20 BC, followed three years later by Lucius Caesar. At Lucius' birth, Dio reports, 'Augustus immediately adopted him together with his brother Gaius... He did not wait for them to attain manhood, but straightaway appointed them as his successors in authority to discourage plotters from conspiring against them.'[11] It is an undertaking clearly at odds with claims of Republicanism; so too the title *princeps iuventutis*, 'Prince of Youth' or 'Leader of Youth', with which Augustus endowed Gaius. In the event it scarcely mattered: Lucius died in AD 2, Gaius two years later. In both cases rumour suggested malevolence on the part of Augustus' wife Livia. No explanations are provided of how Livia poisoned victims scattered across the breadth of the Empire. On 26 June AD 4, Augustus made his final adoption, on this occasion of Livia's elder son, his stepson Tiberius Claudius Nero. It was not a choice born of affection. Unlike his predecessors in Augustus' scheme, Tiberius offered a record of achievement which appeared to fit him for the role of *princeps*. Augustus masterminded awards to Tiberius of *maius imperium* and tribunician power equal to his own. At a moment of uncertainty, it was the most he could do to ensure the continuance of his own system of government in the hands of a member of his own family.

Augustus was a hypocrite. Mark Antony had known it. He taunted Augustus with the knowledge of those double standards by which he criticized Antony's affair with Cleopatra at the same time as himself sleeping with a bevy of married women across Rome. Suetonius states, 'That [Augustus] was given to adultery not even his friends deny.' Antony chose as an example of Augustus' feet of clay his 'taking the wife of an ex-consul from her husband's dining room before his very eyes into a bedchamber, and bringing her back to the table with her hair in disorder and her ears glowing'. As we will see, it was an act of cavalier fornication worthy of Gaius. So too was the punishment he demanded of his favourite freedman Polus, whom 'he forced to take his own life because he was convicted of adultery with Roman matrons'.

Yet Antony was dead while Augustus lived. Both shared talent, charisma, riches. Both were capable of decision, strategy, ruthlessness. But it was Augustus who, in the phoney war of the latter period of the Second Triumvirate, made political capital in Rome. Among Augustus' talents was his ability to

satisfy appearances, a guiding principle of his principate, part of
that policy which blended emollience with self-serving. 'There's
beggary in the love that can be reckoned,' Shakespeare's
Antony tells Cleopatra with splendid carelessness: Augustus
was never so unguarded. In Suetonius' account, his domestic
policy as *princeps* included reviving 'certain obsolescent rites
and appointments: the augury of the Goddess Safety, the office
of Flamen Dialis, the Lupercalian Festival, the Secular Games
and the Cross-Roads Festival'. His policy embraced consciously
archaic elements, a *billet-doux* offered by the first servant of the
Republic to the glories of its vanished past. He rebuilt temples.
He took measures to revive ancient cults. He sought to restore
the prestige of priesthoods and reinvigorate religious observance
with reverence and awe. His reinvented Secular Games of 17 BC
included his sacrifice of a pregnant sow to Mother Earth, an
act attributed by Virgil to Rome's legendary founder Aeneas,[12]
and the 'Centennial Hymn' specially composed for the occasion
by Horace. In bright Roman sunshine on a day of early
June, twenty-seven boys and twenty-seven girls implored
the firmament for moral renewal: 'Goddess, make strong our
youth and bless the Senate's decrees rewarding parenthood
and marriage, that from the new laws Rome may reap a lavish
harvest of boys and girls.'[13] As a prayer it was pretty and pious
and pertinent. Propagandist, too. But its hope was vain, and
hopelessly impractical, for it sought to regulate private lives by
bill, an incursion of the state behind Rome's closed doors.

The previous year the *princeps* had determined on a course of
moral renewal. His focus was not his own ambulatory libido
but the sexual habits of Rome's upper classes, louche, loose-
living and lustful. As Augustus himself makes clear in the *Res
gestae*, it was the legislative aspect of that broader policy of
old-fashioned conservatism which found physical expression

in his spur to a city-wide religious renaissance. 'By new laws passed on my proposal I brought back into use many exemplary practices of our ancestors which were disappearing in our time, and in many ways I myself transmitted exemplary practices to posterity for their imitation.'[14] (He does not stipulate the nature of his own 'exemplary practices'.) The initiatives of 18 BC targeted women's fidelity and the birth rate. The *lex Iulia de adulteriis coercendis* addressed the sexual constancy of married women and, for the first time in Roman history, made adultery a criminal act (with stronger penalties inevitably for the errant wife, who potentially faced banishment; and an obligation for the wronged husband to institute immediate divorce proceedings). The *lex Iulia de maritandis ordinibus*, revised in AD 9 as the *lex Papia Poppaea*, penalized unmarried men and childless couples in an attempt to increase the birth rate. Augustus evidently felt little need to lead by example. There are no indications that he adapted his own sex life along the lines he prescribed for others, while his marriage to Livia, herself a model of old-fashioned rectitude in no need of reform, was childless, despite surviving for more than half a century. In the first instance, Augustus' token lip-service to his moral crusade made an example of his daughter Julia, whom he promptly married again following the deaths of her first and second husbands, Marcellus and Agrippa.

He could hardly have chosen worse. Handsome, witty, haughty and irreverent, Julia was unsuited to embodying moral precepts. She had inherited a streak of wilful sensuousness to rival her father's. Her indiscretions were of long vintage: during her marriage to Agrippa, she conceived a passion for Tiberius which would be disappointed in their eventual loveless union. Her misdemeanours embraced full-scale affairs and casual encounters: Seneca records the rumour that at night in the centre of Rome she offered herself as a tart to any passer-by. Augustus responded with incredulousness to the news of her unmasking; fury succeeded disbelief. 'A calamity broke out in the emperor's household which is shameful to narrate and dreadful to recall,' Velleius reports. 'For his daughter Julia, utterly regardless of her great father... left untried no disgraceful deed untainted with either extravagance or lust of which a woman could be guilty... and was in the habit of measuring the magnitude of her fortune only in the terms of licence to sin, setting up her own caprice as a law unto itself.'[15] Incandescent and dizzy with shock, Augustus discussed Julia's downfall even in the senate. Then he expelled his only child from Rome. Her destination was the volcanic island of Pandateria in the Tyrrhenian Sea. Despite popular demonstrations in her favour, Augustus never relented. He never saw his daughter again and left instructions that her body be barred from his mausoleum. It was a cruel and ironic ending to a policy intended to champion the family; and offers startling confirmation of the importance attached by Augustus to appearances (when it suited him) and to obedience within his own household.

Augustus was sixty-one years old at the time of Julia's disgrace, a greater age in Rome than today. For nearly four decades he had occupied a place of singular prominence in Roman public life. With vigour he had dedicated himself to restoring Rome's fortunes after the tardy cataclysms of civil war which reached back into his 'father's' lifetime and beyond. Some of his policies were practical: he fixed soldiers' pay and organized the Praetorian Guard; he moved to minimize corruption in elections; he created new appointments to enable more men to take part in the administration of the state – supervisors of aqueducts, of public buildings and of the roads. He conjured up romantic visions of the Rome of his forefathers, enforcing toga-wearing in the

Forum, teaching his daughter and his granddaughter spinning and weaving, and himself taking the lead in filial devotion to his mother and his sister. He was affable and approachable in his mien: when a senator he scarcely knew fell blind and resolved to commit suicide as a result, 'Augustus called on him and by his consoling words induced him to live.' Most of all, he defined the role of *princeps* as one of service, an old-fashioned idea in which the greater good of the greater number was seen to count for more than personal gain: 'May it be my privilege to establish the state in a firm and secure position, and reap from that act the fruit that I desire; but only if I may be called the author of the best possible government.' His personal contribution included measures for fire and flood protection, restoration of the Via Flaminia and his unparalleled programme of public building. Observers noticed that he was tired, Julia's downfall a turning point. It was followed by the deaths of Gaius and Lucius Caesar and then, equally dramatically, Augustus' banishment in AD 8 of Julia's daughter, Julia the Younger. Augustus' granddaughter was accused of adultery like her mother; in her case suspicion of conspiracy further muddied the waters. Her brother was involved in the same plan, Agrippa Postumus, the last remaining son of Julia the Elder and Agrippa. Then the following year, in his third year of campaigning in Germania, Quinctilius Varus lost all three Roman legions under his command in a disastrous encounter with Germanic tribes in the Teutoburg Forest. Augustus may have suffered something approaching a nervous breakdown, albeit he appears to have recovered with time: 'they say that he was so greatly affected that for several months in succession he cut neither his beard nor his hair, and sometimes he would dash his head against a door, crying: "Quinctilius Varus, give me back my legions!"'

So much had changed in Rome; some things not at all. Deep-engrained in the city's psyche was that mistrust of female power which Octavian had exploited to destroy Cleopatra. At the moment of Augustus' death, it found expression in a lurid vignette which makes better television than history.

It was August AD 14 and the emperor, travelling in Campania, fell prey to a recurrence of an intestinal complaint which had plagued him for some time; in its wake, attacks of chronic diarrhoea, difficult to manage on the road or at sea. Augustus altered his plans. He headed for Nola. His house there, by chance, was the same one in which his father, Gaius Octavius, had died. He asked that his bed be placed in the very room in which Gaius breathed his last. The instinct was one of peacefulness more than mawkishness: this then was the end. 'Since no care could withstand the fates,' writes Velleius Paterculus, 'in his seventy-sixth year… he was resolved into the elements from which he sprang and yielded up to heaven his divine soul.'[16]

But it is not to be. Into this atmosphere of gentle fading away, a single source interjects a jarring note. Dio claims poisoning, Livia the culprit, her purpose to speed Tiberius' progress to the purple before Augustus could change his mind and nominate as his principal heir his grandson Agrippa Postumus – insolent, brutish, possibly mentally deficient. 'So she smeared with poison some figs which were still ripening on trees from which Augustus was in the habit of picking the fruit with his own hands. She then ate those which had not been smeared, and offered the poisoned fruit to him.'[17]

Poisoning plays its part in our story. A convicted poisoner called Locusta removes obstacles from Nero's path to the throne.

Those crimes were well known to Dio, writing in the second century. Velleius died too soon to hear the rumours – misdeeds attributed to Augustus's great-granddaughter Agrippina. His Livia is not present at Augustus' death, hers is not the applause the dying actor invites. Instead, Velleius' Augustus dies 'with the arms of his beloved Tiberius about him, commending to him the continuation of their joint work'.[18] He escapes poisoning – even the toxic knowledge of the nature of Tiberius' continuation.

TIBERIUS

(42 BC–AD 37)

'Ever dark and mysterious'

Tiberius could see in the dark. His eyes were unusually large and afforded him, albeit for short periods only, vision while the world slept. For Tiberius was preoccupied with seeing. In a society of informers and conspirators, to see all was to know all. His studied contrariness as emperor, a determined equivocation, even obfuscation, in his speech and his written communication, denied anyone insights into the real workings of his mind, imposing a sort of blindness, 'for he thought it bad policy for the sovereign to reveal his thoughts,' Dio relates.[1]

He was addicted to astrology, that study of the aspect of celestial bodies in the interests of foresight; and feared the unseen, be it an assassin's hand, whispering malcontent or eructations of thunder. Fatalistic, self-contained and stern, for nine years as emperor he lived in isolation on Capri, 'particularly attracted to that island because it was accessible by only one small beach, being everywhere else girt with sheer cliffs of great height and by deep water'. Augustus had loved it too: its approach and its moorings afforded neither secrecy nor hiding-places. Previously Tiberius had chosen temporary exile on Rhodes. Its approaches were similarly exposed. Among the small group of highbrow intimates who formed his companions there was the Alexandrian astrologer Thrasyllus. Sources record the two men staring out to sea, each in his different way preoccupied by the challenges of the present, the promises of the future. Thrasyllus' was the position of greater vulnerability: Tiberius valued him only for his clairvoyance and threatened to kill him for a mistaken prophecy. Gifted or otherwise, Thrasyllus combined sang-froid with what looks remarkably like charlatanism: his predictions came true and he feathered his own nest by confirming Tiberius' dependency on second sight.

Augustus' heir, in the summer of AD 14 Tiberius 'almost struggled longer to refuse the principate than others had fought to obtain it'.[2] Formerly his stepfather's partner in government, invested in the year before the old man's death with *imperium*, powers of censorship and tribunician power matching Augustus' own, Tiberius saw too clearly the challenges implicit in Augustus' bequest. Hostile sources interpret his reluctance as hypocrisy, diffidence an affectation. They take advantage of his invisibility on his island retreat to weave around his name a tissue of lurid rumours – 'criminal obscenities... almost too vile to be believed', according to Suetonius, foremost among them that little boys called 'minnows' were trained to follow him when he swam and, darting between his legs, nibble and lick and suck his genitals. Similar tittle-tattle plagued Tiberius in life. During the trial of Votienus Montanus, he was forced to listen to a witness recount just such calumnies. It was the price he paid for his compulsive secrecy. The Tiberius of the ancient sources is more lecherous hypocrite than seer, paranoid and cruel, irresponsible in government, without visionary qualities.

As time would show, his concerns were well placed. The burdens of Augustus' 'restored Republic' were too great for this first hereditary *princeps*, Rome's third Caesar. We will never know the truth of his sex life but understand already that, in cataloguing sexual misdemeanours, the ancients exacted recompense from their great men. In the accounts of both

Suetonius and Tacitus, Tiberius emerges as tyrannous and cold-hearted. He delights in torture and the arbitrary exercise of power. In order to enjoy firm, young flesh without protest, he breaks the legs of those who resist his fetid advances. It is a metaphor for his treatment of dissent at the highest levels of Roman society. His punishment is to be castigated with depravity: paedophilia, incontinent lusts, joyless rape, urges too terrible for satisfaction anywhere but in exile – the stuff of film-makers and warped voyeurs, the shadow side of the sun, nightmarish and, with a degree of detachment on the reader's part, impossible to countenance given what else we can deduce of his character. Such smears would become a repeating pattern in the historiography of the twelve Caesars. In this instance, Suetonius is the prime offender.

This man who loved trees and hard liquor (hot wine without water, the origin of his nickname among his troops: Biberius Caldius Mero) was nevertheless diligent and assiduous in the discharge of his duty. He was commonsensical and practical. When the Tiber burst its banks, he did not echo the widespread response that here was an omen, but 'thinking that it was due to the great over-abundance of surface water, appointed five senators, chosen by lot, to constitute a permanent board to look after the river, so that it should neither overflow in winter nor fall in summer, but should maintain as even a flow as possible all the time'.[3] He required provincial governors to act with moderation, avoiding greedy plunder, instructing them 'that it was the part of a good shepherd to shear his flock, not skin it'. He understood power not as his right or privilege but as a responsibility, himself 'the servant of the senate, often of the citizens as a whole, and sometimes even of individuals'. Even before his accession he enjoyed rare distinction – *dignitas* and the foundations of personal *auctoritas* (which could increase only with Augustus' death). Successful campaigns in Illyricum, Pannonia and Germany made Tiberius the foremost general of his generation. His hard-won victories erased the shame of those Roman standards lost in Germany by Varus; earlier, his diplomatic efforts had secured the return of standards lost by Crassus in Parthia in 53 BC. 'Most charming and valiant of men and most conscientious of generals,' Augustus acclaimed him in a letter preserved by Suetonius. 'I have only praise for the conduct of your summer campaigns, dear Tiberius, and I am sure that no one could have acted with better judgement than you did amid so many difficulties and such apathy of your army.' Tiberius' reply does not survive.

'I treat all his actions and words as if they had the force of law,' he claimed after Augustus' death. We ought not to overlook the possibility of irony, an element of dissembling. Faithful in public to Augustus' formula for power, Tiberius privately discounted that genius humbug's explanation that, first among equals, he had done no more than restore an earlier status quo. He regarded the principate as Augustus' creation, a construct already fully developed, his own role one of custodianship for his lifetime. This explains Tiberius' numismatic programme, his policy (particularly at the Lugdunum mint) of reissuing Augustan coin types in order to assert the continuity at the regime's heart; a commemorative issue celebrating Augustus' divinity is a lone innovation.[4] For this 'greatest of generals, attended alike by fame and fortune', spent his life in thrall to his domineering stepfather who became his father by adoption, 'veritably the second luminary and the second head of the state', 'the most eminent of all Roman citizens save one (and that because he wished it so)', in the syrupy account of Velleius Paterculus.[5] Denied any choice in the matter, Tiberius expended long years in Augustus' service and, afterwards, in safeguarding

Augustus' settlement. At his stepfather's request he divorced a wife he loved to marry a sneering and snobbish harlot who cuckolded him with strangers in full view of Rome's night-time revellers; he adopted as his heir his nephew Germanicus in place of his own son.* He was a big man, strong, taller than average, well proportioned, with a handsome face in his youth, broad shoulders and hands capable of crushing a boy's skull. But he regarded the gift of empire, forced upon him by Augustus, who had the direction of so much of his life, as 'a wretched and burdensome slavery'. While the primary sources admit cynicism, nothing in his record suggests that Tiberius ever changed this view of the principate. Pliny the Elder described him as 'tristissimus hominum', the saddest or gloomiest of men;[7] in Tacitus' portrait he is 'stern', reserved, adept at concealment: 'he had his words and looks under strict control, and occasionally would try to hide his weakness... by a forced politeness.'[8] To his contemporaries he appeared taciturn; even ascetic in the matter of self-fulfilment. His death inspired joy in place of lamentation, perhaps in his own heart most of all.

Above all Tiberius lacked charm. It was part of a larger, conscious detachment from those around him. Dio describes his 'most peculiar nature', his anger 'if anyone gave evidence of understanding him... he put many to death for no other offence than that of having comprehended him'.[9] The contrast with his predecessor is marked. Affable and wily, Augustus had recast the government of Rome as a public celebration of civic-mindedness displayed in building and restoration programmes, large-scale spectacles and the heightened profile of his own family. Tiberius,

---

* This latter may not have been as great a sacrifice as we suspect. Dio describes Tiberius' son Drusus as 'most licentious and cruel, so cruel in fact that the sharpest words were called Drusian after him'.[6]

haughtily patrician, did not trouble to win hearts and minds. He slashed the budget for public games, reducing actors' pay and capping the number of gladiators, omitted to complete a single building project and, distancing himself from his troublesome relations, many of whom he executed, eventually concealed himself from sight. (This neglect of grass-roots popularity was a failing later repeated by the equally aristocratic, equally austere Galba.) High birth and, when it suited him, a superstitious attachment to portents endowed Tiberius with a sense of entitlement which did not require the endorsement of popular consensus. Although his career prior to the purple encompassed troughs as well as crests, 'that strong and unwavering confidence in his destiny, which he had conceived from his early years because of omens and predictions' never left him. It is one of the many ironies of our story that Augustus, embracing autocracy, courted popular support, while Tiberius, at heart faithful to the Republican oligarchy his ancestors had served through five centuries, baulked at currying favour, 'headstrong and stubborn' in his attitude towards the commons as his family had always been. 'Let them hate me, provided they respect my conduct,' Suetonius reports him as repeating from time to time. It is a statement of remarkable aloofness. The first 'Julio-Claudian' thanks to his adoption by Augustus, Tiberius was always the Claudian (arrogant and cruel) and never the Julian (mercurial, given to flashes of genius).

As Romans would readily have understood, he was a product of his background. A descendant twice over of the family immortalized by Livy as *'superbissima'*, 'excessively haughty', he was the son of Tiberius Claudius Nero, whose name he shared, and Livia Drusilla, daughter of a Claudius Pulcher, twin branches of the same Claudian *gens*. His family was among the grandest in Rome and unique in its Republican achievements:

a record of twenty-eight consulships (the first held in 493 BC), five dictatorships, seven censorships, six triumphs and two ovations. Although his father, a shiftless opportunist with an unerring capacity for backing the wrong horse, opposed Octavian and found his way onto the list of the *proscripti*, his mother married Nero's tormentor in 39 BC when Tiberius was only three. Following his father's death, from the age of nine Tiberius lived in the household of the most powerful man in Rome. Yet paternity left its imprint. He grew his hair long at the back, a style affected by Claudians, as if eager to assert loyalties more fundamental than those arising from cohabitation. And despite a philhellenism which increased over time, including an admiration for Greek intellectuals, his nature betrayed old-fashioned Roman qualities of austerity, continence and self-discipline (in themselves a powerful riposte to Suetonius' inventory of sexual miscreancy). These were Republican virtues, paraded by Augustus in the deliberate simplicity of his lifestyle, which Tiberius also followed (he had a taste for radishes and cucumber and, particularly, pears): in Tiberius' case, they were part of a larger admiration for the political system they had once upheld. In time, these genetic sympathies – which found expression in funeral games held in honour of his father and his grandfather – would be balanced by Tiberius' personal admiration for Augustus, a response compounded of reverence and awe. His resistance early in his principate to using the title 'Augustus', save in letters to foreign potentates, arose partly from Republican distaste, partly from a sense that he was unworthy to take on to such an extent the mantle of his adoptive father. He regarded with wariness those personal, king-like awards stockpiled by Augustus; eschewed the civic crown at his door which, Republican in origin, so nearly symbolized the truth of the latter's Roman revolution; resisted the obeisance of senators and colleagues and refused the appellation 'Father of his Country'. 'Of many high honours,' we read, 'he accepted only a few of the more modest.' His motives were not wholly ideological. Dio recounts a telling incident. A few men began wearing purple clothing, something which had previously been forbidden. Although Tiberius took measures to stop them, he 'neither rebuked nor fined any of them'.[10] His upbraiding took the form of a symbolic gesture, a dark woollen cloak flung across his own clothes. It was as if it were the loneliness of the principate which disturbed him: at one level the camaraderie of shared purple clothing did not offend him. In self-imposed exile on Capri, living without many of the trappings of empire, he found escape from that loneliness.

※

In the spring of 12 BC, Dio reports, 'Portents were noted in such numbers... as only normally occur when the greatest calamities threaten the state.'[11] The calamity in question was the death of Augustus' leading militarist, Agrippa. In its wake another, more personal calamity. It took the form of divorce and was the desire of neither husband nor wife. In this case, the husband was Tiberius, his wife Vipsania Agrippina, daughter of the dead man. The couple had been married for seven years, following an engagement of a further thirteen years. Engagement, marriage and divorce were all political, all instigated by Augustus whose motive, as we have seen, had been to ensure Agrippa's loyalty while bypassing him in the succession in favour of Octavia's son Marcellus. In the spring of 12 BC, Tiberius was rising thirty, his wife twenty-four. They had a single son, Drusus, and Vipsania was heavily pregnant. The combined effect of her father's death and her own enforced divorce from Tiberius cost Vipsania the baby she was carrying. For politics aside, the marriage of Tiberius and Vipsania had proved notably happy.

But Augustus did not permit happiness to impede the course of political expediency. With Agrippa dead, Tiberius' marriage to Vipsania lost its *raison d'être*. At the same time, the emperor's daughter Julia, his principal dynastic bargaining tool and milch cow, found herself once again a widow. Augustus knotted loose ends by uniting the Julian and Claudian elements of his family through the marriage of Julia to Tiberius. Agrippa's death therefore brought Tiberius 'closer to Caesar, since his daughter Julia, who had been the wife of Agrippa, now married [Tiberius],' Velleius Paterculus records without elaboration,[12] the chief concern of Tiberius' apologist his hero's advance towards the throne. If we accept this explanation, the marriage may well have given pleasure to Tiberius' ambitious mother Livia. It pleased Augustus too, and the highly sexed Julia, who Suetonius claims had harboured an adulterous passion for the handsome, well-built Tiberius during her marriage to Agrippa. But it brought lasting pleasure neither to Tiberius nor to Vipsania. The latter married Augustus' friend Gaius Asinius Gallus Salonius, senator and future consul. She bore him at least six sons, two of whom were accused of conspiracy under Claudius. Tiberius and Julia had a single child, who died in infancy. The death of that child shattered the fragile comity of what began as a successful, even happy partnership between two people who, temperamentally at odds, had nevertheless known one another most of their lives and spent much of their childhood in the same house. Afterwards amity swiftly dissipated. This arose possibly as a result of Julia's infidelities, more probably over disagreements about women's place in politics, since Julia, ever mindful of her position as Caesar's daughter, did not share her new husband's essentially Republican interpretation of the unseen role of women. Tiberius and Julia subsequently lived apart. Their separation may have rekindled the former's affection for Vipsania, which Suetonius suggests outlived their marriage. 'Even after the divorce [Tiberius] regretted his separation from [Vipsania], and the only time that he chanced to see her, he followed her with such an intent and tearful gaze that care was taken that she should never again come before his eyes.' Four decades later, Tiberius exacted revenge of sorts, instructing the senate to imprison Vipsania's second husband Gallus without sentence, without execution or the means of suicide.

Since the ancient sources do not countenance the possibility of personal development or change, their authors evince no interest in the long-term effects on Tiberius of his unchosen separation from Vipsania. Nor of the indignities of Julia's condescension – Tacitus' assertion that, weary of early amorousness, she disdained him 'as an unequal match',[13] Claudian blood no rival to her own Julian heritage with its associations of divinity. In the aftermath of marital breakdown, when Julia courted disgrace, 'turning from adultery to prostitution', as Seneca has it, 'seeking gratification of every kind in the arms of casual lovers',[14] Tiberius turned his back on Rome and departed, like the Divine Julius before him, for Rhodes. It was the first of two self-imposed periods of exile and resulted in estrangement from Augustus, temporary career meltdown and a degree of personal danger. Tiberius explained his move – for which he received permission only after a four-day hunger strike – as arising from a desire not to overshadow or otherwise stand in the way of the careers of Augustus' heirs, his grandsons Gaius and Lucius Caesar (the eldest of Julia's sons by Agrippa). He also cited 'weariness of office and a desire to rest'. The effects of divorce and troubled marriage surely informed that last desire. After Julia, Tiberius did not marry again. He did not take a mistress and, following the death of his brother Drusus in 9 BC, forged no new relationship of intimacy. The exception was his elevation of a ruthless philandering equestrian whose heart 'lusted for supremacy', Lucius Aelius Sejanus.[15] Prefect of the Praetorian Guard and, for a time, with Tiberius' sanction, scourge of Rome's upper classes, Sejanus cannily exploited Tiberius' emotional dislocation, that fear of assassination which bordered on misanthropy. His brief but bloody career (from which no one benefited) was a high price to pay for the isolation Tiberius embraced as the consequence of two broken marriages.

———

The Tiberius who set sail for Rhodes in 6 BC was conspicuously endowed with honours – as Suetonius described him, 'at the flood-tide of success... in the prime of life and health'. In addition to tribunician power and *maius imperium*, which exceeded the *imperium* awarded to provincial governors, he had twice held the consulship, following quaestorship and praetorship, and won triumphal insignia (in 12 BC), an ovation (10 BC) and a triumph (7 BC). He was thirty-six years old. Despite Augustus' choice as his heirs of offspring of his own blood, it was his stepson Tiberius who could claim the position of imperial second in command. It was not enough. Jealousy of Gaius and Lucius Caesar may have played its part; so too a Republican revulsion against the dizzy honours accorded to these 'Princes of Youth'. But none of the sources records any aspiration on Tiberius' part to usurp Augustus' place. His manner of life on Rhodes was unassuming, 'a modest house and a villa in the suburbs not much more spacious', a virtual abandonment of those tribunician powers which Augustus pointedly neglected to renew on the grant's expiry in 1 BC; a rejection even of Rome itself manifest in his espousal of Greek costume in place of the toga. Granted, Tiberius ultimately chafed to return: that wish arose as much from fear that his life was in danger as from eagerness again to exercise power in the capital. Tiberius' exile on Rhodes offers our strongest indication that the protests of AD 14 – his hesitancy in the face of supreme power – were not the 'barefaced hypocrisy' of the ancients' assessment, but a genuine reservation concerned either with the principate's monopoly of power or with his own reluctance to assume so wide-ranging and overwhelming a battery of responsibilities.

Once Tiberius' portraits resembled those of his mother Livia. Eyes, nose, mouth, even facial shape were all assimilated to that careful iconography developed for Augustus' wife following the grant of sacrosanctity in 35 BC. Later portraits of Livia's son vary: in place of the rounded cheeks and button chin, the long, straight nose and rosebud lips that distinguish Livia's imagery, emerged a less defined appearance, closer to the idealization of Augustus' portraiture. It was not an accident. On 26 June AD 4, Tiberius was adopted by Augustus alongside the youngest son of Julia and Agrippa, Agrippa Postumus. At a stroke, the Claudian became a Julian, reinvented and re-envisioned. What remains is the discernible downturn of those unsmiling lips, token of that excessive sadness noted by Pliny.

The dynamics of power on the Palatine had changed. With Gaius and Lucius Caesar both dead, Lucius succumbing inexplicably at Massilia in AD 2, Gaius dying on 21 February AD 4 of a wound received the previous autumn at the siege of Artagira in Armenia, Augustus adopted his stepson. Father and 'son' were sixty-six and rising forty-six respectively. Their tie was not, on Augustus' side, one of affection but need. 'Alas for the Roman people, to be ground by jaws that crunch so slowly!' was the verdict of the ageing *princeps* on the tight-lipped, often silent Tiberius. 'I am also aware,' Suetonius mischievously reports, 'that some have written that Augustus so openly and unreservedly disapproved of his austere manners, that he sometimes broke off his freer and lighter conversation when Tiberius appeared.' With an ill grace, Augustus justified his action 'for reasons of state'. Six years previously, belatedly aware of her flaunting promiscuity (and perhaps suspecting conspiracy), he had banished his daughter Julia, having first dissolved her marriage to the exiled Tiberius without consulting the latter. This high-handed jettisoning represented a nadir in Tiberius' fortunes. Reversal would be accompanied by a ten-year grant of tribunician power (double the usual allotment), which made Tiberius Augustus' co-ruler as well as his heir.[16] In keeping with Augustus' dynastic preoccupations, future portraits of Tiberius asserted that relationship in three dimensions, incorporating elements of his own official physiognomy. This physical 'kinship' underlined the older man's adoption of the younger: it was a strategy for assuring the succession of which Tiberius himself would be the ultimate beneficiary (Augustus was not concerned with the possibility of Tiberius' future reluctance in the face of that glittering prize). On the surface, Tiberius' life had reverted to the first phase of Tacitus' epitaph: 'It was a bright time in his life and reputation, while under Augustus he was a private citizen or held high offices.'[17] His initial services to Augustus were military. Rebellion in Pannonia kept him on the Danube for three years; thereafter troubles in Germany claimed his attention.

'The first crime of the new reign,' Tacitus famously asserted, establishing at the outset a chronology of malpractice, 'was the murder of Postumus Agrippa.'[18] Augustus had died at Nola on 19 August AD 14, Agrippa Postumus shortly after. Tiberius denied involvement in his stepson's death. Instead, attended in Rome by the Praetorian Guard, on 4 September he called a meeting of the senate to discuss the nature of his 'father's' funeral honours. He did not, at that stage, permit debate about the succession. Like Julius before him, Augustus was rewarded with deification and Tiberius, shy of titles, became the son of a god. The death of Agrippa Postumus left Tiberius sole heir to the Empire: so swift a resolution could only inspire rumour. After a further, protracted debate, in which he protested his own inadequacy in the face of so overwhelming a task – 'Only the intellect of the Divine Augustus was equal to such a burden' is Tacitus' transcript of his hesitancy – Tiberius accepted from the senate the award of all Augustus' formal powers. Since Augustus had taken pains to invest Tiberius with these powers anyway, he may have regarded elaborate preliminaries as a necessary procedural nicety, a case of dotting *i*'s and crossing *t*'s. Such an approach is in keeping with his apparent wish throughout the first years of his reign to involve the senate in imperial decision-making – 'consulting them about revenues and monopolies, constructing and restoring public buildings, and even about levying and disbanding the soldiers', according to Suetonius – and to assert the desirability of independent thought and action on the senate's part, as with his nomination of only four of a possible twelve candidates for the first praetorship elections of the reign. It was an assertion (of which Augustus would have approved) that the powers of the *princeps* existed in the gift of elected representatives of the state. In time, future emperors would reiterate Tiberius' reluctance with more hypocrisy and less justification. (In later instances, no one repeated Quintus Haterius' question, 'How long, Caesar, will you suffer the state to be without a head?' That avowal that choice belonged not to the senate but to the new *princeps* was ultimately superfluous – and, in time, repeatedly submerged in the role of the military.)

But if the new emperor genuinely fought shy of this greatness thrust upon him, the troops who accompanied him revealed an alternative truth of constitutional developments in Rome. Their loyalty belonged to him, their concept of the good of the state already embodied in the person of the *princeps*. In Tacitus' account, evasions and denials in the senate house notwithstanding, Tiberius had already written to Roman legions across the Empire. This undertaking acknowledges the practical foundation in armed force of Julio-Claudian hegemony. The motive of Tacitus' Tiberius was 'fear that Germanicus, who had at his disposal so many legions, such vast auxiliary forces of the allies, and such wonderful popularity, might prefer the possession to the expectation of empire'.[19] From the outset the author interprets supreme power not as a benefit to the state but as a personal possession worth fighting for. At the same time he establishes in the reader's mind Tiberius' jealousy of his nephew, who is also his son and his stepson. The unravelling of that relationship – at one level a variant on the convention of the wicked stepmother, which already existed on the classical stage – will provide the dynamic of the first years of his reign. This dominance of Rome's public life by family politics encapsulates Tacitus' objections to the replacement of a system of elected magistrates by government by a single faction, the heirs of Augustus.

In the short term, both Germanicus and the army occupied Tiberius' thoughts. Soldiers in Pannonia mutinied on hearing the news of Augustus' death; messengers carrying reports of their revolt arrived in Rome ahead of Tiberius' first meeting with the senate.[20] Similar unrest broke out among the legions of the Rhine. Under the command of Germanicus, it was to Germanicus rather than Tiberius that the Rhinish legions declared their loyalty; they also demanded improved pay and conditions. Germanicus quelled their uprising with vain promises. In theatrical fashion, he threatened to kill himself and publicly sent away from the camp his wife Agrippina, the youngest daughter of Julia and Agrippa (and thus, formerly, Tiberius' stepdaughter), and the couple's two-year-old son Gaius, whom the troops called 'Caligula', a walking and prattling legionary mascot who would afterwards become the least military of emperors. Despite Tacitus' insinuations, it looked like loyalty on the part of Tiberius' heir. Significantly, it was an interlude which served to heighten the profile of husband and wife alike. In Pannonia, order was restored by Tiberius' violent, booze-glugging son Drusus. On this, his first overseas assignment, Drusus received no special award of powers: instead he was assisted by the joint Praetorian prefect Aelius Sejanus (of whom more later) and a contingent of the Praetorian Guard.

———※———

Around 1614, the Flemish painter Peter Paul Rubens produced a double portrait of Germanicus and Agrippina. The artist was approaching the full maturity of his talents. He had already completed *The Massacre of the Innocents*, inspired by events in St Matthew's Gospel, and *The Recognition of Philopoemen*, based on one of Plutarch's *Lives*. His thoughts returned to Rome, where he had spent several years of the previous decade. It was there that Rubens had begun his collection of ancient cameos and engraved gems. The double-bust format of his finished portrait – the two sitters presented in profile, Agrippina's image uppermost and central, Germanicus glimpsed behind his wife – recalls similar cameos. Germanicus' profile, with its distinctively 'Roman' aquiline nose, echoes a drawing of a cameo Rubens made as part of a larger, abandoned project of illustrations of objects in his own collection.

In this simple-seeming image, the couple appear bold in their resolve and flushed with the beauty of moral rectitude. The pearlescent glow of Agrippina's pale skin and the enamelled luminosity of Rubens' paint conjure a gem-like translucency. The portrait's shimmering surface and pale highlights invest husband and wife with a quality that is more than human. The heroism of Rubens' vision is entirely in keeping with the portrayal of Germanicus and his wife which survives in written accounts inimical to Tiberius. As we shall discover, events about to unfold – in the main, unresolved and ambiguous – invested the couple with legendary status. In life and in death, they provided a rallying point for Tiberian dissidents. Such was the extent of their popularity and the long-term currency of their magnetism that, in little over two decades, a homicidal maniac wholly unqualified for government became Rome's fourth Caesar. The principal claim to power of the emperor Gaius lay in his illustrious and charismatic parents.

<hr />

Cruelty and tyranny dominate the presentation of Tiberius within hostile sources: twin impulses, the former is enlisted in the service of the latter. Ditto those martyrs on whom the ancient authors insist, material proof of Tiberius's viciousness. From within the imperial family first Agrippa Postumus, imbecilic and sluggardly, then Germanicus, Tacitus' hero, handsome if spindly legged, histrionic, with a weakness for the trappings of rank, a man in whom charm probably held the upper hand over capability. At Augustus' instigation, Tiberius had adopted his nephew Germanicus as his son. He became at a stroke the brother of Tiberius' surviving child from his marriage to Vipsania, Drusus the Younger. The brothers-cousins were further united by Drusus' marriage to Germanicus' sister Livilla. Germanicus ascended the ladder of magistracies with bravura, comfortably in advance of the minimum age qualifications; Drusus' record was more dogged – a case of history repeating itself, Germanicus in Marcellus' place, Drusus in Tiberius's (like father, like son). And so it proved. For in AD 19, to widespread consternation, Germanicus suddenly died. Poison and witchcraft were the rumour, blame attributed to Tiberius himself.

The emperor had grown jealous of his dashing but apparently loyal nephew. Germanicus' response to the mutiny of the four Rhine legions in AD 14 had been a series of campaigns within Germany. Victorious, nonetheless all exacted a heavy Roman death toll; none resulted in significant gains of territory. Veteran of no fewer than nine periods of military service in Germany, Tiberius recalled Germanicus to Rome. He may have doubted the long-term success of his nephew's policy: certainly he was more interested in stabilizing than extending the German frontier. He rewarded Germanicus with a triumph and partnership in his consulship of the following year. He then dispatched him to Syria, foremost among Rome's eastern provinces, his capabilities enhanced by a grant of *maius imperium* which matched that once bestowed on Tiberius by Augustus.

At the same time, Tiberius appointed a new governor to the province. Gnaeus Calpurnius Piso, a man of high estate and Republican sympathies, had previously served as proconsul of

Africa. There his chief distinction consisted in unwarranted brutality towards his own men.[21] Arrogant and old-fashioned in outlook and behaviour, he was connected to Tiberius through a shared consulship in 7 BC, and to the emperor's mother Livia, who was a close friend of his wealthy, independent-minded wife, Munatia Plancina. Tacitus suggests that husband and wife received separately from Tiberius and Livia unofficial commissions concerning the younger couple. Their role amounted to surveillance: the historian does not provide evidence.

Germanicus and Piso did not meet until late in AD 18, when a disagreement over relative status within the province, understandable given Piso's role as governor and Germanicus' *maius imperium*, caused open conflict. Both men appear to have reached their own conclusion. Germanicus departed for Egypt; in his absence, Piso countermanded his recent orders. That inflammatory course of action was discovered by Germanicus on his return to the province the following spring. Overt hostility at that point soured the men's relationship to such an extent that, when Germanicus fell ill, he suspected Piso of poisoning him and ordered his immediate departure from Syria. While Piso frittered away his days on Kos, on 10 October at Antioch the affronted Germanicus died.

In Rome news of his death had an electric effect. Agrippina had ordered her husband's living quarters to be searched: inevitably the haul revealed evidence of witchcraft and magic spells – bones, charms, crude human likenesses, tablets engraved with Germanicus' name. Germanicus' last wish was for justice for Piso and Plancina. Rumour, taking wing, strengthened the bonds between the governor and his wife and Tiberius and Livia. Few doubted Piso's guilt. Agrippina landed at Brundisium (Brindisi) in company with her children, bearing the urn of Gaius' ashes, and embarked on what became a triumphal progress to Rome. Attended by grief-stricken crowds, her mourning odyssey inspired widespread support and set the seal on Germanicus' martyrdom and her own role as faithful and suffering widow. Tiberius and Livia were conspicuously absent from the torch-lit service of interment of Germanicus' ashes in the Mausoleum of Augustus. That absence further augmented unfavourable rumour. When the trial began, Livia intervened in Plancina's cause and successfully secured her acquittal. Tiberius made no efforts on Piso's behalf bar ordering the repair of those public statues of the erstwhile governor destroyed by an angry mob. 'Let no notice be taken of my own sorrow, or the tears of Drusus,' he addressed magistrates. 'This case should be tried in the same manner as any other.' The accused man committed suicide after correctly assessing the popular mood: at one point a lynch mob gathered outside the hearings.

The aftermath of Germanicus' unexpected death represents a watershed in Tiberius' reign. Agrippina conceived a violent hatred for the man who had once been her stepfather: over time that feeling increased and hardened; it gathered in its wake others who nurtured grievances against the emperor. Her loathing included fear, so that she dare not eat at Tiberius' table without first entrusting her food to a taster; and shaped the relationship of Tiberius and Agrippina's children, with almost universally unhappy results. The suspicion felt by Agrippina, a member of Tiberius' extended family and a palace insider, found an echo in a wider unease among Romans concerning the emperor's benevolence. Given Tiberius' refusal to indulge in acts of crowd-pleasing, the mysterious death of his handsome and popular heir – the only member of his family capable of challenging him for the throne – became a focus for wide-ranging apprehensions. In Tiberian historiography, the events surrounding Germanicus' death provided justification for that overwhelmingly negative characterization of Augustus' successor which has become the stuff of legend. Tiberius' contemporary, Philo, an Alexandrian Jew, commended his gift of peace 'and the blessing of peace to the end of his life with ungrudging bounty of hand and heart' with which he endowed the empire.[22] Suetonius, Tacitus and Dio, concerned more exclusively with life within Rome and, in particular, senatorial Rome, present instead a man whose every action is open to negative construction.

In Suetonius' case, this second Tiberius, visible for the most part only during his sixties and seventies, poses problems for the writer. For Suetonius subscribes to the ancient belief in the immutability of character (despite the repeated volte-faces and circumambulations of several of his twelve subjects). Thinking on his feet, he pinpoints evidence of cruelty in Tiberius' childhood. As Tacitus states more explicitly, that cruel impulse which defines the 'real' Tiberius only ever slips from view as a result of conscious dissimulation. Suetonius offers us instances of enlightenment and benignity on Tiberius' part – his patience 'in the face of abuse and slander, and of lampoons on himself and his family'; his belief in freedom of speech and thought in a free country – trusting that we will formulate our own conclusions. Occasionally he guides our hand: 'Little by little he unmasked the ruler, and although for some time his conduct was variable, yet he more often showed himself kindly and devoted to the public weal.' Insinuation aside, this is the layman's 'lost' Tiberius, a diligent and conscientious public servant. He has been overshadowed by that geriatric pervert who enjoys underwater the tickle of small boys' tongues against his cock, a monster created by scandal mongers and partly of Suetonius' own invention. In this instance, Suetonius cannot have it both ways. Two factors come to his assistance: the ascendancy of Sejanus and Tiberius' retirement to Capri. The latter suggests the ending of one chapter and the beginning of another and facilitates a shift in tone and change of narrative gear. Before that, the former, like a playwright's *deus ex machina*, intervenes to unknot the apparent contradictions between Suetonius' two Tiberiuses: this Sejanus is a catalyst. Henceforth, the villain in Tiberius will prevail.

———

In September AD 23, Tiberius disguised his grief at Drusus' death. He curtailed the period of formal mourning, while his behaviour soon after towards a visiting deputation suggested that he had already forgotten his bereavement. We have learned to mistrust Tiberius' public emotions. Two years previously he had made his son consul for the second time; the following year he awarded him tribunician power. He also entrusted Drusus with guardianship of the elder sons of Germanicus and Agrippina, his heirs in the next generation, a move which went some way towards sidelining Agrippina and minimizing what Tiberius undoubtedly regarded as her malign influence. He acted in accord with a pattern established by Augustus. With Germanicus dead, Drusus became his father's heir: office-holding and grants of power paved the way for the succession; the whimsicality of fate demanded an heir in the second generation. Inspiration for these developments lay in pragmatism rather than affection. As so often in Augustus' quest to ensure the succession, it was not to be.

In the event, Tiberius appeared to have chosen an alternative helpmeet in government. A speech given by the emperor in the senate in 20, while Drusus was still alive, suggested that Tiberius had chosen to place his trust in the man who had recently succeeded his father as prefect of the Praetorian Guard: Lucius Aelius Sejanus. For the next decade of Tiberius' reign, it was Sejanus rather than any member of the imperial family who came closest to exercising power. For a period he did so with the *princeps'* full consent. In time, of course, his fall matched his rise.

His name has become a byword for ambition. Sejanus was born of Etruscan equestrian stock but adopted into the senatorial family of Quintus Aelius Tubero in Rome. Hard-working and opportunistic – Tacitus reports him as selling his sexual favours to 'a rich debauchee, Apicius', presumably in the interests of advancement – he preferred following his father's career to embarking as a new man on the *cursus honorum*. He became a friend of Gaius Caesar's. Afterwards 'he won the heart of Tiberius so effectually by various artifices that the emperor, ever dark and mysterious towards others, was with Sejanus alone careless and freespoken'.[23] Sejanus had joined his father as co-prefect of the Praetorian Guard, a position which facilitated privileged access to the emperor. That access increased after Tiberius transferred all nine units of Praetorians, six of which had previously been stationed outside Rome, to a single barracks near the Viminal Hill.[24] This development also augmented the political influence of the Praetorian prefecture, as Sejanus quickly grasped following his father's promotion to the prefecture of Egypt. He embarked on a policy of making himself indispensable to Tiberius. Chief among his malign practices was his orchestration of a network of paid informers, *delatores*, who provided the evidence required to institute criminal proceedings for treason (*maiestas*). Partly through Sejanus' influence, these trials became a feature of Tiberius' reign and, targeting the senatorial class above others, grounds for that schism between emperor and senate which survives in the intense dislike of Tiberius in all the major

sources bar Velleius Paterculus. Sentences were characterized
by their severity and cruelty (an impulse Suetonius attributes
to Tiberius on the grounds that his cruelty did not diminish
following Sejanus' downfall). Nothing less than terror afflicted
Rome's senators; within that loosely enclosed fraternity terror
bred mistrust. For the shady underground network of *delatores*
operated outside senatorial convention. Their scaremongering
encouraged a degree of paranoia on Tiberius' part too, which
in turn increased his reliance on his Praetorian bodyguard.
Openly Tiberius began to acknowledge this cynical upstart as
'the partner of his toils'. He endorsed the erection of statues
of Sejanus not only in the public spaces of the capital but at
legionary headquarters across the Empire (only the legions in
Syria resisted this piece of misplaced flattery, abstinence which
later earned them rewards).

All this happened following Germanicus' death but during
Drusus' lifetime. The predictable result was resentment on
the part of Drusus, 'who did not conceal his hatred and
incessantly complained "that a stranger was invited to assist
in the government while the emperor's son was alive. How
near the step of declaring the stranger a colleague!"'[25] Sejanus
avenged himself for Drusus' dislike by seducing the latter's wife
Livilla. If we believe Tacitus, he also took the opportunity of
killing Drusus, administering a slow-working poison through
the agency of a eunuch called Lygdus. (Dio attributes this
information to Sejanus' ex-wife Apicata, who distributed blame
equally between Sejanus and Livilla, partners in crime; hitherto
dissipation had been regarded as the most likely cause of Drusus'
sudden and mysterious demise.) With Drusus dead, Sejanus
came clean about the extent of his ambition: in AD 25, he asked
Tiberius' permission to marry his mistress Livilla. Tiberius
declined. Drusus' death had made Germanicus' elder sons, Nero

and Drusus, Tiberius' heirs. The emperor withheld permission for remarriage from Agrippina as well as Livilla, denying both the opportunity of producing alternative heirs or strengthening the focus of opposition. In 23, Nero and Drusus were still young: Sejanus understood that in time their influence would rival his own. Tiberius' refusal of 25 demonstrated that that influence was not boundless. He responded with a campaign of calumny and aggression directed against Agrippina and her sons, his purpose to isolate Agrippina from power to his own advantage. Agrippina's life, and those of Nero and Drusus Caesar, all fell forfeit to Sejanus' ambition and Tiberius' brooding mistrust. By the two men's joint agency, the pool of Tiberius' potential heirs shrank to two: Gaius Caesar, youngest son of Germanicus and Agrippina, and Tiberius Gemellus, Tiberius' grandson via Drusus. Suetonius claims this outcome as Tiberius' intention all along: 'He had advanced [Sejanus] to the highest power, not so much from regard to him, as that he might through his services and wiles destroy the children of Germanicus and secure the succession for his own grandson, the child of his son Drusus.' It is an oversimplification apparently refuted in Tiberius' fragmentary lost autobiography, in which he claimed Sejanus' plots against the children of Germanicus as the grounds of the former's downfall,[26] and ultimately discarded even by Gaius, who possessed the greatest grounds for enmity.

———

The Villa Jovis occupies rocky terraces of a steep hill on the northeastern tip of Capri. Despite the proliferation of distinctive white houses which today freckle the island's wooded heights and downs, its dazzling views of Klein-blue sea, tree-lined shores and sheer cliffs have survived two millennia mostly unscathed. It was here, to this craggy eyrie impossible of invisible assault, one of twelve villas on Capri inherited by Tiberius from Augustus,[27] that Tiberius retreated following his departure from Rome in 26 to dedicate temples of Jupiter and Augustus at Capua and Nola.

He offered no explanation. Granted there had been that year an unsatisfactory altercation with Agrippina, who accosted him with the taunt of her Augustan blood as he sacrificed to Augustus. (The strain of Sejanus' programmatic attacks on her friends and relations, including, most recently, her kinswoman and close friend Claudia Pulchra, both emboldened and undermined Germanicus' widow.) Vexations too continued to dominate Tiberius' relationships with his imperious mother Livia, the senate and Rome's political classes. For the first two years of Tiberius' reign, Suetonius claims, the emperor never left Rome. Throughout its slow termination, he would never return there. He surrounded himself with savants and stargazers. It was a quiet coterie, unlikely on the face of it to seek gratification in the pornographic paintings, the young girls dressed as nymphs or the adolescent boys of easy access schooled in the arts of Eastern erotica which Suetonius conjures for the septuagenarian's twilight years. Dilatory in his acceptance of supreme power in 14, Tiberius had at length succumbed with a suggestion that he might in the future set aside the burdens of office: 'Until I come to the time when it may seem right to you to grant an old man some repose.' On Capri, an older, bald and stooping Tiberius, his face a patchwork of plasters covering those sores and inflammations which had plagued him lifelong, found repose of sorts. It did not encompass any cessation in the business of empire nor, the sources aver, any lessening of the emperor's pernicious cruelty. Tourists in Suetonius' time could see the spot from which transgressors, 'after long and exquisite tortures', were hurled headlong into the sea while Tiberius looked on; sailors waited below, armed with oars and boat-hooks to beat the last vestiges of life from the tumbling bodies. On rainy days Tiberius encouraged unsuspecting dinner-guests to gorge themselves on wine. Then he bound their cocks so tightly it was impossible to piss, a double torture he had devised himself.

It was government by letter and, given the contortions and convolutions of Tiberius' prose, an unsatisfactory arrangement. While Tiberius remained the fountainhead, Sejanus wielded malevolent influence as his conduit. Intermittently the senate struggled to interpret the imperial wish dispatched by courier from Capri: inspired by experience rather than hope, it selected severity over moderation on those occasions. Distance did not lessen the force of Tiberius' anger directed against those he suspected of plotting against him. But he recognized the usefulness of an intermediary prepared to act as fall guy for inevitable opprobrium. Decidedly he was not finished with Sejanus yet. Nor was Sejanus' own task complete. In Tiberius' absence he raised the stakes against Agrippina and her family, placing spies among their friends and relations. Sejanus himself played a double role, courting Agrippina and offering tokens of his friendship in the form of incriminating advice. Agrippina kept her head, but she was treading water, safeguarded only by the continuing influence of the aged Livia. When Livia died in 29, 'the fury of the pair [Tiberius and Sejanus] was unmuzzled'.[28] Tacitus claimed that as long as Livia lived there was good in Tiberius as well as evil: without the restraint of Livia's presence, and with the apparent encouragement to brutality of Sejanus, 'he expressed only his own personality – by unrestrained crime and infamy'.[29] Despite angry popular demonstrations in their favour, Tiberius ordered the banishment of Agrippina and her eldest son Nero; the following year Drusus was imprisoned in Rome. Only two likely candidates for the principate remained to succeed Tiberius: Agrippina's third son, Gaius, then nearing eighteen, and the eleven-year-old Tiberius Gemellus.

It must have seemed to Sejanus that he had reached the point of no return. He was declared Tiberius' fellow consul for 31, an unprecedented award for an equestrian who had held none of the magistracies of state, and invested with proconsular power. On two previous occasions during his reign Tiberius had held the consulship: with Germanicus in 18 and Drusus in 21. Both men at the time were his heirs.

For so long Sejanus had held his nerve. Higher and higher his dizzying ascent had carried him. If he stooped now to make sacrifice to the gods, he surely misread the message coiled in bleeding entrails. For into this tale of ambition, corruption and death stepped a fairy godmother. She was a Roman matron of exemplary virtue. Tiberius' widowed sister-in-law and Livilla's mother, her name was Antonia. Josephus claims that Antonia wrote to Tiberius. Among the claims she made was that Sejanus had turned his attention to Gaius as the final significant obstacle in his way.

It was at last a chink of light shone through that curtain which Sejanus had hung before Tiberius' eyes. The ageing emperor, embattled and embittered, saw so many things now. Perhaps even that he himself was in danger of becoming Sejanus' pawn, a stepping-stone in an ambitious upstart's bid for power. 'Sejanus was growing greater and more formidable all the time,' Dio reports, 'so that the senators and the rest looked up to him as if he were actually emperor and held Tiberius in slight esteem. When Tiberius learned this, he did not treat the matter lightly or disregard it, since he feared they might declare his rival emperor outright.'[30] With circumspection and the utmost secrecy he made plans to topple his former ally. For the boy's safety, he summoned Gaius to Capri. He appointed a replacement Praetorian prefect, Quintus Naevius Cordus Sutorious Macro. To prevent Sejanus' suspicions, he awarded the favourite further honours: a priesthood shared with his son. At the same time, Tiberius invested Gaius with the same priesthood. He sent Macro to Rome. There, encountering Sejanus, Macro informed him of the imminence of the award of tribunician power; he also secured his own position with the Praetorians and delivered to the senate that letter in which, to universal astonishment, Tiberius denounced Sejanus. He was condemned and strangled on the same day. Then his body was taken from the Mammertine prison and displayed on the Gemonian Steps. For three days a people steeped in hatred vented fury and disgust at the remains of this man whom the principate had encouraged to aim too high. Tiberius made excuses, as we have seen. But Sejanus' death did not save Agrippina or Drusus. With Nero already dead, mother and brother followed him to the grave.

Instead more killing. It was a sort of madness, an espousal on the senate's part of an alternative reality for which neither rules nor guidebook existed. First to die: Sejanus' family – unsavoury details, an infant daughter Junilla, who, because no precedent existed for the execution of a virgin, was raped by the executioner with the noose around her neck. Afterwards further attacks by the *princeps* on senatorial ranks, more than half the major judicial proceedings of Tiberius' reign compressed into his final six years.[31] Vengeance against Sejanus' supporters and accomplices was a dastardly, elemental force. Bruttedius Niger, Publius Vitellius, Sextius Paconianus, Gaius Annius Pollio, Gaius

Appius Silanus, Gaius Calvisius Sabinus, Annius Vinicianus, Geminius the knight: on the list stretches, no connection with Sejanus too slight to merit the death sentence. 'Every single one of those who were condemned to death heaped all kinds of abuse upon [Tiberius],' Suetonius tells us: 'his anxiety of mind became torture.' Sleepless nights became the price of tyranny: it is an historical convention.

Eventually the clouds lifted. On Capri in the villa gardens there were cucumber frames. Tiberius acquired a small pet snake and fed it himself. He retained his grip on the Empire, loathed in Rome but still a competent and conscientious administrator, his *auctoritas* (as great as once Augustus' had been) a binding force across wide-flung provinces. In 33, he resolved the greatest financial crisis of his reign by distributing 100 million sesterces in three-year, interest-free loans. New currency minted to meet the demand proclaimed the roll-call of Tiberius' titles. But the pictorial element of these last Tiberian coins was all concerned with Divus Augustus,[32] the numismatic iconography of Augustus' ascent heavenwards. It expressed in miniature a truth of Tiberius' principate, the earnestness of his fidelity to that settlement Augustus had carved out for himself more than half a century earlier. But Tiberius deceived himself. His abandonment of Rome for Capri amounted to a dereliction of Augustus' most careful charade: that the *princeps* was the servant of the state, first among equals, a Republican in purple clothing. For all his lip-service to Augustus' settlement, in ruling by edict – letters of instruction to the senate from the Villa Jovis – Tiberius dispensed with the illusion of service and consensus. His power, as Sejanus had realized, was absolute.

Tiberius died on 16 March 37 on the mainland at Misenum, the ancient port of Campania. Death occurred in a villa which had previously belonged to Lucius Lucullus, that leviathan figure of the late Republic known as 'Xerxes in a toga'. He was seventy-eight. His pet snake had already died, devoured almost before his eyes by an angry swarm of ants. Given the fervour with which his death was anticipated in the senate house and on the streets of Rome, it is no surprise that varying reports proliferate. The immediate cause of death was fever; exhaustion and old age can safely be added to the mix. Faithful to a lifetime of concealment and dissimulation, Tiberius struggled to disguise his true condition and carry on as normal. (A more popular ruler could have laid claim to indomitability.) In the presence of the leading physician of his generation, Charicles, Tiberius' shamming was recognized for what it was. The end came peacefully, whether we believe Suetonius' report that he fell dead beside his couch, strength suddenly failing him, or Tacitus' version. After a false alarm, when delighted sycophants rushed to congratulate Gaius, Tiberius regained consciousness. Amid the toadies, a panic-stricken dispersal; stupefied silence Gaius' only response. In that moment of dashed hopes, Macro seized the initiative and ordered that the old man be suffocated with his bedclothes. No fight ensued: Tiberius was old and tired, the blankets were simply heaped upon him. No one protested. Not even, in the event, Tiberius himself. He left behind him a treasury replete with almost three billion sesterces, the result of his long and careful husbandry of imperial resources. As we shall see, it was not enough to fund that four-year act of repudiation in which his successor sought to deny his memory. The tyranny and cruelty had only just begun.

GAIUS CALIGULA

(AD 12–41)

───✦───

'Equally furious against men
and against the gods'

No more pretence. No more crocodile tears for a Republic broken and discarded than for the death of an absentee emperor hated and feared (although appearances were satisfied in the splendid funeral Gaius granted Tiberius and, in time, himself threatened by conspiracies, he would reassess his opinion of the behaviour of a predecessor similarly threatened. Indeed, for episodes of his reign, a deliberate historical amnesia on the part of Rome's fourth Caesar, posterity's 'Caligula': a refusal to kowtow to precedent or to humour senatorial memories of a vanished Golden Age of oligarchic rectitude and influence.

In Gaius' nostrils, Tiberius' cynical adherence to that illusion Augustus had fabricated of government by a continuing system of elected officials, the *princeps* 'first among equals' (a leading citizen in a company of leading citizens), smelt as stale as his corpse. Always frank to the point of offensiveness, he despised its untruths. Not content to be hailed as 'Greatest and Best of Caesars' – equally unsusceptible when the mood took him to flattery and to plain speaking – he craved autocracy and made significant strides towards achieving it. That radical shift formed the dynamic of Gaius' reign. It shaped his behaviour towards senate and commons. It inspired his creation of a personal mythology. It alienated the writers of ancient history so comprehensively that, for modern readers, Gaius – imprecisely but consistently dismissed as insane – lies lost in a fog of fact and fable which we may never navigate with certainty.

His youth had been one of suffering and circumspection, his prominent and popular family suspected by Tiberius of dangerous designs. With Tiberius dead, a new dawn promised. There would be only one way from now on, in appearance as well as fact: Gaius' way. No 'dominion of the senate and the people of Rome' as celebrated in Augustus' *Res gestae*.[1] No senatorial involvement in public finance, public works, military recruitment or correspondence with client kings as fostered by Tiberius.[2] Not even lip-service to good relations between emperor and senators. 'Let them hate, provided they fear' became the broad-brush policy applied to all classes, where fear was the clear blue water that separated governor and governed. Invested with legal power by the senate on his accession and enjoying the support of the army through family connections – as well as a timely payment of 2,000 sesterces to members of the Praetorian Guard made on his behalf by the Guard's prefect, Macro – Gaius nevertheless crucially lacked *auctoritas*: he could not, like his predecessors, claim to rule through personal authority or as a reward for services to the state. Without experience, he was simply himself. Within himself, he decided, lay the grounds of his distinction. It was an attitude unconducive to compromise. In March 37, the accession of Tiberius' successor was managed without opposition. His reign began in happy emollience, a policy of inclusiveness and consensus applied to commons and senate alike. It would prove short-lived. In Gaius' reign there were no happy endings – either for Gaius or for his Rome. Like fellow epileptic Julius Caesar before him and Galba, Otho, Vitellius and Domitian after, in time this miscreant emperor would die a thousand deaths, victim of a frenzy of killing: his jaw split, his groin ripped by swords, his body bludgeoned, battered, butchered. Irony destroyed him: a bloody and agonizing end for a sick-minded tyrant who had revelled in the bodily and mental anguish of many who ought never to have been his victims.

At the outset the beloved son of a beloved father, Gaius was the first of Rome's emperors to exult in his own eminence. (He was also the first to gain the throne exclusively through the hereditary principle, his sole qualification for office descent from Augustus via Julia and Agrippina the Elder.) He began by pursuing plaudits, praise and pity (the last survivor of three sons, both parents killed, his family beloved of Rome's masses). It was so easy with a carrying wind, 'for Tiberius', as Josephus tells us, 'had brought a vast number of miseries on the best families of the Romans',[3] none more so than Gaius' own. Tiberius' death was greeted with joy, Gaius' accession with rapture among the Roman crowd and, in the senate house, a qualified optimism which its members took pains to disguise as joy. Dio describes the twenty-four-year-old emperor wooing the senate with promises of power-sharing and a little-boy-lost version of himself as the son and ward of the city fathers;[4] he abolished treason trials and unpopular taxes, recalled exiles, destroyed incriminating papers. A conciliatory gesture: he adopted his co-heir, Tiberius' grandson Tiberius Gemellus, as his son. (Later he would have him killed, invoking with grim cynicism the legal power of life and death possessed by a father over his sons: *patria potestas*.) In Suetonius' account, the fledgling ruler 'tried to rouse men's devotion by courting popularity in every way'. His efforts verged on the theatrical but, emphasizing themes of family piety and the unstinting generosity of the emperor, met with notable success. Primary and secondary sources agree – witness Eustache Le Sueur's painting of 1647, *Caligula Depositing the Ashes of his Mother and his Brother in the Tomb of his Ancestors*, a heroic, understatedly moving image despite painter and viewer's knowledge of the emperor's imminent degeneration into madness and badness.

Too soon, seduced by visions, Gaius outgrew initial joy. Without compunction he shattered every good opinion. Indifferent to any estimation bar his own, he cultivated contentment in his very callousness, the actions by which he lost Rome's love more theatrical than those by which once he had sought to keep it. 'Would that you had but a single neck,' he told a hostile crowd repelled by his orgiastic delight in slaughter and his apparently insatiable desire for the sight and scent of blood and money;[5] by then Romans knew better than to doubt his desire to kill them one and all. It was as if he had decided to turn the world on its head: an iconoclasm of misery and mistrust. In the beginning, he made payments to the people of those generous legacies left by Livia (suppressed by Tiberius) and Tiberius (suppressed by the senate), as well as his own early donatives made on two occasions; later he imposed swingeing taxes and cut off supplies of free grain. In the beginning, championing the people's pleasure, he sponsored public games and festivities, even appearing as a gladiator himself; later, on a day of broiling heat, he locked the crowd in the theatre and withdrew the awnings that sheltered them from the sun. (Mistreatment of spectators at the games always bodes ill. Dio later accuses Domitian of confining the crowd in the circus during a storm so violent that, drenched and freezing, several caught colds and died.[6])

In the beginning, he elevated his family, offering decent burial to those who had died and honours to those who remained – the same privileges for his grandmother Antonia as those once enjoyed by the elderly Livia, including the title 'Augusta', public prayers for his sisters, a shared consulship for his uncle Claudius; later, he is accused of poisoning Antonia or driving her to suicide; he exiled his sisters on suspicion of conspiracy and killed his widower brother-in-law Lepidus whom Dio claimed was his lover;[7] he dunked Claudius in the Rhine simply for being Claudius. Unsurprisingly, his plummet through the opinion polls was rapid. That downward journey revelled in bloodshed, torture and casual carnality. Scholars impose a tentative coherence by discerning a chilling, cruel humour behind Gaius' atrocities: as an alternative morality it falls flat. Today his hair-raising record provides lurid inspiration for playwrights, film-makers and pornographers. It is a wanton legacy in default of any other. 'For any great or royal work that he did, which might be for the present and for future ages,' Josephus sniffs, 'nobody can name any such.'[8]

Dio characterizes Gaius as a compound of contradictions, his only consistency inconsistency.[9] So, having at first forbidden Romans to set up images of him, he afterwards offered himself for public consumption to be worshipped as a living god in temples on the Palatine and Capitoline Hills. His ambitions were grandiose: he appeared in the guise of Hercules, Neptune, Bacchus and Apollo; with recourse to wigs he even impersonated Venus, Juno and Diana. The sources preserve a rumour that he went so far as to try to seduce the moon, thirsty for a new sort of thrill as pale, cool light flooded his palace bedroom. One temple contained a life-size golden statue of Gaius. In a practice designed to blur boundaries between the mortal and immortal figures of the emperor, it was dressed on a daily basis in clothing like his own. Only the smoke of sacrifice dimmed its brightness: guinea-hens, peacocks, pheasants, woodcock and even flamingoes burned in appeasement of this charade-loving charlatan.

Apparently capricious, that attention-seeking volte-face was typical of Gaius' inability to reconcile irreconcilables: that conjunction of excessive timidness and extreme assurance which Suetonius placed at the root of his mental weakness. In time the man who regarded Rome's pantheon with contemptuous offhandedness appeared at the seaside playground of Baiae in 'a crown of oak leaves... and a cloak of cloth of gold'; on other occasions he carried a trident, a caduceus or a thunderbolt, accessories of the gods. Was he testing the perimeters of his newfound power – enjoying an elaborate joke at the expense of Roman credulousness and senatorial sycophancy – or asserting the unassailability of the *princeps*' position by 'borrowing' heavenly attributes? Was this talent-show approach to public worship in fact a deliberate policy designed to underline Gaius' own eminence, his fitness to reign by dint of qualities that were more than human, denied to the common herd? If so, events would unveil the hollowness of vainglorious posturing. Perhaps these amateur dramatics should be interpreted as no more than the youthful *jeux d'esprit* of a man who had schooled himself to rely on his own resources for amusement – 'a huge bullshitter', as a brave cobbler once described him to his face;[10] alternatively as an exercise in wish-fulfilment perpetrated by one who, even in his youth, was condemned by his appearance to mockery. (To mention the word 'goat' in the presence of the bald but hairy-limbed emperor was a capital offence.) Both answers provide grounds for our pity. With their emphasis on mental instability, the sources do not comment. Enough to register that in spirit these were the very gestures which, less than a century earlier, had cost the Divine Julius his life; the same self-aggrandizement which once had marked out Mark Antony as Rome's ideological enemy, seduced by equations of kingship and divinity associated with the East. Time had moved on since the Ides of March and Mark Antony's defeat at Actium. Things change, even attitudes. Gaius the madman, with a taste for female footwear and formative years spent among Eastern princelings in the household of Antony's daughter Antonia, may have been the first in Rome to realize those changes' full extent.

If only, like Augustus, he could have espoused abstemiousness, restraint in any aspect of his life. Then he might have survived. Instead he was consistently extravagant in his appetites, with an appetite for extravagance. Cassius Dio accuses him of spending more than three billion sesterces in the space of two years,[11] Seneca of blowing the annual tribute of three provinces (ten million sesterces) on a single dinner.[12] Such extravagance embarrassed the imperial treasury: lust for money was just one ground for his wayward killings. And his appetites ranged widely. According to the sources, he 'had not the slightest regard for chastity, either his own or anyone else's'. He opened a brothel in the palace. He married four times in quick succession: only his last wife, Caesonia, lacking beauty but sexually accomplished, leaves any imprint. He indulged incestuous passions for all three of his sisters (a common complaint against unpopular emperors, but one more closely associated with Gaius than others); his favourite sister, Drusilla, became the first woman of the imperial house to be deified. Though he expelled from the city Rome's most notorious male tarts, he himself was buggered by Valerius Catullus until the latter confessed himself worn out. The simple truth is that, in an amoral age, Gaius fucked with abandonment. Unlike Tiberius, he eschewed even the decency to shelter indecency from prying eyes on an island hideaway like Capri. Unlike Augustus, dissimulation was not among his faults. He cuckolded husbands at dinner-parties to which both husband and wife had been invited. The wife enjoyed in a neighbouring room, Gaius' post-coital small talk with his guests included a frank assessment of her charms and performance, her husband compelled to silent acquiescence in fear of his life.

In vain did Macro the Praetorian prefect remind him of the dignity of his office: within a year he had silenced Macro's carping. Ditto Silanus, the father of his short-lived first wife, Junia Claudilla: Gaius' father-in-law paid heavily for appearing to aspire to the role of *éminence grise*. There were token concessions. Like Tiberius before him, Gaius assimilated his portraiture to that of Augustus, as a bust in Copenhagen's Ny Carlsberg Glyptotek attests. Save a petulant pursing of the lips and a thickening of the nose – the latter possibly the result of heavy drinking – his features closely resemble those of the classicized, idealized imagery of his ageless forebear. Later he would insist that statues of the gods share his own Augustan physiognomy. Gaius evidently needed Augustus' reflected glory to underpin the legitimacy of his rule and explain the foundation of his divine pretensions: his official iconography merges his features with those of his great-grandfather. But he did not seek to emulate Augustus' record and translate visual comparisons into the spheres of policy-making or reputation. He resisted comparisons with the 'young Augustus' as a slur on his youth and inexperience.[13] From a distance, it looks like contrariness; it may have been laziness or lack of interest.

The full story of this unhappy hell-raiser and his maniacal abuse of power is not confined to Suetonius' famous assessment of a double career as emperor and monster. Quite as remarkably, it illustrates the durability of the Augustan settlement in the face of mental instability, murder and megalomania. In 37, the Romans took to their hearts a 'star', a 'chick', a 'babe', a 'nursling' – a young man whose whole life had been lived under the principate and in the shadow of family politics. Such terms of endearment did not remain long on the lips of the mob. Gaius was a cuckoo in the nest, a wolf in lamb's clothing: as Tiberius had predicted, a viper in Rome's bosom and brimful of poison; Phaeton destined to lose control of the sun-chariot and burn the entire Roman world. But his death was not the means of restoring the Republic. Instead, the last remaining adult male of his family inherited that ragbag of powers which Gaius had misused so spectacularly, the office stronger and more durable than the man.

Revisionist scholars choose to pity him; the ancients, memories still sharp, delve less deeply. Their primary focus is not cause but its spectacular effects. Suetonius buries Gaius beneath a highly flavoured millefeuille of gossip and scandal, layer upon layer of arid lust and senseless viciousness. His *Life* is punctuated by anecdotes and hearsay. It includes recollections from his own childhood of tidbits dropped by his grandfather, as if his grandfather's insights and his own memory of stories overheard in his earliest years merit the authority of the written word. Accomplished storytelling, it is questionable history and slapdash biography, even according to the ancients' nugatory estimation of life-writing as a genre. It did not arise by accident. Deconstructed, Suetonius' Gaius reveals himself as a composite of would-be didactic literary models and conventions: an ersatz Icarus hell-bent on flying too close to the sun, an unrepentant Prodigal Son; Lucifer glorying in his fall from grace; the degenerate sport of an exemplary father.

Fast forward two millennia, and Suetonius' victim has yet to escape. He never will. Gaius was a historical travesty: the 'Caligula' of the sources is a legend. He will survive as long as the abuse of power remains a human impulse, continually reinvented, like Cleopatra a convenient and enduring archetype; and as long as prurience revels in stories of excess which, just possibly, contain grains of truth. In his *Natural History*, Pliny the Elder recorded Gaius' enjoyment of bathing in perfumed oils; like the Cleopatra of Augustan propaganda, he dissolved pearls in vinegar and drank them; such was his passion for gold that, anticipating the princes of Renaissance Europe, he sponsored costly, fruitless experiments in the alchemy of base metals.[14] Unlike Suetonius' tone of high censoriousness, Pliny's list centres Gaius' predilections within a contemporary culture of sumptuous superfluity: his prodigality was distinctive but not remarkable, a failing of its time. Nor were its implications necessarily as serious as the sources suggest, since the evidence denies any serious financial crisis at the beginning of the next reign. Rationality is not enough. More often in the rumours recorded about this cruel and insolent despot, Gaius' historiography has permitted no excuses. He is condemned by the facts (such as they can be traced)... condemned alike by fictions.

His reign was brief: three years, ten months and eight days. Suetonius enumerates its duration as if marvelling at its continuance for so long. We too are right to be surprised: given the catalogue of atrocities attributed to Gaius, his survival in power for almost four years is unexpected. It suggests that much of what we accept as intrinsic to his story may be later accretions added by a hostile tradition, or events which occurred in private, unknown either to many senators or to the majority of Romans.

The emperor's death, as so often in the *Lives of the Caesars*, is presaged by portents. Phidias' statue of Jupiter at Olympia, on the brink of being dismantled and removed to Rome at Gaius' particular request, burst into peals of laughter. The room of Gaius' palace doorkeeper was struck by lightning, a meteorological outburst associated with the gods' displeasure and one of which the emperor himself was terrified, hiding under tables at its onset. Meanwhile Gaius bungled a sacrifice in the temple. Killing a flamingo, he splashed the bird's blood onto his clothes, priestly ham-fistedness traditionally a signifier of something adrift. For Suetonius, this otherworldly corroboration of Gaius' unfitness to govern is the ultimate vindication. It is also, unusually in the context of this account, surplus to the historian's requirements. Gaius had spared no effort to stockpile his offences against Rome. The result, by January 41, was an atmosphere of fear and loathing in which desperate men were prepared to embrace desperate measures. As Josephus has Gnaeus Sentius Saturninus tell an emergency meeting of the senate in the aftermath of regicide:

> this Gaius... hath brought more terrible calamities upon us than did all the rest [of the emperors], not only by exercising his ungoverned rage upon his fellow citizens, but also upon his kindred and friends, and alike upon all others, and by inflicting still greater miseries upon them, as punishments, which they never deserved, he being equally furious against men and against the gods.[15]

From the sources (with their senatorial sympathies) emerges a sense of a city worn out by the murderous caprices of its madman ruler, the gods alienated, nature in revolt: a kettle too close to boiling to require the tinder of the numinous.

But the twenty-eight-year-old Gaius was worn out, too. He slept only three hours a night. Even that rest was fitful and disturbed. Dark, disquieting dreams rent the stillness. He fell prey to night terrors. Unable – unwilling? – to linger in bed, he shifted about the palace, sitting or standing, sometimes quite still, his head thumping, prone to fainting. Along the marble colonnades with their view of the Forum and the slumbering city he trailed – like the figures of Julius Caesar and Calpurnia in Edward Poynter's 1883 painting *The Ides of March*, his eyes fixed on the sky and the distant horizon where the sun must rise. Sometimes he cried out, desperate for the dawn. All his cries were prayers that night would end. Little wonder that we read that his eyes and temples were hollow, his face naturally forbidding.

For an empire that never rested, an emperor unable to sleep. But while the empire's 6,000 miles of frontier were patrolled by legions and its provinces administered by an imperial bureaucracy which had evolved over time into a sequence of highly efficient government satellites, no one fully shared with Gaius the burdens of the purple. He would not have wished it. Yet it was an unrealistic weight to place on the shoulders of a man whose infirmities were not only mental but physical, and whose undignified enthusiasm for tragedians and circus performers outweighed his interest in the day-to-day business of imperial rule.

'The empire was not given to himself, but to his father Germanicus,' Seneca tartly observed of Gaius.[16] In March 37, it was a truth universally acknowledged. Gaius himself took no pains to disguise or deny the hereditary nature of his elevation. On the contrary, his consciousness of a distinction grounded in descent – indissoluble, impossible to gainsay – explains that conviction of unanswerability which characterizes much of his interpretation of the principate. He even sought to 'improve' his bloodline, preferring to erase the humbly born Agrippa, husband of his grandmother Julia the Elder, and instead to imagine his mother Agrippina as the daughter of an incestuous father–daughter relationship between Augustus and Julia.

Gaius Julius Caesar Germanicus, born on 31 August AD 12, was the youngest surviving son of Germanicus Caesar and Agrippina the Elder. He was thus a great-grandson through the paternal line of Mark Antony, Livia and the latter's first husband Tiberius Claudius Nero and, through his mother, of Augustus himself. This heavyweight inheritance would prove a highly charged genetic amalgam. It conferred on Gaius Julio-Claudian ancestry and proximity to divinity. Embracing both victor and victim of Actium, it facilitated scattershot loyalties on the part of a young man determined to cherry-pick only those aspects of Augustus' Roman revolution which suited him.

But Gaius' heredity was more than a tracery of bloodlines, a painted stemma on the walls of the family atrium. His inheritance encompassed heroism and villainy, Empire-wide acclaim, the loyalty of Rome's armed forces, and deep wellsprings of popular sentiment which his mother had taken pains to manipulate in her children's favour. In Roman minds, the melding of aristocratic clans predisposed Gaius to a sequence of inherited traits: Julian swagger and even genius; the cruelty, hauteur and distinction of the Claudians; Mark Antony's feckless prodigality; the amiability of Germanicus. So richly scented a brew ought to have stimulated reflection. Seneca, we have seen, placed the emphasis on Germanicus. That and, we can add, the absence of any alternative candidate from within the imperial family.

We know Germanicus' story. Consul at twenty-six, he had been a distinguished military commander whose popularity surpassed that of his uncle Tiberius. A probable candidate for *princeps*, he campaigned successfully in Pannonia and Dalmatia and on the Rhine, earning comparisons from Tacitus with Alexander the Great. In Germany, the infant Gaius shared in his father's renown. Dressed by his mother in a tiny soldier's uniform, he became an unofficial legionary mascot and on one occasion helped prevent revolt in the ranks. It was the troops who called him 'Caligula', 'Little Boots', in reference to his miniature soldier's boots. The incident of the mutiny in 14, like the soldier's pet name (which he himself hated), has entered the emperor's mythology, though he himself can hardly have remembered it. What adhered was the affection of the military. In 19, it was not enough to save Germanicus. As we have seen, he was probably poisoned by Piso in Syria on the instructions of Tiberius, who afterwards stayed away from his funeral. His grieving widow certainly thought so. Agrippina understood enough of the world to exploit family tragedy for subsequent advancement. The principal beneficiary of her plotting, which brought about her own death and that of her two elder sons, was her smallest chick, Gaius.

In the third quarter of the eighteenth century, at the request of the archbishop of York, a Pennsylvania-born history painter trained his sights on Agrippina. *The Landing of Agrippina at Brundisium with the Ashes of Germanicus* occupied Benjamin West for several years. At the cleric's request it was inspired by a passage from Tacitus' *Annals*:

Agrippina… worn out though she was with sorrow and bodily weakness, yet still impatient of everything which might delay her vengeance, embarked with the ashes of Germanicus and her children, pitied by all. Here indeed was a woman of the highest nobility.[17]

In keeping with contemporary ideas of the dignity of history painting, West depicted a scene of noble pathos. Dressed in white, her head covered and bowed, Agrippina cradles her husband's remains. She is surrounded by the survivors of the couple's nine children – the same children who, two years earlier, had ridden in Germanicus' chariot in his triumph over the Germans[18] – and by a supporting cast of mourning Romans. Centre-stage, the objects of popular adulation, Germanicus' sons and daughters could not be expected to resist inflated perceptions of either their misfortune or their public significance.* From Brundisium the party travelled to Rome. The seven-year-old Gaius attended his mother in her triumphal progress, her pilgrimage of reversal and revenge.

As it happened, Agrippina was not so noble that she was not prepared to stage-manage pity to attain that vengeance and, in doing so, to make herself such a thorn in Tiberius' side that the emperor banished her to Pandateria, site of her mother Julia's exile. She died there in 33, four years before Tiberius, after an unsuccessful attempt to starve herself to death which resulted in force-feeding and a beating so severe that she lost an eye. It was a dismal, gut-wrenching, inhuman end, which nevertheless assured her the commendation of a historical tradition otherwise opposed to the petticoats aspect of Julio-Claudian government. Taken in conjunction with Germanicus' murder, and the arrests of Gaius' elder brothers Nero Caesar

---

* Five years later, West returned to the plight of Agrippina and her children in the more overtly sentimental *Agrippina and her Children Mourning over the Ashes of Germanicus*. In this image it is the liveliness and cherubic good health of the couple's younger children, who again occupy the painting's central space, which highlight the suffering of their drooping, milk-skinned mother.

and Drusus Caesar, both of whom were also starved to death (Drusus after having been reduced to eating the stuffing of his bed), it amounts to a family inheritance decidedly less enviable than Seneca may lead us to assume. In the atmosphere of rank suspicion which characterized Tiberius' court, Gaius' crowd-pleasing paternity was as much curse as blessing.

From tragedy, pragmatism. Gaius was nineteen when he was summoned to Capri. His grandmother Antonia promoted the move, her intention to safeguard him from Sejanus' evil attentions. There he schooled himself in emotional costiveness, a stranger to complaint, 'ignoring the ruin of his kindred as if nothing at all had happened, passing over his own ill-treatment with an incredible pretence of indifference,' as Suetonius relates. Afraid to react publicly to the misfortunes of his family, Gaius adopted a policy of stupefying self-control every bit as calculated as the ageing emperor's wiles. Following Tiberius' death, he made a correct assessment of the propaganda value of the memory of Germanicus, Agrippina and their depleted brood. Reprising the laudable emotionalism of Agrippina's act of homage as recorded by West, he travelled to Pandateria and Pontia to reclaim the remains of his mother and his brother Nero (no traces of Drusus' body could be identified). He purposely chose a period of stormy weather, harnessing nature's spring-time histrionics to his tableaux of elemental grief. In Rome, claiming that he had transferred the ashes to new urns with his own hands, he interred them with great solemnity in the Mausoleum of Augustus. It was a process of denying Tiberius. Gaius chose not to position himself within the newly emergent continuum of Rome's emperors, but in a specifically dynastic context: the heir to the divine blood of Augustus through a family notable for its greatness. In elevating, and justifying, this dynastic element of the principate – in its explicitness something new in Rome – he both legitimized his own rule and sanitized his accession (which had, after all, been willed by Tiberius). He also laid down problems for the future, among them the claim to the throne of Lucius Domitius Ahenobarbus, afterwards known as Nero, a grandson of Germanicus able like Gaius to invoke a family history of grandeur and tragedy.

In July 37, the mint at Lugdunum (modern Lyons) received instructions about the new reign's coinage. On the obverse sides of the coins, a portrait of Gaius. Three reverse types included a head of Germanicus, the relationship of father and son explained in the surrounding inscription; a bust of Agrippina the Elder, ditto; and a radiate head of Augustus bearing the legend 'The Divine Augustus, Father of his Country'. At the mint in Caesarea, this tendency was more explicit: one design featured Germanicus on both sides of the coin, another Germanicus on the obverse, Augustus on the reverse, Gaius in both cases unglimpsed.[19]

The implications were clear. In his coinage as in his official iconography and his public religious observances, Gaius extolled his distinguished ancestry. In celebrating those qualities to which he laid claim as child and great-grandchild, he appealed directly to that affection for Germanicus, Agrippina and Augustus which persisted across the Empire. He also aligned himself with Augustus' divinity. It was a statement of belonging on the part of a man who, save a quaestorship in 33, was a stranger to the *cursus honorum* as well as to military experience and achievement. The support of the armed forces, associated with Gaius' family since the time of Julius, was summoned through the memory of Germanicus, cherished as a soldier cut off in his prime by an associate of the hated Tiberius. Gaius' numismatic exploitation of his father's memory is a further refutation of Tiberius and his one-time henchman Sejanus, alloy-based legerdemain linking the new emperor directly with Augustus by a process of elision. It was the same impulse which, six months into his reign, inspired him to dedicate the new Temple of Augustus in the Forum. After twenty-three years, Tiberius may or may not have completed construction of the temple which the senate had voted the deified Augustus on his death. Gaius' two-day ceremony included a choir of aristocratic children, 800 lions and bears slaughtered, horse-races and a banquet for senators and their wives. In bricks and mortar prominent in the heart of Rome, it associated the new emperor with his most illustrious forebear. The Roman equivalent of a commemorative tea-towel, coins issued by the mint bore an image of a large-headed Gaius in front of the temple sacrificing a bull. On the reverse, appropriately, sat a veiled personification of Piety.

As always, the inescapable hand of the past took as much as it gave. Gaius inherited from his father the ungainly combination of a long body and long, thin legs. A programme of vigorous riding had countered this unwieldiness in Germanicus' case, spindle-shanks less obvious than the aura of martial heroism. We do not read of the conceited Gaius exercising. So promising at the outset, his inheritance could have transcended physicalities. The life he led undermined a body already weak and wrought havoc with a mind besieged by demons. If the sources approximate truth, the ingredients of his downfall would challenge the strongest constitution: excessive alcohol, lack of sleep, an addiction to sex and a seeming determination to steel himself against every compassionate or feeling impulse. Voyeuristic in his sadism, compulsive in his need to view mental and physical torture at close quarters (the spectator now, as once in Tiberius' palace on Capri his unnatural self-control had provided the spectacle), he was the author of his own demise. At such a remove in time, the extent of his mental weakness cannot be estimated. The Alexandrian Jewish philosopher Philo, in a first-hand account of Gaius' behaviour, indicates caprice and unpredictability but not madness, and attributes these weaknesses to an illness in October 37 brought about by 'a life of luxury': 'heavy drinking and a taste for delicacies, an appetite insatiable even on a swollen stomach, hot baths at the wrong time, emetics followed immediately by further drinking and the gluttony which goes with it, indecent behaviour with boys and women.'[20] It hardly matters whether we second Philo – or prefer Suetonius' more egregiously lascivious explanation (which fails to take account of the reign's chronology) that the trouble began with a mind-altering aphrodisiac administered by Gaius' promiscuous fourth wife Caesonia.

For a twelve-month period at the beginning of his reign, Gaius issued one of the most famous coins of Roman imperial history. It was a bronze sesterce bearing images on the reverse of his three sisters, Agrippina, Drusilla and Julia Livilla. The standing female figures personified a trio of those abstract qualities which the Roman mindset – pagan, superstitious, earnest in its religiosity but robustly practical – invested with significance: Securitas, Concordia and Fortuna. It was the first appearance on Roman coinage of identifiable (and identified) living female figures, a distinction denied even to Livia, but the coin did not survive Drusilla's death in 38. In inspiration it celebrated that bounty with which the apparently malleable Gaius of the first months of the reign wished to endow Rome: security, harmony and fortune. That aspiration did not survive its year-long currency.

None of these qualities characterizes Gaius' legacy. From disharmony arose his murder. The loss of any sense of security in Rome created that atmosphere of fear in which conspiracies flourished. (Gaius also took measures to ensure that senators actively feared him.) His greedy possessiveness about the blessings of fortune expressed his monarchical outlook, token of his belief in the *princeps'* special position above that of the loftiest Roman noble. Quickly, a coin which had once extolled the virtues of the emperor's exemplary family and broadcast his good intentions in three dimensions acquired a grim irony. Conditions changed in the course of Gaius' reign, including relationships within the imperial family. By the end of 39, with Drusilla already dead, Gaius banished Agrippina and Julia Livilla. In their wake, security, harmony and fortune departed too.

The ideological vacuum created by the overthrow of traditional virtues provided fertile soil for the emergence of Gaius' demonic mythology. Much of what we read may be true. Some of it is probably imaginative scaremongering on the part of writers determined to blacken his memory beyond redemption. But all of it has on occasion been regarded as the truth. That Gaius' life survives in the manner it does in the ancients' telling – a quasi-veracity dense with caliginous anecdote – is connected to that climate of profound unease which provided the backdrop for his particular theatre of the macabre.

Was it true that he commended a tortured actor for the euphoniousness of his screams? Did he really lessen the food bill of wild beasts in the circus by feeding them prisoners in place of butcher's meat? What prompted Gaius to insist that a father witness the execution of his son, or that Publius Afranius Potitius, the senator who in October 37 had offered to die so long as Gaius recover from his illness, make good that promise and commit suicide? Was he serious in suggesting the consulship for his favourite horse, Incitatus, or was his intention another joke at the senate's expense? Did he laugh or wince after ordering the executioner to chop off the hands of a slave caught stealing and to hang the severed body parts around the slave's neck as he remained in attendance at the party? Again, at one level it scarcely matters. These are merely brushstrokes in the broader depiction of Gaius' reign, an imagery in which he himself, wittingly or otherwise, was complicit.

———

It was early in 39 when Gaius made a speech to the senate which, with good reason, unnerved Rome's upper classes. He did not claim authorship for himself, but attributed it to Tiberius:

> Show no affection for any of them and spare none of them. For they all hate you and they all pray for your death; and they will murder you if they can. Do not stop to consider, then, what acts of yours will please them nor mind it if they talk, but look solely to your own pleasure and safety, since that has the most just claim.[21]

The emperor had lately been reading papers relating to treason trials of the previous reign. These were the same papers which, in 37, abolishing the charge of *maiestas* to widespread relief, Gaius had promised to destroy unread. Perhaps their destruction would have served both emperor and senate better. For the papers related to Tiberius' treatment of Gaius' mother Agrippina and his brothers Nero and Drusus. Their revelations startled and enraged him. On the evidence they contained he saw that

Tiberius had been forced to condemn Agrippina and her sons as conspirators. Some of that evidence was contributed by men who continued to frequent the senate. They were the same men who, for the last two years, had added their voices to the chorus of praise with which a craven senate habitually greeted Gaius' actions and innovations. For a moment, the world jolted on its axis. For so long Gaius had been accustomed to consider Tiberius the architect of his family's downfall. Too late he recognized the distribution of blame. To a stunned senate house, Gaius made plain his discovery and his deliberations. Then, chillingly, he quoted what he claimed were Tiberius' own words to him on senatorial duplicity and dislike. He ended with what, in Dio's account, is a classically Tiberian statement of nihilistic menace: 'For no man living is ruled of his own free will; only so long as a person is afraid does he pay court to the man who is stronger.'[22] The same day, determined to inspire unease, he restored treason trials to the Roman statute books.

The senate's response – to vote annual sacrifices to Gaius and formalize veneration of the emperor's cult – failed to impress. As the senators had deceived Tiberius, so they would deceive Gaius too. He was aware already of rumoured conspiracy. Before the year was out, he would act on just such a hunch, adding to the death toll among Rome's aristocracy.

It was not a case of groundless paranoia. Nor is this its significance. The revelations of those 'burnt' papers drove a wedge between Gaius and the senate. They convinced him of the rightness of a policy which discounted senatorial consultation in favour of monarchical government by himself and a chosen coterie of personal advisers, including an influential freedman called Kallistos. And so an irony is revealed. Regret for the political influence it had enjoyed under the Republic encouraged the senate to flatter the *princeps* in order to maintain those vestiges of power it retained (and perhaps build on that platform in an attempt to regroup). In doing so, it succeeded only in further undermining its position by revealing a querulous cowardice which proved to Gaius his good sense in mistrusting so debased a body of men and discounting their counsels in favour of friends and former slaves.

For his part, Gaius emerges from the sources as determined to stamp out opposition wherever it raised its head. From now on, the focus of his principate was absolutism: an urgent need to retain his throne, enforce submission and further elevate his own position by an unrelenting emphasis on his divinity. It was a high-risk strategy both at home and abroad. In Judaea, for example, his insistence that a cult statue of himself be erected in the temple in Jerusalem brought the Jewish world close to conflagration. Although Gaius' advisers included anti-Semitic Alexandrian freedmen, his policy was only partly mischievous: the Empire must accept his godliness. (Eventually Gaius softened his line towards the Jews, concluding that they were 'sadly misguided rather than wicked; and foolish in refusing to believe that I have got the nature of a god'.[23])

His actions had acquired a symbolic dimension. He devised what Suetonius describes as 'a novel and unheard-of kind of pageant'. Across the three-mile span of the bay at Baiae he created a floating temporary 'bridge', a costly and impressive feat of engineering. It was in fact a pontoon of boats and ships in two lines, closely anchored and supporting a dirt track 'fashioned in the manner of the Appian Way'. Gaius rode across it, dressed in the breastplate of that legendary absolutist, Alexander the Great. On the following day, for the diversion of spectators who included delegates from Parthia, he raced a chariot across his sea-borne bridge. He was followed by friendly attendants and the entire Praetorian Guard.

Unsurprisingly, this puzzling and unique set piece of Roman public theatre – in which, with that easygoing brutality which is such a part of Gaius' principate, spectators lost their lives after drunkenly falling into the sea from their vantage-points on surrounding hills and cliffs – did little to diminish the emperor's *folie de grandeur*. Instead, it may have steeled his hand to undertake the only military campaign of his reign, a 'joke' in Tacitus' assessment, played out along the banks of the Rhine.

In the autumn of 39, Gaius left Italy to cross the Alps. Although he travelled in an enormous and luxurious convoy, carried in a litter with eight bearers and followed by Praetorians, his progress was rapid. For his purpose was not principally, as Suetonius tells us, the recruitment of additional Batavian warriors for his German guard, nor, as Dio suggests, the need to shore up a bankrupt treasury with plunder from Spain and Gaul, but the quashing of a conspiracy which Gaius could not ignore.

Travelling with the emperor were his sisters, Agrippina and Julia Livilla, and Drusilla's widower Lepidus. Their first destination was Upper Germany, where, by the end of October, Gaius had executed the imperial legate, Lentulus Gaetulicus, on suspicion of treason. Although the facts are confused, Gaetulicus was probably suspected of plotting to assassinate Gaius and replace him with Lepidus, at that point Gaius' most likely heir. Inevitably, Lepidus too paid for this disloyalty with his life (in his case, he was charged with adultery with his sisters-in-law rather than direct involvement in scheming to become Rome's fifth Caesar). Agrippina and Julia Livilla were commanded to accompany Lepidus' remains back to Rome – presumably an intentional parody of the elder Agrippina's triumphal progress from Brundisium – before being sent into exile, their possessions auctioned by Gaius to the highest bidders. Meanwhile Gaius, largely idle with the quarter-of-a-million troops he had assembled around him, staged a sequence of imaginary 'raids' across the Rhine, posting his own men as 'enemies', then chasing and capturing them. He accepted the senate's congratulations on these warlike antics and seven acclamations by the troops as *imperator*. The timely defection to the Romans that autumn of a British prince called Amminus enabled Gaius to claim that he had conquered the inhospitable island during this northern progress, an achievement for which he was rewarded with the name 'Britannicus'. In an act of future significance, he appointed as Gaetulicus' replacement in Upper Germany a hatchet-faced grandee called Servius Sulpicius Galba.

Gaius spent the autumn in Lugdunum, gambling and money-grubbing. Restored, bored or perhaps simply reluctant to return to Rome, he then embarked on an escapade which sealed beyond recall his reputation for madness and folly. The 'invasion' of Britain did not progress further than the southern shores of the English Channel. Instead, with his soldiers lined up on the beach, Gaius ordered them to fire their catapults into the ocean and gather seashells as the spoils of their victory. It is a much-debated incident, which appears to embody Suetonius' taunt of extreme assurance and excessive timidness. Whether the soldiers in fact refused to embark for Britain, and Gaius instructed them to fill their helmets with shells as a reprimand for cowardice, we cannot know. Suffice to say that his reputation no longer permitted any benefit of the doubt.

The senate… Lepidus… Agrippina… Julia Livilla… and now, perhaps, those troops who had always adhered to the family of Germanicus: Gaius' isolation was growing. That bronze sesterce on which the emperor's sisters masqueraded as Security, Harmony and Fortune had already been discarded by the mint. But it was not only Rome which was denied their benison.

Despite his bluster and bravado, Gaius himself was reaching a position where it was clear that he too had forsaken all.

———

In the end, after a flurry of senatorial executions and escalating uncertainty among all classes across the capital, assassination from within palace ranks. Gaius had been foolish to taunt Cassius Chaerea, tribune of the Praetorian Guard, with effeminacy. Had the emperor, in his godly role-play, overlooked the goddess Roma herself? Perhaps then, as much of his behaviour suggests, he had not been sufficiently mindful of *virtus*, that Roman definition of manliness in the form of man's ideal behaviour whose cult image exactly matched that of Roma herself. Once, *virtus* had been Romans' defining quality. Cicero described it as 'the badge of the Roman race and breed':[24] a prohibition against male submission, the bar to Roman troops' surrender even in the face of certain defeat. Granted, the bulkily masculine Chaerea, with a distinguished service record behind him, spoke in high, lisping tones. But he cannot have relished being called 'Lassie' by an emperor so conspicuously his inferior in *virtus*, nor the obscene gestures Gaius made in full view of Chaerea's men when the latter kissed his hand in obeisance. His disaffection smouldered and finally boiled over into hatred. When Gaius was murdered on 24 January 41, in a covered passage leading from the theatre to the palace, Chaerea swung the first blow. His co-conspirators included his fellow Praetorian tribunes Sextus Papinius and Cornelius Sabinus and Praetorian prefect Marcus Arrecinus Clemens. Gaius' own principal response, despite the years of suspicion, was surprise. His wife and daughter died at the same time, the blood-smattered Caesonia in one account boldly extending her neck to the assassin's blade.[25] A common soldier dispatched the infant Julia Drusilla. With an utter brutality well matched to Gaius', he dashed out her brains against a wall.

<hr />

No ease could be expected of so violent a death. In the Lamian Gardens, high on the Esquiline Hill close to the Gardens of Maecenas, Gaius' troubled spirit haunted Rome's early-spring nights.

The gardens were imperial property, given to Tiberius by Lucius Aemilius Lamia, legionary commander, imperial legate and city prefect. Former cavalry officers, the Lamiae were among those who had benefited from the principate. Raised to the senate by Augustus, the family earned at least two consulships, one under Augustus himself, a second, suffect appointment under Domitian. In January 41, their name was again synonymous with loyalty.

Secretly, stealthily, the mangled remnants of Gaius' body had been transported across the city to this hilltop refuge. A pyre was quickly improvised and the body partly burned. Charred remains were interred in a shallow grave. As in life, Gaius battled restlessness. The gardens' caretakers, Suetonius tells us, soon became familiar with the sight of his ghost.

He might never have found peace were it not for his sisters Agrippina and Julia Livilla. Returning from exile in the aftermath of Gaius' death, they oversaw the body's removal, cremation and appropriate burial. It was a remarkable act on the part of women once banished by a brother lost to all claims of love and faithfulness. But Agrippina the Younger was indeed a remarkable woman. In 41 she was not finished with Rome's emperors. As we will see, her own fate would prove no happier than that of her tyrannous, misguided brother.

CLAUDIUS

(10 BC–AD 54)

'Remarkable freak of fortune'

CLAVDIVS, Lugduni in Gallijs natus. Imperauit ann.XIII. mens VIII. di.XX. sedente Petro, ueneno sublatus an.Chr. LIV.

Historian turned history-maker, Claudius struggled with speech but wrote Greek with cumbersome prolixity. With the voice of a sea creature, throaty and raucous, he was virtually unintelligible, Seneca claimed; Pliny the Elder counted him among the hundred most scholarly authors of the day. Disgraced by 'a horrible habit under the stress of anger of slobbering at the mouth and running at the nose, a stammer, and a persistent nervous tic', Claudius devoted the wastelands of his youth, when Rome ignored him, to an activity which took no account of his physical shortcomings and which Dio praises as suitable training for the principate: writing history. (He also devoted his time to taverns and tarts.) A scion of the imperial house, his tutors were appropriately eminent: Livy and Sulpicius Flavus. He possessed from birth an exceptional memory, from exceptional circumstances the time and leisure for solitary study. The result was twenty volumes on the history of Etruria, homeland of his first wife Plautia Urgulanilla (granddaughter of a confidante of Livia); an account of the old enemy Carthage written in eight volumes; and forty-three volumes in Latin devoted to the recent history of Rome, with tactful omissions concerning the civil war, the Proscriptions and the roots of Augustus' settlement. (This last was read by Tacitus.) More remarkably, this limping master of 'feeble and far-fetched jokes'

spun out his autobiography to eight volumes. Length took no account of paucity of incident. His contemporaries rubbished the undertaking for its poor taste.

Pedant and thinker, while harvests failed, the emperor Claudius spearheaded the introduction of three new letters to the Roman alphabet (two corresponded to the modern letters W and Y); it was a short-term innovation which did not survive him. Like so many in his high-living family in this period of excess, he was lustful, gluttonous and hard-drinking, 'impatient of celibacy', driven to a point of bodily suffering by the need to satisfy urges that were in equal measure libidinous and greedy. (So extreme were the attacks of heartburn which succeeded his overindulgence that he confessed to having considered suicide frequently.) More than sex and alcohol, his passion was the schoolmaster's weakness for instruction. He bombarded Romans with pithy edicts on subjects from grape harvests to cures for snakebites (the sap of yew trees, apparently): his proposals included a decision to legitimize farting at dinner-parties, after he heard about a man who had endangered his health by attempting to restrain himself. Despite the public readings of his books sponsored during his reign, his only written work to gain wide circulation was a treatise on dicing. It hardly mattered. Despite Gaius' posturing with wig or caduceus, the 'Clau-Clau-Claudius' of Robert Graves's popular fictions was to become the first of Rome's Caesars who was openly worshipped in his own lifetime. This 'monster whom Mother Nature had begun to work upon but then flung aside' (his mother's disillusioned assessment) alone among his siblings became a living god.

His Cinderella story includes, famously, his discovery by soldiers behind a curtain and subsequent acclamation as emperor; in the conquest of Britain in 43, completing what Julius Caesar had begun, shaking head and buckling knees did not prevent his appearance at Camulodunum (Colchester) in the guise of conqueror mounted on an elephant. Indeed, this physical wreck, dismissed by one doctor as 'a very battleground of diseases', would allow the troops to salute him in the manner of a victorious general as *imperator* no fewer than twenty-seven times; in his role of *princeps*, by contrast, he accepted only the titles 'Augustus' and 'Caesar' and never became officially *imperator* of Rome. 'He possessed majesty and dignity of appearance,' Suetonius allows, 'but only when he was standing still or sitting, and especially when he was lying down.' Among surviving portraits is a statue of a seated Claudius discovered in the theatre of the Etruscan city of Caere, today housed in Rome's Vatican Museums. The greater part of that image consists of an improbably muscular torso worthy of the *Ignudi* of Michelangelo. The emperor compelled to immobility was a novel form of heroism.

'When [Claudius'] sister Livilla heard that he would one day be emperor, she openly and loudly prayed that the Roman people might be spared so cruel and undeserved a fortune.' It is a sibling reaction typical of that dysfunctionalism engendered in Augustus' heirs by the scramble for power. (Livilla may have coveted the throne for her husband, Marcus Vinicius, or her own sons.) As it happened, misfortune was not the lot of the sixty million inhabitants of Claudius' empire. His victims were senators and, in particular, knights. Some thirty-five of the former and as many as three hundred of the latter received death penalties during the thirteen years of his reign. ('This man, my lords, who looks as though he could not hurt a fly, used to chop off heads as a dog sits down,' as Augustus laments in Seneca's satirical *Apocolocyntosis*, 'The Pumpkinification of Claudius'.) It was the latest chapter of post-Republican Rome's tortuous dialogue between senate and Palatine, which only Augustus had arbitrated with consistent success and which Claudius, moving ineluctably towards military-backed absolutism, failed to resolve.

Despite the misgivings shared by the senate and his family, Claudius governed with conscientiousness and a degree of wisdom for much of his reign. Characteristically, Suetonius accuses him of lack of moderation in his passion for women: he applied the same wholeheartedness to the business of empire, working 'even on his own anniversaries and those of his family, and sometimes even on festivals of ancient date and days of ill-omen'. He completed the annexation of Britain; he extended and overhauled membership of the senate, in 47 invoking the ancient office of censor to do so and cudgelling Rome's conservative upper classes into accepting colleagues from the provinces, specifically Gallia Comata; he improved the lot of the ordinary Roman by building a harbour at Ostia to ensure the safe arrival of the imported grain supply and prevent food shortages, as well as by completing two new aqueducts, the Aqua Claudia and the Aqua Anio Novus, at a cost estimated by Pliny the Elder at 350 million sesterces: together they supplied almost half the city's drinking water. In his coin issues he celebrated a virtue that was both inarguable and uncontentious: Constantia, personifying the steadfastness, persistence and perseverance of the emperor. It was a suitably unshowy claim on the part of a man whose political experience prior to 41 was virtually non-existent and who, despite the notable careers of his father Drusus and his brother Germanicus, lacked military experience entirely. 'By dulling the blade of tyranny, I reconciled Rome to the monarchy,' claims Graves's Claudius in *Claudius the God*. It was only partly true. (Certainly, in entrusting tasks to imperial freedmen, Claudius spared himself some of the opprobrium of unpopular decision-making.) With greater trust in the legions which had made him *princeps* than in the senators who had hesitated to confirm their *fait accompli*, Claudius treated Rome's political classes with traditional respect. Like all his immediate predecessors, he denied them the means of effective dissent.

━━━◦◦◦◦━━━

In the absence of the relevant passages of Tacitus' *Annals*, and in light of question marks over the surviving version of Dio's account and the loss of lives of Claudius by Pliny the Elder, Fabius Rusticus and Cluvius Rufus, Suetonius bequeaths us the only full-length account of Claudius' life to survive from antiquity.[1] Its enjoyment ought not to preclude a degree of cautious scepticism on the reader's part. For in one of his more richly coloured biographies, Suetonius presents that series of apparent contradictions which, taken in aggregate, have contributed to Claudius' historiographical reputation as a 'problem' emperor, his legacy ambiguous, ripe for just the sort of red-top sensationalism which adds piquancy to Graves's novels and their subsequent televisation. Suetonius' fifth Caesar combines physical frailty with academic rigour, timidity with barbarous cruelty, clear thinking with overwhelming susceptibility to the self-interest of unofficial close advisers, notably his wives and freedmen. Both his strengths and his weaknesses are strident. He inspires conflicting responses: more than inconsistent, he appears to be compounded of irreconcilables. Early studiousness prior to the throne later gives way to buffoonery; physical infirmities regulated by high office, he apparently jettisons aspects of right thinking.

His ascent to the purple, a case of the swish of the curtain, is one of the best-known vignettes of the layman's Rome, more dramatic than convincing. In 1871, it inspired an equally well-known painting, *A Roman Emperor, AD 41*, by Dutch-born classical painter Lawrence Alma-Tadema. Alma-Tadema painted pot-boilers. His large-scale snapshots of Roman life and history enjoyed immense popularity and were acclaimed in the artist's lifetime for the accuracy of their archaeological details. In *A Roman Emperor, AD 41*, it is the narrative, not the decorative impulse, which predominates. An old and ugly Claudius cowers behind a curtain, where he is discovered by a soldier. We join the scene at the moment the centurion draws back the heavily fringed drapery to expose Gaius' grim-faced uncle to the obeisance of a motley crowd of soldiers and court beauties. Claudius is revealed half in shadow, right of centre. Occupying the centre of the painting are a mound of richly draped dead bodies and a marble herm, its base suggestively stained with crimson handprints. The painting contains a single image typical of Roman heroism: the dignified profile of the herm.[2] It also offers a potent riposte to the legend of 'innocent' serendipity surrounding Claudius' accession. To seize his destiny, the unprepossessing Claudius must step over those ornamental corpses. He must also overcome that fear which contorts his face – surely born of a sense of his own unworthiness which, in Alma-Tadema's image, the viewer shares.

But *A Roman Emperor, AD 41* was not Alma-Tadema's only depiction of Claudius' transition to pre-eminence. Four years earlier he had painted *Proclaiming Claudius Emperor*. In this earlier, quite different image, the composition is inspired by paintings of the Annunciation by Fra Angelico, Filippino Lippi and Botticelli. A youthful Claudius kneels in supplication before a bowing soldier, begging for his life. Other soldiers look on, their faces rapt with joy. The painting depicts the prequel to an unambiguously happy ending, the moment Claudius emerges from his curtained hiding-place to a brighter destiny. In both compositional and symbolic terms, Claudius occupies the Virgin Mary's place. Inscribed on the frame of Botticelli's Annunciation were words from St Luke's Gospel: 'The Holy Ghost shall come upon thee, and the power of the Highest shall overshadow thee.' In this first image of Claudius, Alma-Tadema draws on the visual language of good and evil, blessings (in the form of benefactions promised by the youthful figure of Claudius) following the curse of Gaius' short reign. It was an historical inaccuracy, of course, and not without melodrama and a heavy dollop of sentiment. More than this, *Proclaiming Claudius Emperor* cannot be reconciled with the painter's later revisiting of the same scene. Unable to negotiate the contradictions of Suetonius' Claudius, a Victorian crowd-pleaser offered the gallery-visiting public both sides of the story, verdicts wholly at variance.

Claudius ought to have been born for distinction. In the first instance, that role fell to his brother Germanicus, in time soldier and popular hero. His father Drusus, Livia's younger son, was a favourite of Augustus and also of the senate for the reason that 'he made no secret of his intention of restoring the old-time form of government, whenever he should have the power'; Augustus asked the gods to make Gaius and Lucius Caesar resemble Drusus. But Drusus died in 9 BC, the year after the birth of his youngest child, Tiberius Claudius Nero, known as Claudius. In place of power, he had to make do with posthumous glory, while the fortunes of his immediate family, lacking any trace of Julian blood, were overshadowed for the next decade and a half by the careers of Tiberius and the sons of Julia and Agrippa. Claudius' mother was Antonia, daughter of Mark Antony and Augustus' sister Octavia, a woman of irreproachable reputation whom we have witnessed intervene with Tiberius on behalf of Claudius' nephew Gaius and, in doing so, play her part in the inception of that troubled psychopath's premiership, not to mention Sejanus' downfall; Antonia successfully resisted Augustus' pressure to remarry after Drusus' death. Claudius inherited from his family a share in the popularity of Drusus and Germanicus, which extended to a predisposition in his favour on the part of Rome's legions independent of his own lack of military prowess. By contrast, his record as emperor demonstrates little of Drusus' overt Republicanism, while his private life falls short of Antonia's faithful vigil.

Almost from birth, Claudius 'suffered so severely from various obstinate disorders that the vigour of both his mind and his body was dulled'. Suetonius' description has troubled successive generations of readers, who have diagnosed Claudius' complaint variously as congenital cerebral paralysis, prenatal encephalitis, multiple sclerosis, meningitis and poliomyelitis;[3] his most recent biographer suggests a nervous disorder called dystonia.[4] Crucially, despite Claudius' tottering walk, the single foot he may have dragged behind him, and his difficulties in off-the-cuff speech with its attendant spluttering and drooling, the sources do not indicate physical deformities: it is a mistake to envisage an unnuanced portrait which conflates this skilful administrator and enthusiastic fornicator with images of Quasimodo or the Richard III of Shakespearean amateur dramatics. The ancients may have accorded significance to the circumstances of his birth: as Drusus dedicated an altar to Divus Augustus in Lugdunum, the first of its kind in Gaul, a Sicilian slave disguised as a waiter produced a dagger and flourished it behind his neck. Terror jolted Antonia into premature labour. She appears never to have warmed to this child born of a moment of fear. First fears may also have impacted on Claudius: as emperor his terror of assassination and conspiracy was sufficiently acute to turn his thoughts on occasion to abdication.

To Claudius' grandmother Livia Augustus wrote:

> The crux of the matter is (how best to put this?) whether he has full command of his faculties. If he is going to be physically or mentally handicapped, he (and therefore we) might easily become a laughing stock. There are going to be constant problems if we have to keep deciding if he can officiate here, or carry out duties there. What we need to decide is whether he is basically competent to perform in a public capacity.[5]

Careful in deliberation, that propagandist emperor would answer his own question. In AD 12, acting jointly with Tiberius, Augustus decided to exclude Claudius categorically from Roman public life. Given the limited significance both men later accorded Claudius in their wills and Tiberius' refusal of Claudius' request for a magistracy in 14, it was evidently not a decision of which either repented. (Augustus' prohibition extended to portraiture: in portrait schemes like the reliefs of the Ara Pacis Augustae, Claudius is a shadowy presence, sketched in whispers in the background, present only to avoid the conspicuousness of absence.) For longer than usual Claudius remained in his mother's house, under the tutelage of a brutish guardian, a one-time mule-train commander, who abused him physically. If we accept Suetonius' claim that the latter's 'express purpose' was to '[punish] him with all possible severity for any cause whatever', that programmatic bullying proceeded with Antonia's consent. Such unmaternal harshness was a family-wide policy: 'His grandmother [Livia] always treated him with the utmost contempt, very rarely speaking to him.' She admonished him in short, loveless missives, or, more impersonally, through messengers. In a further act of indignity, Claudius' coming-of-age ceremony, the public donning of the *toga virilis*, happened in clandestine fashion under cloak of darkness with minimal trappings. It is little wonder that the object of this hole-in-the-corner indifference should immerse himself so thoroughly in the alternative reality of historical research. On Claudius' part, it was an acknowledgement of defeat and a retirement from the political mêlée which rejected him; both served him well. The illusion of incapacity insulated him against conspiracy. Following Germanicus' death in 19, Claudius appears to have successfully avoided declaring any public allegiance during the lengthy and dangerous antagonism between Tiberius and his sister-in-law Agrippina: he is unlikely to have been canvassed for his opinion. Instead, that analysis which is central to the historian's task replaced the first-hand experience of Roman politics his family took pains to deny him. It also generated a lifelong interest in the esoterica of Republican convention and the mores of previous generations of Romans. It is this period of research, part of the life he led after '[abandoning] all hope of advancement and [giving] himself up to idleness, living in obscurity now in his house and gardens in the suburbs, and sometimes at a villa in Campania', which afterwards inspired those aspects of his principate which suggest a conscious archaism, like Augustus' revival of lapsed cults and temple restorations. Claudius, for example, established a 'Board of Soothsayers'. 'The oldest Italian art,' Tacitus reports him saying, 'ought not to die out through neglect.' He looked less kindly on the (non-Italian) Druids, whose 'cruel and inhuman' cult in Gaul, prohibited by Augustus to Roman citizens, he outlawed entirely. In the same period, restless in pursuit of diversion, he did not neglect the city's drinking dens.

In the event, Claudius did attain the consulship. The year was 37, the term from 1 July until 31 August; Claudius was forty-six. The new emperor Gaius exploited family loyalty to consolidate the legitimacy of his rule: Claudius was virtually a lone male relation. Two years later, Gaius forsook the illusion of a nephew's affection, hurling Claudius into the Rhine in response to his message of congratulation on the former's detection of Gaetulicus' conspiracy. Smarting with bludgeoned *amour propre*, Claudius may have held fast to a portent of better things to come which Suetonius associates with his consulship: entering the Forum for the first time with the fasces of office in 37, he was singled out by a passing eagle which landed on his shoulder. Certainly there was little else in his life to encourage ambitious hopes. He cannot have conceived of the consulship (with a promise of a second term in four years' time) as a springboard to ultimate power; he lacked prestige, authority, even – as Dio indicated – any experience of having been tested at all in any noteworthy position. It was, as he himself afterwards acknowledged, his trump card: only the appearance of dim-wittedness shielded Claudius throughout the purges of Tiberius, Sejanus and Gaius. There were those who did not believe this assumed stupidity. One wrote a book, *The Elevation of Fools*. Its thesis, Suetonius tells us, was 'that no one feigned folly'.

———∞———

Alma-Tadema's paintings hint only obliquely at the atmosphere in the immediate aftermath of Gaius' murder. Despite the anxious facial expression of the youthful Claudius of *Proclaiming Claudius Emperor*, the terrified grimace of the older Claudius in *A Roman Emperor, AD 41*, those motionless bodies and the bloody handprints of the same image, these paintings are too decorous to conjure effectively the chaos compounded of terror and exhilaration which overtook Rome. A panic-stricken populace converged on the Forum. In the Temple of Jupiter, senators gathered, their moment of decision – denied them for so long – come at last. Consuls transported the state treasury to the Capitol for safe-keeping. In an atmosphere dizzy with possibilities, senators 'resolved on maintaining the public liberty' by abolishing the principate; others, like Gaius' brother-in-law Marcus Vinicius, husband of Julia Livilla whom Claudius would recall to Rome, proposed their own candidacy. Dio's image of a senate at odds with itself suggests that few of its members had dared anticipate the eventuality in hand. 'Many and diverse opinions were expressed; for some favoured a democracy, some a monarchy, and some were for choosing one man and some another.'[6]

Uncertainly, Claudius made his way from the imperial box. It was the last day of the Palatine Games. 'He withdrew to an apartment called the Hermaeum,' Suetonius tells us. 'A little later, in great terror at the news of the murder, he stole away to a balcony hard by and hid among the curtains which hung before the door.' What happened next has a quality as anecdotal as historical. In Suetonius' version, after a day and a night in the Praetorian camp, Claudius found himself emperor by dint of the senate's vacillations – 'the tiresome bickering of those who held divergent views' – and the calls of the entire city mob, whose chanting brooked no denial. In this version, the soldiers kill Gaius out of fury: their support for Claudius is a later decision, perhaps swayed by the popular mood, certainly encouraged by Claudius' own promise to them of a reward of 15,000 sesterces each for their support (he afterwards made a smaller financial award every year on the anniversary of his accession).[7] An alternative version by Josephus has the Praetorians choosing

Claudius as Gaius' successor in a hastily convened meeting following the murder on the Palatine. In this case, Claudius' removal to the Praetorians' camp is the means of guaranteeing his safety until the senate can be called upon to ratify the soldiers' choice.[8]

The net result for Claudius, whatever the degree of his involvement in the process, was the same. By what Suetonius calls a 'remarkable freak of fortune', the fifty-year-old Claudius, noted for his absent-mindedness and the political obscurity of his life to date, became Rome's fifth Caesar through the armed support of the Praetorian Guard. The emperor's crack fighting force had demonstrated incontrovertibly that they could make – as well as unmake – their leader. In both versions of the story, the senate's endorsement of Claudius' accession is laggardly. They hesitate… and falter in the face of bolder forces. It is a telling reservation and not tactful. It will linger in the memories of ruler and ruled. Time will reveal the exact nature of senatorial acquiescence and the feelings inspired by the Guards' irresistible initiative. The senate's acceptance of Claudius as *princeps* in 41, despite his undoubted status as minority candidate, bespeaks a truth Augustus had been at pains to conceal. Impossible any longer to perpetuate that hoary fiction of a restored Republic. There had been those that winter afternoon who dreamed of restoring the Republic Suetonius and Dio agree. Soldiers thought otherwise. And Claudius – to the manner born, heredity his sole distinction – did not resist the siren call of destiny.

The concerns of Rome's newest *princeps* were twofold: the Empire's wellbeing and his own safety. The measures he took to ensure the latter encompassed symbolic acts intended to bolster the legitimacy of his claim to power as well as active steps to protect him from assassins and conspirators. Suetonius describes his timidity and suspicion as notorious:

> he never ventured to go to a banquet without being surrounded by guards with lances and having his soldiers wait upon him in place of the servants; and he never visited a man who was ill without having the patient's room examined beforehand and his pillows and bed-clothing felt over and shaken out.

Visitors to the palace, regardless of the nature of their business, were rigorously searched. Only towards the end of his reign did he permit a less intimate frisking of women and children. Conscious that he owed his throne to the simple fact of physical survival, ever mindful of the swingeing depredations to Augustus' family tree of the previous two reigns, and apprised, from his reading of history, of the vulnerability of prominent lives, Claudius' anxiety in the face of possible attack was extreme. Perhaps the nature of his nervous condition exacerbated his response. After an equestrian was discovered in the Temple of Mars armed with a hunting knife while Claudius sacrificed, he tearfully begged the senate's protection, proclaiming with purple pathos that there was no safety for him anywhere. We need not doubt Claudius' sincerity – nor in several cases the sincere intent of the instances of opposition which punctuate his rule from the outset: the suspected conspiracy of Asinius Gallus and Statilius Corvinus, confirmed by Suetonius and Dio; the unnamed equestrian who lay in wait for Claudius outside the theatre brandishing a sword-stick; the man who broke into the palace at night and, dagger in hand, found his way to Claudius' bedchamber.

Of greater significance both to Claudius' future outlook and, given the nature of his response, to attitudes to his principate among senatorial circles was the attempted uprising in 42 of Lucius Arruntius Camillus Scribonianus, governor of Dalmatia, which Suetonius described as a rebellion amounting to civil war. This five-day conspiracy of senators who the sources claim as former potential successors to Gaius, chief among them Scribonianus himself and Annius Vinicianus, collapsed, Dio asserts, because the Dalmatian legions, 'when Scribonianus held out to them the hope of seeing the Republic restored and promised to give back to them their ancient freedom, suspected that they should have trouble and strife once more, and would therefore no longer listen to him.'[9] Claudius duly rewarded the legions with the name 'Claudian, Loyal and Patriotic' and further gifts of money,[10] sagaciously blind to the element of pragmatism that had governed their actions and the decisive role of ominous weather conditions. So far, so good. But in his determination to stamp out lingering embers of Scribonianus' revolt, he embarked on something like a witch-hunt, which offered informers a bonanza and resulted in large numbers of executions, women as well as men in Dio's account. The repressiveness of Claudius' reprisals disconcerted those concerned most nearly, namely Roman senators and their families, precisely that group which for the past year had demonstrated reservations about Claudian rule. In a response which extended to denying the condemned even ordinary funeral rites, Claudius could no longer lay claim to moderation: although she was ultimately pardoned, a wife called Cloatilla found herself on trial for burying her husband.[11] It was vindictive and petty-minded, closer to Gaius' model of leadership than Augustus', and gave rise to rumours of a 'cruel and bloodthirsty disposition' which revelled, among other diversions, in scenes of torture and execution.

Unsuccessful it may have been, but Claudius was unsettled by Scribonianus' conspiracy. It indicated the extent of personal dissatisfaction with his rule, and the failure of his policy, in the face of senatorial intransigence, of legitimizing his claim to power by emphasizing family connections. The wholly Claudian Claudius had set in motion the process of awarding divine honours to his grandmother Livia, wife of the adopted Julian Augustus, and in addition to games given in memory of his father Drusus, had similarly honoured his mother Antonia, herself Augustus' niece. Early coin issues reiterated this litany of distinguished and useful descent, commemorating Drusus, Antonia and the Divine Augustus. It was unavoidable, given the nature of Claudius' claim to the throne. It was evidently not enough.

———◦◦◦◦———

But Claudius was not insensitive to the feelings of the senate. An assiduous (even officious) jurist, when it suited him he cultivated an illusion of something approaching stakeholder government. He requested the senate to voice independent judgements, this insistence on the appearance of free-thinking his own version of Augustus' 'collaboration' of *princeps* and magistrates. Punctiliousness in the matter of traditional courtesies created that ersatz equality by which he meant to woo senators, etiquette in the service of deception. He avoided the bulldozer approach of his nephew Gaius: his intention was never Eastern-style monarchy. To this end he overruled the senate's proposed awards following the birth of his only son three weeks after his accession; Claudius' third wife, Valeria Messalina, was not created Augusta nor did the couple's son, afterwards called Britannicus, receive the honorific 'Augustus'. Such resilience in the face of apparent senatorial sycophancy (whatever the truth of that body's feelings) countered claims of tyranny. It also attempted to reassure Romans that the role of the emperor's wife was appropriately circumscribed. This too was a deceit.

Claudius had had two previous wives before his marriage to Valeria Messalina (he had also been engaged on a further two occasions: his second would-be bride died on their wedding day). His divorce of his first wife Plautia Urgulanilla included charges of adultery and sensational, if unconfirmed, rumours of murder: not of Claudius but of Plautia's sister-in-law. The circumstances of that death – a fatal fall from a window – were sufficiently provocative to necessitate the involvement of the emperor Tiberius. Claudius' second wife, Aelia Paetina, was a connection of Sejanus. Their marriage was of relatively short duration, its purpose presumably negated by Sejanus' fall. By early 39 at the latest, Claudius had married the youthful Messalina, who was less than half his age. As a great-granddaughter of Augustus' sister Octavia through both her father's and her mother's families, she would afterwards reinforce those claims to power made by Claudius on the grounds of Augustan pedigree. The couple's marriage coincided with Claudius' emergence under Gaius to a position of greater prominence.

Distinction takes many forms. Messalina could undoubtedly lay claim to high birth. It would not prove her chief attribute. Amoral, rapacious, manipulative, deceitful, interfering, fecund and above all spectacularly oversexed, she emerges from the sources as a byword for feminine transgression. We assume that she was beautiful, though thanks to the *damnatio memoriae* which followed her death, no certain contemporary images of her survive: certainly she exercised sexual power bordering on bewitchment over the susceptible Claudius. (Perhaps she was a cause of that insomnia which led him to fall asleep during his working day, often when he was hearing cases in court.) In his *Natural History*, Pliny the Elder records a competition instigated by Messalina with 'one of the most notorious women who followed the profession of a hired prostitute' to see who could take the largest number of sexual partners in a single session. Predictably – else the story should hardly have survived – Messalina won with a tally of twenty-five.[12] In a well-known passage of character assassination, Juvenal related nocturnal sorties made by Claudius' wife to a Roman brothel. There, while the *princeps* slept, she worked in a blonde wig, with gilded nipples, under the trade name 'She-Wolf'. All the sources agree that Messalina suffered from an addiction. Juvenal describes her unrosily after such a session as 'still burning with her clitoris inflamed and stiff... exhausted by the men but not yet satisfied... a disgusting creature'.[13] Such images would undoubtedly have shocked the empress's contemporaries: so marked a predisposition, were it known, could hardly have earned her the award of the title Augusta from the senate, however debased.

At the outset of Claudius' reign, Messalina received public honours, including a grant of statues and a place alongside the Vestal Virgins at the theatre. When Claudius celebrated the triumph of Britain in 44, she took a prominent place in the procession in a special carriage behind him. It might have continued thus, but Messalina's cravings apparently drove her to actions which, impacting on upper-class life in the capital, merged distinctions between her public and private lives, politicizing her libido in a way which could only end badly. At this point she becomes the bejewelled nude of a Gustave Moreau watercolour, skin pale as whey, a diadem in her hair, so dizzy with her own erotic delusions that she scarcely notices the ardent youth whose neck she cradles; blind to the Rome beyond palace windows, the claims of rank, motherhood or

Claudius' happiness. Examples like this of overspill into the public arena of the peccadilloes of his wives would become one of the principal criticisms of Claudius' reign. In Messalina's case, it offended another precept of Augustus' revolution: the promotion of imperial women as exemplars of outstanding moral virtue, the role Livia, Octavia and Antonia had embraced.

At first Messalina adhered to Augustan convention. But she busied herself in pointless conspiracies. Her motives may be lost for ever. She enlisted in her cause Claudius' powerful freedmen: Pallas (his treasurer), Narcissus (his secretary) and that opportunistic relic of the previous regime, Kallistos. Marcus Vinicius, brother of the conspirator Vinicianus, was apparently poisoned for resisting Messalina's advances, a story which includes too many unprovables for comfort. Earlier Messalina's jealousy probably lay behind the second banishment of Vinicius' wife, Julia Livilla: on this occasion Gaius' sister starved to death. The Gaulish consul Valerius Asiaticus died so that Messalina could gratify through theft her craving for gardens in Rome which Tacitus reports him as 'beautifying with exceptional lavishness'.[14] Asiaticus' trial behind closed doors, with every appearance of a stitch-up, earned senatorial antipathy for both Messalina and Claudius; his phlegmatism in the face of imperial caprice gave the regime's opponents a valuable martyr.[15] By contrast there may have been dynastic reasons for getting rid of Appius Silanus, a connection of the Claudii, at the beginning of the reign. 'Messalina and Narcissus put their heads together to destroy him,' Suetonius records. They invented dreams in which both saw Appius kill Claudius. It was enough to ensure his hasty execution. Claudius took naïvety to extremes in reporting the affair to the senate and importuning thanks for his freedman. Such proofs of uxoriousness did not enhance senators' views of the emperor's capabilities nor of the good practice of his government. Over time they also eroded Messalina's popularity to an extent which boded ill for her son Britannicus. For as there existed within the imperial family men and women equally closely related to Augustus as Claudius and Messalina – and therefore equally qualified to rule – there existed in the next generation a young man whose claim to the principate came close to matching Britannicus'. His name was Lucius Domitius Ahenobarbus and he was the son of Agrippina the Younger, who so far, unlike her less fortunate sister Julia Livilla, had resisted Messalina's fury. At the Secular Games held by Claudius in 47, the year Agrippina became a widow for the second time, Domitius received applause more lusty than that accorded to Britannicus, his junior by five years. It was a sign of things to come.

Before that, Messalina's downfall. Sluttishness alone did not undo the emperor's well-born wife. As she cherry-picked the flower of Roman manhood (the sources would have us believe), diverted alike by aristocrats and the ballet dancer Mnester, she distracted Claudius with a stream of pretty maids and serving wenches. Until, in the autumn of 48, Messalina succumbed to momentary madness. Taking the opportunity of Claudius' absence from Rome, she 'married' a consul designate, Gaius Silius, who, in Tacitus' account, meant to adopt Britannicus and usurp Claudius' throne. She did not do so discreetly in a secret room of the palace but in a formal service conducted in semi-public surrounds. Afterwards she followed her indiscretion with a revel that sounds like a Bacchic *fête champêtre*. The outcome provides an example of dishonour among thieves. The same freedmen who had once forwarded her schemes of vindictiveness and greed turned against Messalina: they persuaded two of Claudius' mistresses to report her to the emperor. As news seeped out that Claudius was returning to Rome, the wedding throng dispersed and Messalina herself hastened to Ostia to intercept Claudius and explain herself in person. She was forced to hitch-hike in a garden refuse cart. The encounter of husband and wife proved unsatisfactory, thanks to the intervention of an implacable Narcissus. Messalina won a temporary stay of execution, but was later killed on Narcissus' instructions before Claudius had a chance to relent. In the best Roman tradition, her mother Domitia Lepida looked on with apparent dispassion, having already tried to persuade Messalina to commit suicide.

Suetonius exploits the corollary to this puzzling and extraordinary interlude to illustrate Claudius' absent-mindedness: the emperor, who does not respond to news of his wife's death other than by requesting more wine, 'asked shortly after taking his place at table why the empress did not come'.

Claudius was months short of his fifty-seventh birthday. In contrast to earlier periods of his life, the first seven years of his principate had seen a marked stabilization in his physical health (which may suggest a psychosomatic aspect to his illness); it was now that the period of deterioration began. Until now there had been notable successes. Aulus Plautius' campaign in southern England had brooked no resistance in claiming a fabled new province for the Empire. In the triumph voted to him by the senate the following year, Claudius had briefly enjoyed intimations of that glory once associated with his father and brother; coins depicted images of a fallen Britannia. Similarly successful were early campaigns on the German frontier (against the Chauci and the Chatti) and Suetonius Paulinus' campaign in Africa (for which the senate also voted Claudius a triumph:

on that occasion he demurred). Largely without bloodshed he had extended Roman citizenship in the provinces. He had rebuilt the Circus Maximus and the Theatre of Pompey and celebrated these public works with lavish unveiling ceremonies. He had commissioned the draining of the Fucine Lake in an attempt to increase available arable land. At the unveiling of the new harbour at Ostia, Pliny records, the assembled crowds were treated to the unlikely sight of the emperor leading an attack on a killer whale. The animal had become trapped in sandbanks. Claudius ordered that nets be strung across the harbour mouth. He then boarded a ship in the company of the Praetorian Guards and exhorted them to action as they showered the stranded animal with lances, to the delight of the viewing public.

On the debit side, he had failed to overcome that senatorial antipathy which had greeted his accession. Despite his much-vaunted respect for the senate, his paranoia in the face of conspiracies real or imaginary had resulted in frequent executions. Claudius had also persistently perpetuated that process of senatorial marginalization which had been a feature of all his predecessors' reigns. Dispensing with consultation in several areas of government, he had organized the imperial administration into a number of informal ministries, each under the control of one of his own freedmen: Narcissus, his secretary, the minister of letters; Pallas, the finance minister; Kallistos, who helped Claudius with judicial matters; and Polybius, to whom Seneca said, 'You owe the whole of yourself to Caesar', who effectively controlled imperial appointments but was nominally minister of culture and the emperor's librarian. The loyalty of freedmen, as Seneca indicated, was to themselves and Claudius alone. It was not a recipe guaranteed to garner senatorial good graces and it gains short shift in surviving sources. Suetonius regards it as part of a larger pattern of malign influence which characterizes the entirety of Claudius' principate: 'almost the whole conduct of his reign [was] dictated not so much by his own judgement as that of his wives and freedmen, since he nearly always acted in accordance with their interests and desires.' In the ancient sources, this is central to any assessment of Claudius' reign: it underpins his reputation for folly and injudiciousness. It is an unfair dismissal, shaped at least in part by succeeding events. For the most powerful influence of Claudius' principate was Agrippina the Younger: her will to power was of an indomitability Claudius could not resist. And Agrippina was the mother of the emperor Nero. Susceptibility is a human frailty. In those writers we consider 'primary' witnesses, among them Suetonius and Tacitus, that susceptibility by which Claudius overlooked the claims to the throne of his own son Britannicus in favour of his stepson Nero acquires a quasi-criminality in the light of aberrances to come.

A competition. The competitors the emperor's freedmen. The prize a bride for Claudius and untrammelled influence for the winner. Three competitors, Narcissus, Kallistos and Pallas, each with their own candidate for the *princeps'* shaking hand. Narcissus favoured Claudius' former wife, Aelia Paetina; Kallistos backed Gaius' ex-wife, Lollia Paulina. But it was the judgement of Pallas which prevailed. The woman who became Claudius' fourth wife, after an adjustment to the incest laws, was his thirty-something niece Agrippina the Younger, youngest daughter of Claudius' brother Germanicus (hero and martyr) and Agrippina the Elder (heroine and martyr) and a great-granddaughter of Augustus. Among the baggage she brought to the marriage was an upbringing scarred by family feuding – and her son Domitius Ahenobarbus. Tactfully, soldiers of the Praetorian Guard overlooked Claudius' suggestion after Messalina's death that they kill him if he decided to marry again: they may have been won over by Agrippina's Julian credentials and upright reputation compared with Messalina's lurid disgrace. Flirtation played its part in Agrippina's winning suit: Suetonius describes her as ensnaring the emperor with her wiles (kisses and endearments), a suggestion which raises questions about the role of Pallas' pimping and, by extension, the veracity of the literary tradition of a three-way race masterminded by the freedmen.

But what sex was to Messalina, so the story goes, power was to Agrippina. She was not distracted by bodily appetites: arrogance and an undeviating focus steadied her performance. She engineered the exile of her rival Lollia Paulina and subsequently her suicide, and banished one Calpurnia, whose good looks had momentarily turned Claudius' head. She also rewarded Pallas by becoming his mistress. He repaid the compliment by suggesting on Agrippina's behalf that Claudius adopt Domitius Ahenobarbus. In 50 the emperor complied, winning votes of thanks in the senate for his misjudgement. The adopted Domitius Ahenobarbus changed his name to Nero Claudius Drusus Germanicus Caesar. Agrippina became the first wife of a living emperor to be styled Augusta; her public prominence increased accordingly. Nero took the *toga virilis*, was nominated *princeps iuventutis* ('Prince of Youth'), and, in 53, married Claudius' daughter Octavia. For Britannicus, an intelligent boy who, unlike his father, saw the way the wind was blowing, the outlook was bleak. Even his slaves were taken from him. As a final indignity, his 'brother' Nero buggered him. How Claudius envisaged his blood son's incorporation into Agrippina's scheme is not clear: Nero was adopted in the first instance as a guardian for Britannicus, a fiction of short duration. After long years outside the fold, Agrippina's pursuit of her personal agenda was systematic and undeviating, 'a rigorous, almost masculine despotism', in Tacitus' assessment. Like Messalina before her, she played on Claudius' horror of conspiracy as a means of eliminating rivalry. Unlike Messalina, she never lost her head. At the critical moment, she acted with ruthless decision.

'Careless talk costs lives,' posters once admonished. Too late would Claudius learn the truth of that wartime injunction. He was ageing quickly. There had been signs of a slackening of his faculties, weakness his new wife seized upon to consolidate her position and extend her sphere of influence. Claudius had announced to his freedmen 'that it had been his destiny... to have wives who were all unchaste, but not unpunished'. Then in public he gave signs once again of favouring Britannicus over Nero. These were dangerous indiscretions in 54. Agrippina was prepared to countenance neither her own punishment nor Nero's disenfranchisement from the purple. She acted swiftly and with deadly resolve. She poisoned Claudius with mushrooms and gruel, assisted by a convicted poisoner called Locusta, Halotus the eunuch taster and a doctor lacking scruples named Xenophon. Locusta poisoned the mushrooms, which Halotus gave to the emperor. At first diarrhoea saved Claudius – that or his habitual drunkenness. With the mushrooms expelled or otherwise ejected, Xenophon administered a second draught in a bowl of gruel, or on the tip of a feather inserted into the sleeping emperor's throat. It was a poison chosen with care, neither too fast nor too slow in action. And on the second occasion it worked.

But posterity was not hoodwinked. Agrippina's murder of Claudius as Britannicus' majority loomed transformed her into the quintessence of the scheming stepmother. In time her villainy was matched only by that of the son she served. She would pay for the crime of regicide. 'Never yet has anyone exercised for good ends the power obtained by crime,' Tacitus commented in a different context.[16] So, in Nero's case, it would prove to be. By then Agrippina had completed the hat-trick: sister, wife and mother of men who ruled the world. In doing so, she revealed another secret of the principate: that the person of the *princeps* could be a conduit for the ambition of third parties. It was a dangerous development. Especially, in Roman eyes, when that person was a woman. The casual reader does not doubt that Agrippina murdered Claudius: the historical sources come too close to consensus for refutation. It is a tale spiced by misogyny, by sexual politics, by fears of a world turned upside down, by the sensationalism of the natural order subverted. It is the story of an emperor turned lightning conductor. As we will discover, it was an appropriate introduction to the reign of Claudius' successor.

NERO

(AD 37–68)

'An angler in the lake of darkness'

His pack mules shod with silver, Nero travelled far from Rome. To Greece and back again, though metaphorically he flunked the homeward journey. Philhellenism was not a virtue in the Caesars' Rome. This philandering poetaster cherished 'a longing for immortality and undying fame'. He sang, raced, fiddled and fucked his way to ignominy, all in public view: in private he kicked and he killed. His infamy lives yet. The Greeks rewarded him with prizes. 'They alone,' he said, 'were worthy of his efforts.' Only the Greeks had an ear for music. But Nero's 'Greek' tastes embraced more than singing or the cithara. One of his spouses was a young boy called Sporus. Nero had him castrated, so that he could serve him lifelong as his 'wife'. (Sporus was indeed loyal to the end, a rare example of fidelity in this story.) He also married his freedman Doryphorus: in this case it was Nero who played the wife, 'going so far as to imitate the cries and lamentations of a maiden being deflowered' as Doryphorus set to work. Riding in a carriage with his mother, Nero offended even that primordial relationship: stains on his clothes betrayed the guilty couple. (Happy, then, that this spendthrift emperor, who fished with a golden fishing net, never wore the same clothes twice.) Nero's was a reign of histrionic excess: thanks to Monteverdi and Handel, its tortuous and hazardous relationships survive today in the opera house.

After his death his memory was condemned by decree of the senate: his historiography offers rich pickings for scandal-mongers. Perversion, incest and murder notwithstanding, for the layman he is damned by his response to Rome's biggest bonfire night: the emperor who, in AD 64, made music while his people perished and the city tumbled to torches of fire.

He was born feet-first, an unlucky sign in Rome, and his birth was attended by portents promising murder and a throne (perhaps a convenient afterthought on the part of our chroniclers). In addition to 'acts of wantonness, lust and extravagance', his topsy-turvy career, standing his world upon its head, embraced 'avarice and cruelty'. Suetonius describes him once as beguiled by dreams of the lost treasure of Queen Dido (when his rest was not shattered by nightmares, haunted by the ghost of the mother whom by then he had killed). That mythical booty was promised to him by a Roman knight, who had glimpsed it in huge caves in Africa. Such cavalier promises were the stuff of life to Nero, the quotidian replaced by poetry, dreams in place of action: illusions – or delusions – of grandeur. When he sat down to dinner in his brand-new palace, the Golden House, the ceiling revolved, a heavyweight mechanism operated by nothing more complex than water. Through a tracery of ivory panels flowers and perfume rained down upon the emperor's guests. In Nero's Neverland, albeit the man himself stank mightily (his skin pocked with blemishes, 'his body marked with spots and malodorous'), for twelve hours at a stretch life could be a bed of roses. His banquets were day-long affairs. He rose only to cool himself down in snow-chilled water or warm himself up, never in the interests of business. Like Gaius before him, Nero was emperor part-time. As elderly senators were quick to note, he was the first *princeps* of Rome to employ a ghostwriter for his speeches. His choice, made for him by his mother, fell upon no less a luminary than writer and philosopher Lucius Annaeus Seneca. At the time it may have been sensible: later it looked like detachment – even worse, like play-acting.

His horrible father, Gnaeus Domitius Ahenobarbus, 'a man hateful in every walk of life', committed incest with his sister, killed a boy for kicks and, in full view of the crowds in the Forum, gouged out the eyes of a colleague who criticized him. Vicious and untroubled by public contempt, he is a challenge to historians' impartiality. As a young man, his son Nero roamed the streets after dark, disguised by a wig or cap or dressed as a slave. In company with friends and members of his guard, he raided brothels, smashed and looted shops, and attacked passers-by with blows and daggers. In 56, he came close to losing his eyes in such an encounter: a senator called Julius Montanus took the opportunity of darkness to avenge himself on an affront made by Nero to Montanus' wife. With grim complacency Domitius had claimed that no one of whom he was father and Agrippina mother could be anything but a scourge and a terror to the public. And so, in a shadowy alley-way in the second year of Nero's reign, it seemed to be. But Nero's cruelty did not long delight in casual violence. Chariot-racing, wrestling bouts, acting and singing competitions cooled the heat of his temper. By contrast the killings of his reign were directed at political opponents. Unlike his three immediate predecessors, we have no reason to assume that Nero particularly enjoyed their deaths.

In time, he threatened that he would blot out the entire senatorial order 'and hand over the rule of the provinces and the command of the armies to the Roman knights and to his freedmen'. Whether he meant it or not, it was a plan the ancients could not permit. The result may be a fictionalized Nero emerging from the styluses of the earliest writers, an archetype of evil offensive to the national myths of the Republic still dear to Tacitus et al. Little wonder this senate-hater is accused of sexual incontinence and tyranny. Such, we know, are the aspersions cast by our sources upon their political opponents. The story repeats itself: Julius, Tiberius, Gaius, even Claudius. In Nero's case, much of his startling waywardness may be true: there is a homogeneity to the sources' extremism which is persuasive in itself.

Nero is alone among the twelve Caesars in succeeding to the throne without political experience: even Gaius and Claudius managed a magistracy apiece (Gaius the quaestorship, Claudius a consulship). Instead, at the outset, he ruled with the assistance of a philosopher of academic bent who delighted 'in boys past their prime' – Seneca;[1] and a guardsman with a deformed arm who had begun his career as overseer of estates belonging to Livia – Burrus. It was a notably successful arrangement. The hostile nature of the sources makes it difficult to form an accurate assessment of Nero's own capabilities. On the face of it, this seventeen-year-old of violent temper was ill placed to negotiate unaided the challenges of the principate – an arbitration between determined and implacable factions advocating arguments he may not have understood. All we can conclude with certainty is that, at a certain point, he put behind him Seneca's lessons. 'Cruel and inexorable anger is not seemly for a king,' the latter wrote in the treatise *On Mercy* at the beginning of Nero's reign: the good ruler is one 'whose care embraces all, who, while guarding here with greater vigilance, there with less, yet fosters each and every part of the state as a portion of himself; who is inclined to the milder course even if it would profit him to punish'.[2] Nero's downfall embraced a failure of vigilance, the duty of care neglected or misapplied: it is partly attributable to his lack of interest in 'each and every part of the state'.

At the outset, however, a 'milder course'. The poet Calpurnius Siculus hailed the return of the Golden Age, an era of tranquillity and peace. Coins in Alexandria acclaimed Nero as the New Augustus. Nero asked the senate's permission to erect a statue to his father Domitius (family piety satisfied); he declined a senatorial grant of his own statues in gold and silver.[3] Like Gaius and Claudius emperor by descent, with no claims of merit or *auctoritas*, he stated 'that he would rule according to the principles of Augustus', a deliberate avoidance of the complex legacies of Augustus' successors; according to Suetonius, he missed no opportunity for acts of generosity and mercy or displays of affability. He signed a death warrant with a heavy heart and the lament, 'How I wish I had never learned to write!' Briefly he made use of his status as son of the deified Claudius, no more a believer in fact than those senators who had jeered at Claudius' elevation or the audiences who applauded Seneca's satirical dramatization, the *Apocolocyntosis*, performed during the Saturnalia of 54. Four decades after Augustus' death, his remained the only model of government by *princeps* sufficiently successful for imitation. It was an indication of a deeply fissured system and the impossibility of extending indefinitely one man's vision. For a young man untrained in government, already betraying signs of distraction, it was a toxic prescription. Nero may have been doomed to fail. Perhaps he is a victim as well as a villain.

His early aversion to bloodshed, as we shall see, evaporated. So too that stage-fright which, at the beginning of his reign, preserved his imperial dignity. (By the time of his death, Dio tells us, he was making desperate, but nevertheless serious, plans to earn his living as a lyre-player in Alexandria.[4]) Song, slaughter, sex, subversion and a search for sensation became the stuff of his supremacy. As Edgar describes him in *King Lear*, 'Nero is an angler in the lake of darkness.' In the end he simply ignored unpalatable truths. Inertia cost Nero his throne, ever after dismissed as fiddling while Rome burned. The lake of darkness yielded only further depths of black.

With hindsight, diverted by the rainbow hues of ancient scandal mongering, it is easy to dismiss Nero's principate as an interlude of madness, when every extremism thrived and the business of government took second place to the spectacular unravelling of one man's fancies. The emperor himself certainly took a novel line on Roman leadership. But Nero was not Gaius. His interpretation of the principate was distorted not by mental instability but by wilfulness, distraction and a misinterpretation of the political power base of his position. He pursued an agenda of stage performances, chariot-races, singing competitions and, in the form of his Golden House in Rome, an architectural extravaganza of unprecedented magnitude and lavishness. These efforts wowed crowds in Italy and Greece. Yet real influence remained the possession of a traditional senatorial elite, which was alienated by behaviour it regarded at best as undignified, at worst as un-Roman and subversive. Where we are misled by the sources – written by upper-class conservatives – is in accepting their verdict of a Nero who was universally detested. On the contrary, those public demonstrations of profanity exposed Nero to a larger audience than any previous Roman ruler. In conjunction with his sumptuous generosity in the matter of public games and spectacles, they won him the foundations of a large, partly apolitical following and created those well-springs of popular feeling which survived his death and were afterwards exploited in the short reign of his former confidant Otho. Decades after Nero's suicide, a 'false' Nero was reported in the eastern Empire. This second coming set hearts a-flutter. Even in Rome, his tomb in the family grave of the Domitii, on the Pincian Hill in sight of the Campus Martius, was for many springs and summers decorated with garlands of flowers. For a man who had revelled in godlessness, secretly sneering as he expedited Claudius' divine honours, despising all cults bar that of the Great Mother (and even pissing on her statue), it was immortality after a fashion.

It was also suggestive of an approach to love, an ingredient in short supply in any account of Nero's life. His father had died when he was three. His banished mother had abandoned him, leaving him in Rome while she journeyed to temporary perdition. He was brought up by an aunt in straitened circumstances, Domitia Lepida, whom he claimed to revere like a mother but later poisoned in old age in order to lay hands on her estates at Baiae. In Domitia's house his education was entrusted to a dancer and a barber, low-grade tutors for a prince of the imperial house. Rome's sixth Caesar was greater than the sum of these parts. Despite ancient historians' emphasis on heredity – Suetonius furnishes the reader with vivid examples of his family's miscreancy 'to show more clearly that though Nero degenerated from the good qualities of his ancestors, he yet reproduced the vices of each of them, as if transmitted to him by natural inheritance' – we can understand Nero as much as a product of his times as an amalgam of bloodlines. He was fond of quoting a Greek proverb, 'Hidden music counts for nothing.' And indeed his life acquired over time a flaunting, prodigal quality, no light too dim to merit concealment beneath a bushel. To waste and to squander were the hallmark of the great nobleman, he believed: he admired Gaius for nothing so much as the speed at which he ran through Tiberius' carefully hoarded surplus. The last of the Julio-Claudians embodied the weaknesses of a dynasty and a generation. With him died much of that culture of riotous excess which was the antidote to centuries of determined Republican austerity, when sumptuary laws had sought to legislate even the quantities of jewellery a woman might wear.

At a moment when the rule book was being comprehensively challenged, Nero played the lord of misrule, a thrill-seeking potentate who elevated pleasure more than principle and deluded himself that art and life could merge. 'Pleasure is extinguished just when it is most enjoyed,' wrote Seneca in *On the Happy Life*.[5] With no interest in philosophy, an aspect of his education overruled by Agrippina, Nero worked hard to hold that extinction at bay. Intermittently he transformed the capital of empire into a playground of the senses. In 64, assisted by the Praetorian prefect Tigellinus, this emperor, whose 'unshaken conviction [was] that no man was chaste or pure in any part of his body', threw a party which reinvented the Campus Martius, one-time training-ground of soldiers and would-be soldiers, as a giant brothel and drinking den. While Nero cavorted on a purple-draped raft floating in the centre of the Stagnum of Agrippa, naked prostitutes patrolled the shores or languished in gimcrack pavilions alongside virgins and noblewomen all dedicated for one night only to the thrill of easy sex. Taverns ran with wine. Lust and drunkenness contended for the upper hand: rape and violent, bloody orgies were the outcome. Nero himself, rowed by male tarts, underwent a marriage to an ex-slave, Pythagoras, the emperor dressed as a bride.[6] On the shore, brawling led to a handful of killings.

It was a night of ecstatic subversion in which Nero failed to countenance the possibility of reprisals, an outcome similar to that of Messalina's marriage travesty fifteen years earlier. But if the commons revelled in this unashamed pandering to baser instincts, that kernel of steel-spined conservatism which was still engrained in a minority of Roman aristocrats refused to yield to persuasion. Nero's mistake, like that of Gaius before him, was to imagine that he could discount lip-service to a past he did not remember. In ruling without apologies, he exposed the hypocrisy of Augustus' magnificent deceit. But it was he, not Augustus' memory, who suffered. As the civil wars following Nero's death would show, Romans were not yet ready to dispense with the fabrications Augustus had bequeathed them as he robbed them of their liberty. An emperor there must be, the army demanded it. But an emperor whose dialogue with Rome extended beyond salacious gewgaws to a meaningful political exchange, the flexibility to alternate the master's and the servant's part in pursuit of a greater good.

———◦◦◦———

A marble statue survives of Nero as a child. He was not called Nero then, we know, but Lucius Domitius Ahenobarbus, named for his father's family. Around his neck, he wears the gold bulla (locket) of upper-class Roman boyhood; his face is broad, open and untroubled. His eyes – afterwards short-sighted – appear large and somewhat staring. In one hand he extends a document rolled into a scroll. It is an image of adulthood in miniature, patrician precocity, the iconography of the insider. Given its probable date (post-dating Agrippina's marriage to Claudius but preceding the latter's adoption of her son), it is partly an exercise in wishful thinking. Nero owed his career to his mother, as we learn from Dio that she reminded him on at least one occasion. In his veins, as in her veins, flowed Augustus' blood. This was the nominal justification for Nero's pre-eminence, but as the example of countless imperial heirs from Agrippa Postumus to Tiberius Gemellus attested, it was not a guarantee. The path to the purple, as mother and son understood and as we have seen, was not so straightforward.

It was accomplished satisfactorily, however, on 13 October 54. Agrippina stage-managed the announcement of Claudius' death, waiting until the day's resolutely bad omens showed signs of improving. Nero, accompanied by the prefect of the Praetorian Guard, Afranius Burrus, an appointment of Agrippina's, delivered a speech to the Guard written for him by Seneca and promised a generous cash donative. All went smoothly. Murder, mendacity, money and an obdurate mother made Nero emperor.

Far from protesting, the teenage *princeps* acknowledged his indebtedness by giving 'The Best of Mothers' to the tribune of the Guards as the first watchword of the reign. 'He left to his mother,' Suetonius announces, 'the management of all public and private business.' Dio's account suggests that the 'giving' may have been taken from him by that redoubtable parent, a subtle shift in subject and object, active and passive, which is undoubtedly important: 'At first Agrippina managed for him all the business of the empire.'[7] This unorthodox arrangement, unique in Roman history to date and posing insuperable constitutional problems, was recorded in gold and silver coins minted between 4 and 31 December. Nero occupies one side of the coin, Agrippina the other. The position of their twin busts is significant: it is Agrippina who takes the obverse, Nero the reverse, the emperor placed physically and symbolically below his mother. 'My youth has not been steeped in civil war or family strife. I bring with me no feuds, no grievances, no desire for vengeance,' Nero had announced with careful disingenuousness in his accession speech to the senate.[8] Seneca, who also owed his position to Agrippina, may have written the words without irony. But family strife, feuding and grievance lay close at hand. Their source was Agrippina's overweening ambition, testified by those coins created by a mint which we assume that she, rather than Nero, influenced. By 55, a second series of coins had been issued, Nero's bust joining Agrippina's on the obverse side, the emperor's likeness in the position of greater significance: unparalleled honours for the emperor's mother still, but surely a falling-off from the dizzy apotheosis of weeks earlier. So swiftly was the Augusta's supremacy checked.

She may not have been surprised. In Dio's account, Nero's lack of interest in governing the Empire is not something which emerges gradually but a characteristic of his response to the purple from the outset: 'he was not fond of business in any case, and was glad to live in idleness.'⁹ The thirst for power was Agrippina's. Nero's loyalty belonged to those who facilitated his idleness with least hectoring. The major development of the first year of his reign was the transfer of that baton from Agrippina to Seneca and Burrus, described by Tacitus as two men connected by a unity rare among partners in power and, by different methods, equally influential on Nero. 'Burrus' strength lay in soldierly efficiency and seriousness of character, Seneca's in amiable high principles and his tuition of Nero in public speaking.'¹⁰ It is difficult to exonerate Agrippina from all responsibility. Anti-female bias aside, the record of the sources suggests that she wilfully overreached herself.

In late 54, Armenian envoys travelled to Rome. Tacitus relates with indignation Agrippina's behaviour at their reception at court. The Augusta 'was seen to be about to seat herself alongside the emperor and preside over the tribunal with him' when Seneca intervened: his quick-fire suggestion that Nero descend the steps of the dais to greet his mother and thus deflect her advance averted scandal and enabled Tacitus to

breathe freely again.[11] It was a careful rebuke. What we cannot
know is whether Agrippina's action was simply in line with her
customary behaviour during her marriage to Claudius.

At Seneca's instigation, Nero held the consulship in 55. It was
an appointment that brought with it enhanced *dignitas* of a sort
which Agrippina as a woman could not rival. Its award was also,
as she would have understood, in line with the policy followed by
the majority of Nero's predecessors of monopolizing this senior
magistracy in order to assert more fully their own dominance of
the senate. Agrippina's mistake in 55 did not consist of claiming
consulships for herself or opposing Nero's appointment: her
attempted governance was of a more overtly petticoats variety.
She intervened in Nero's first recorded romantic entanglement.

Acte was a freedwoman from Asia Minor. Suetonius lists
the liaison within an inventory of Nero's sexual and marital
misdemeanours and claims that the youthful emperor came
close to marriage with the former slave, 'after bribing some
ex-consuls to perjure themselves by swearing that she was of
royal birth'. But in 55 Nero remained unhappily married to
Claudius' daughter Octavia, whom he had wed, presumably as
a result of Agrippina's machinations, the year before Claudius'
death. Irked by a combination of jealousy and snobbery –
a former slave exerting greater influence in the imperial
household than a granddaughter of Augustus and the emperor's
mother – Agrippina requested Nero to break off the relationship.
Her behaviour lacked the woman's touch or even simple charm.
She dismissed Acte as 'her daughter-in-law the maid' and,
torrential in her anger, trained her attention on Nero's friends
too, loud in her condemnation (among their number was the
future emperor Otho who, as we will see, acquired a history of
playing gooseberry in Nero's flirtations).[12] When Nero refused,
Agrippina resorted to threats. Even given Nero's limited political

acumen, he must have recognized the hollowness of her intimation that, having once made him emperor, she could now imperil that position. Doubtless Seneca discreetly corrected any misapprehensions. Since Seneca had encouraged the liaison with Acte – an indication that, despite Suetonius' demonizing of the relationship, wise, moderate counsellors considered it essentially harmless – the outcome was to push Nero further from his mother and closer to his tutor. A pattern had been set which would last for the next five years, with almost uniformly happy results for everyone bar Agrippina. Temperamentally incapable of quiet retreat, Agrippina briefly adopted a course of dissembling, offering herself in the role of pander and aiding Nero's meetings with Acte. The emperor's friends blew her cover and Agrippina embraced again her preferred mode of attack, making overtures to Britannicus in Nero's place and leaving Nero to draw his own inferences. Nero for his part turned his attention to Pallas, Agrippina's freedman helpmeet and lover, whom he sacked, perhaps on grounds of financial irregularities. It was a double blow for Agrippina. There was worse to come.

Suetonius' *Life of Nero* includes a ghoulish account of a series of experiments in poisoning conducted in the emperor's private apartments at the palace. The poisoner is again Locusta, at Nero's order her intended victim on this occasion apparently Britannicus, 'not less from jealousy of his voice (for it was more agreeable than Nero's own) than from fear that he might sometime win a higher place than himself in the people's regard', a neat dismissal which simultaneously accuses Nero the karaoke king-turned-killer of murder and silliness. Once Locusta had developed a mix strong enough to inflict instant death, Nero made plans to administer it to Britannicus. Predictably the latter 'dropped dead at the very first taste', a result which shocked his fellow diners, including Agrippina and his sister

Octavia. Wholly unconcerned, Nero attributed the mishap to epilepsy.* Dio admits no possibility of death by epileptic seizure. Nero's poison, he claims, turned Britannicus' body livid. Slaves covered the tell-tale blotches with gypsum, but the furtive funeral took place in driving rain, which washed off that thin enamelling of innocence, exposing Nero's guilt. The emperor rewarded Locusta with large estates in the country. No one sought retribution on Britannicus' part; indeed, Tacitus suggests that Nero's popularity overrode any serious examination of the implications of his misdeed. Agrippina was forced to reach her own conclusion on her future wellbeing in the light of Nero's revelation that, in pursuit of his own ends, he (like his mother) baulked at few constraints.

Such a pre-emptive strike on Nero's part represented a momentum of sorts and swiftly acquired an inexorability which looked to deny the Augusta room for rearguard action. First she was deprived of the soldiers who protected her. Then she was removed from the palace. Nero had made plain his intention towards her. She was probably still safe as long as she behaved with circumspection and accepted the new role Nero had determined for her. But as Agrippina survives in the sources – a termagant of tunnel vision tortured by ambition – she was incapable of such a course.

Nero's thoughts had already turned to his musical career. In Britannicus' death he had eliminated one challenger. It was not

---

* Britannicus did suffer from epilepsy: in the event that Nero had killed him with poison, the taunt is spiteful given the recent association of epilepsy with those destined to rule – the Divine Julius and Gaius.

enough. His early education had included a musical component. Now as emperor he summoned the leading lyre-player of the time, Terpnus, to play and sing for him. For many nights, Nero simply listened. Then he embarked on a course of practice and a strenuous training regime which involved abstinence from fruit, regular emetics and self-induced vomiting, and lying on his back under a lead plate in order to strengthen his chest. At one level it testifies to a degree of self-discipline that was alien to Gaius; it also outlines the first stirrings of an obsession.

The combined influence of Seneca and Burrus prevented Nero's wholehearted surrender to his artistic 'vocation' at this stage. 'The senate shall keep its ancient powers,' Nero had asserted in his accession speech. It would become no more than a form of words but in the beginning it implied a two-way compact in which *princeps* and senate both had roles to play. Nero delivered judgements carefully, not as many as Claudius but less capriciously, after deliberating over written opinions; he prevented sons of freedmen from becoming senators, a conservative policy which ought to have won golden opinions among the political classes; and following the killing by one of his slaves of Lucius Pedanius Secundus, former city prefect, Nero upheld unpopular legislation which insisted on every slave in Pedanius' household being killed. After the power struggles of emperor and senate which had characterized recent reigns, the city fathers were surely impressed by Nero resisting so obvious a chance to win popularity at their expense. Either the emperor or his advisers re-examined tax-collecting and, in keeping with another accession-speech promise, Nero distanced himself from the culture of informing. It was a parade of good behaviour managed with something of that amiability to which he laid claim as part of his inheritance from Germanicus. In relation to Rome's upper classes, it served the same purpose as

Nero's accession gift to every Roman citizen of a sum of money which has been estimated as equivalent to a year's supply of wheat (Romans' staple diet).[13]

—— ·⚬⚬⚬· ——

After Acte, a less benign temptress. Once the *egoïsme à deux* of Nero and Agrippina had been unthinking. Jointly they had publicized a story that Nero was defended by snakes. (When Messalina sent assassins to kill Nero in bed, a snake emerged from his pillow and routed the would-be killer. In the process it shed its skin. Agrippina had the skin fashioned into a bracelet, which Nero wore as a guarantee of his safety.) But in Rome, snakes took many forms. The serpent that finally outmanoeuvred Nero's mother bathed in asses' milk to dispel 'all diseases and blights from her beauty'. Graced by every quality save virtue, Poppaea Sabina first became a sexual obsession for Nero, afterwards a wife whom he loved with angry intensity (and as angrily killed) – that aspect of Poppaea's life which survives in Monteverdi's opera *The Coronation of Poppaea* with its emphasis on love. Like Agrippina, discounting baroque opera, Poppaea has fallen foul of history. Her contemporaries disliked her too, publicly demonstrating against her. In 59, Poppaea was married to Nero's fellow reveller Marcus Salvius Otho. Unwilling to share her, Nero banished Otho to provincial governorship in modern-day Portugal. (In doing so, he provided the basis for Otho's later claims to the principate.) Sources describe Poppaea as no more willing to share Nero than he was to share her. The price of her love was Nero's divorce of Octavia – and the removal of Agrippina. In Tacitus' hands it becomes one of the great dramatic set pieces of classical literature. In the history of the principate it represents a critical development. 'Everyone longed for the mother's domination to end. But no one believed that her son's hatred would go as far as murder.' The emperor not only killed his mother but escaped unpunished, the 'happy' outcome celebrated in acts of thanksgiving in shrines and temples and a vote of annual games at the Festival of Minerva. Even senators added their voices to the clangour of untruths, a single arch conservative, Thrasea Paetus, walking out of the senate in protest at this policy of whitewash. Such blanket acquiescence is a symptom of debasement, one ground for that lowly estimate placed on the crown during the year of upheavals which followed Nero's death.

The plan depended on an ingenious if far-fetched contrivance: a collapsing ship. It was the brainchild of Nero's boyhood tutor Anicetus, now commander of the fleet at Misenum. The unpredictability of the sea offered a cloak for dark deeds and Nero invited Agrippina to join him at Baiae to celebrate Minerva's festival. He installed her in a splendid mansion; offshore an equally splendid ship lay becalmed at anchor. That night, in his own house, Nero hosted a banquet of long-drawn splendour. Afterwards he conducted his mother to the jetty for her homeward journey. The brightness of the moon was a blow to best-laid plans, but there could be no retreat. On a millpond sea, stilly reflecting a million stars, the 'accident' happened. Heavy lead weights caused the ceiling of the ship's cabins to fall. There were casualties but Agrippina was not among them. The high sides of her couch protected the Augusta and her waiting woman. Instead, both fell into the sea. The waiting woman, Acerronia, shouted that she was Agrippina and must be rescued. Sailors in Nero's pay battered her to death with oars. Silently, stealthily, Agrippina swam for her life. A fishing boat rescued her and returned her to the house from which all peacefulness had vanished. She saw everything.

Agrippina sent word to Nero of her terrible 'accident' and her survival. He knew already, reduced by the knowledge to a frenzy of panic. Nero summoned Seneca and Burrus for advice, but again it was Anicetus who seized the initiative. When Agrippina's messenger arrived, Nero dropped a sword at his feet and promptly had him arrested on suspicion of trying to kill him. With a convoy of men, Anicetus set out for Agrippina's house. He dispelled the crowds of watchers who had gathered, drawn by curiosity. Then he slew each and every slave who stood between him and the bedroom in which, half in darkness, Agrippina waited with a single maidservant. Through the flickering lamplight, this former employee bent on revenge advanced towards his quarry. The maidservant fled. But Agrippina stood resolute. 'I know my son is not responsible,' she said. 'He did not order his mother's death.' A truncheon blow to the head shortly silenced her. Stunned but still, in Tacitus' account, mistress of the dramatic scenario, schooled in the dynamics of the Roman way of death, she placed her hands above her womb. Two last words: 'Strike here!' Like rain the blows fell.

For the first time in his life, Nero found himself dreaming while he slept. Dark, portentous dreams – in Suetonius' history, the wages of sin, restlessness the tyrant's lot. The emperor was twenty-two. The biographer does not countenance the possibility of remorse. Although his conscience pricked him so hard that he summoned priests to conjure up his mother's shade and beg her forgiveness, he did not utter a single penitent word. When, probably in 64, Nero made his debut on the Roman stage, his repertoire included a song Suetonius calls 'Orestes the Matricide'. It told the story of Clytemnestra's murder by her son. That such a performance should have been contemplated tells us something of the moral temperature of the times, as well as the collapse of that policy once pursued by Seneca and Burrus of distancing Nero's public life of rectitude from his private viciousness.

The year after Agrippina's murder, the appearance of a comet was interpreted as a presentiment of a change of ruler. (A descendant of Tiberius, Rubellius Plautus, was suggested; Nero requested his banishment and killed him later.) Perhaps the ancient authors invented the phenomenon to underscore Nero's unsuitability and demonstrate that alternatives existed within the emperor's own extended family. If so, the time was not ripe. Nero's hold on power remained strong. With Agrippina dead, awaiting immortalization by Handel, he later divorced Octavia on trumped-up charges of adultery and barrenness.* Nero banished Octavia to Pandateria and there ordered her death. Then he married Poppaea. He created her Augusta and the couple had a daughter, who shortly died. Poppaea died too, in 65, after a miscarriage and severe haemorrhaging. The sources preserve a rumour that Nero caused his wife's death, also her miscarriage. Furious at Poppaea for criticizing his late return from the chariot-races, he kicked her repeatedly in the stomach. His reputation permits such an explanation.

⸺◦⊰⊱◦⸺

Throat cancer was the most likely cause of Burrus' death in 62. Having murdered his mother and his brother, Nero could not expect to escape without accusations of poison. Burrus'

---

* Although it was true that in ten years of marriage Octavia had failed to conceive a child, the obvious explanation was not her infertility. The poisonous Anicetus again came to Nero's rescue in substantiating fictitious claims of adultery.

replacements as Praetorian prefect were Faenius Rufus and Gaius Ofonius Tigellinus. The former had acquired a reputation for honesty and efficiency in his organization of Rome's grain supply; the latter proved the dominant personality despite – or perhaps because of – the considerable animosity felt towards him by the senate. Following their appointment, Tacitus claimed, 'decent standards carried less weight... now Nero listened to more disreputable advisers', and Seneca petitioned Nero to allow him to retire, having first offered to give up his fortune.[14] Nero declined both offers, though a plea of illness on Seneca's part had the same effect as resignation; he transferred much of his dependence on his former tutor to Tigellinus, a man whose interests like his own emphasized debauchery at the expense of statecraft. Nero's marriage to Poppaea in the same year had completed the shift in tone of the imperial regime. The new empress's inclination was for magnificence: her funeral would later suggest affinities with Eastern concepts of royal divinity closer to Gaius' preoccupations than those of the Nero of the early years. If it is possible to discern a turning point in the conduct of government in Nero's reign, it occurred in 62. The emperor made further breaks with the past. This was the year of Pallas' death as well as that of Nero's former freedman lover Doryphorus; Tacitus claims poisoning on Nero's instructions in both cases. In a development which presaged a revival in *maiestas* (treason) trials, the emperor expelled from Italy a scribbler called Aulus Didius Gallus Fabricius Veiento, after the latter had written a wittily slanderous spoof will which included Nero among the targets of its mordant maligning. In this case Veiento escaped with his life. But attitudes were hardening on the Palatine. The senate looked on with unease.

Despite his misgivings, Nero's entry into Rome following the death of Agrippina was received with rapture. For the observant there were signs that that feeling was neither universal nor deeply engrained. Suetonius reports Nero's relaxed response to lampoons circulating in the city. Graffiti proliferated: it accused the emperor outright of matricide. It may not have been benign. The most famous event of Nero's principate, occurring in 64, demonstrated the depth of ambivalence which existed towards the emperor ten years after his accession.

On a warm, moonlit night, fire broke out in Rome. It began amid the jerry-built cafés and cook-shops close to the Circus Maximus racecourse.[15] Nero was out of town, at the seaside resort of Antium thirty-five miles away, but hurried back in time either to recite a poem on the fall of Troy or to supervise the fire-fighting operation (only lyre-playing is ruled out categorically). His efforts, which included the demolition of several large granaries in the path of the fire in order to halt its spread, proved unsuccessful. Wind probably fanned the conflagration, which eventually ravaged ten of the city's fourteen districts. In the smoke and whirling soot, rumour too took wing. Observers noted men hurling firebrands, attempting to augment the fire's spread. It may have been a cover for looting. Or they may have acted on higher instructions. The finger of blame pointed at Nero. It was not a response born out of popular affection. 'To suppress this rumour, Nero fabricated scapegoats,' Tacitus explains. 'He punished with every refinement the notoriously depraved Christians (as they were called).'[16] Under the circumstances it was a sensible deflection on the emperor's part. Disasters on such a scale were traditionally interpreted as proof of heavenly disapproval, ominous and threatening. As the embers cooled, Nero concurred with the outpouring of prayers offered to Vulcan, Ceres, Proserpina and Juno; then he executed

Christian prisoners. He fed them, dressed in animal skins, to wild beasts; they were crucified or burned. It was a highly public purge intended to make his point. Still the rumours persisted.

Extending the reach of his aestheticism, Nero exploited the destruction of so much of Rome to institute a city-wide rebuilding programme that was partly designed around future fire-avoidance but also emphasized visual considerations. Dominating this new cityscape was a splendid imperial palace, the Domus Aurea or Golden House. Facilitated by recent clearances as well as land confiscations, it stretched from the Esquiline Hill in the northeast, over the Oppian, Caelian and Palatine Hills, to the Circus Maximus in Rome's southwest quarter.[17] 'Its wonders', according to Tacitus, 'were lawns and lakes and faked rusticity – woods here, open spaces and views there.'[18] Suetonius describes the lake as 'like a sea'. The astonishing size of the Golden House was underlined by the statue of Nero himself erected in the new palace vestibule, a shimmering, golden likeness that rose 120 feet into the Roman skyline. Within the palace complex, rooms were decorated with more gold, walls inlaid with mother-of-pearl and gemstones. Insensitive to the losses of so many Roman townsfolk, Nero announced that at last he was beginning to be housed like a human being. Martial preferred to describe it as 'an arrogant park which deprived the poor of their houses'.[19] The taunting excess of the Golden House – albeit it might in future provide a source of pride for Romans – undid any good opinions Nero had won through his enlightened rebuilding of Rome itself.

It may have contributed to that support from all classes of Romans claimed by Tacitus for a bungled conspiracy against Nero the following year. Although the sources disagree about the identity of the plotters, the 'Pisonian' conspiracy, which may or may not have centred on Gaius Calpurnius Piso, grandson of that Piso accused of poisoning Germanicus, included senators, prominent thinkers and members of the Praetorian Guard (Dio offers Faenius Rufus as well as Seneca). Gossipy in its organization, the plot was betrayed by carelessness on the part of the man chosen to strike the first blow: Flavius Scaevinus.

Nero's retribution ignored Seneca's one-time warning against the unseemliness of cruel and inexorable anger in kings; vanished was that moderacy which had tolerated graffiti and lampoons. He resorted to torture to root out as many of the conspirators as possible. In doing so, he learned unpalatable truths. A military tribune called Subrius Flavius explained his motive for joining the conspiracy in unequivocal terms: 'I have both loved and hated you above all men. I loved you, hoping that you would prove a good emperor; I have hated you because you do so-and-so. I cannot be a slave to a charioteer or lyre-player.'[20] For his part Piso committed suicide. The death of Faenius Rufus created a vacancy in the Praetorian Guard, which was filled by an opportunist on the make, Nymphidius Sabinus. In the long term, the latter offered Nero poor service. Meanwhile, on Nero's behalf, Tigellinus trained his sights on the elimination of future dissent. The senate's victimization was determined, occasionally arbitrary and consistently cruel. Rumour claimed rapacity as a rationale: Nero needed money. Public building work in Rome could not be blamed for the emptiness of the imperial coffers. It was the Golden House, that dream of grandeur, which threatened to impoverish Rome.

———

Other emperors could have claimed the exorbitant cost of war as exoneration. But Nero, Suetonius tells us, was 'so far from being actuated by any wish or hope of increasing or extending the empire, he even thought of withdrawing the army from Britain and changed his purpose only because he was ashamed to seem to belittle the glory of his father [Claudius]'. Trusting in the army's loyalty – his inheritance from his grandfather Germanicus – Nero omitted to visit a single provincial legion. Instead, his government's policy in the provinces was one of reacting to changing circumstances. Significant revolts broke out in Britain (Boudicca's rebellion of 60) and, in 66, in Judaea; in Parthia it was only the skill of Gnaeus Domitius Corbulo which restored Roman honour after the wholesale defeat of Caesennius Paetus in 62. The glory of that reversal cost Corbulo his life. Afraid of his general's eminence, Nero requested his suicide in 67.

The victories Nero craved were not to be found on battlefields; the prizes he valued did not lie among the spoils of conquest. With unprecedented lavishness, his instincts those of the set designer or Hollywood director, in 66 the emperor celebrated victory over Parthia. Then he departed Rome for Greece. He left behind him two freedmen, Helius and Polyclitus, to act as viceroys in his absence. It may have been a calculated snub to the senate. With him, he took his ardent philhellenism and those skills in singing and chariot-racing which he had practised in Rome both in public and in private. His efforts, which at home, as Dio tells us, had inspired laughter, in Greece earned him 1,808 prizes: among them was a prize won in the Olympic Games for a chariot-race in which he had fallen from his chariot. Shameless it may have been, but Greek realpolitik reaped dividends. On 28 November 67, Nero declared the whole of Greece free from Roman taxation. 'To cities other rulers too have granted freedom,' he announced, 'but Nero alone to an entire province.'[21] His return to Rome took the form of a triumph. In Augustus' triumphal carriage he processed through city streets sprinkled with perfume. Ribbons rained like confetti. Contending with the perfume were the scents of sacrifice: victims offered in thanksgiving lined the processional route. Over his purple robe, Nero wore a cloak patterned with stars, on his head the Olympic crown. It was an extraordinary piece of posturing, attributable in Suetonius' version to his need to win popular approval: 'above all he was carried away by a craze for popularity and he was jealous of all who in any way stirred the feeling of the mob.' Such megalomaniac theatricality served only to assert the impossibility of incorporating within traditional Roman mores tendencies that were alien, out of sympathy, a challenge.

He forfeited popularity. He had antagonized the senate and distanced the people by long absence from Rome. His misdeeds were all known, the tally (beginning with those murders in his own family) a long and painful one. He had squandered the riches of empire, the loyalty of troops and commons alike. Not Claudius' divinity, Germanicus' lustre or the distant shadow of Augustus availed him now. In the spring of 68, a provincial governor of high birth and old-fashioned inclinations issued a proclamation repudiating Nero. In the aftermath of Galba's bid for the purple, Dio writes, Nero found himself 'abandoned by everybody alike'.[22]

In the first instance, the historian overstates the case. Nero responded with calmness and indifference to the news of Galba's revolt – and did nothing. Inertia was the expression of his contempt. Was he drugged by detachment, too lost in the echoing chambers of his private world of Greek triumphs to recall himself to the business of Rome? In truth he had been absent for a long time. He declared himself sole consul for the

year, unaware of the irony of seeking refuge in the tatters of
Republican office-holding. He summoned legions from Britain
and Illyricum and made plans to supplement their numbers
with sailors stationed at Misenum. By the time he took decisive
action, it was too late. A part of him wanted it that way. He
wanted to escape to Egypt but there was no one left who
would go with him. The Praetorians had defected, Nymphidius
Sabinus resorting to bribery in their transfer of allegiance to
Galba. In this Rome of the principate, loss of the Praetorians
probably amounted to an insuperable obstacle. In the garden
of Livia's villa at Prima Porta, where a laurel sprig received by
the old Augusta as a portent had grown into a hedge supplying
branches for wreaths, the laurels were dying. There would be no
more crowns for Augustus' heirs, no more garlands for scions of
the Julii or the Claudii; that day was past.

Events were pressing in on Nero. The palace, when at length
he returned to it, stood empty. It had to be so, in Suetonius' story
the figure of a forlorn emperor lost among empty rooms and
echoing corridors repeatedly an image of tyranny unmasked.
Nero fled to the house of a freedman outside Rome. Sporus
was among the small party who accompanied him. Disguised
as a slave, Nero bore little resemblance to the young man who,
fourteen years earlier, had roamed Roman streets at night in
pursuit of easy violence and cheap thrills. An excess of good
living had made him bloated and waddling; the sway of early
good looks was all gone. When the moment came, the surfeit
of self-indulgence even stopped him from steeling himself for
suicide.

He played the last scene badly, this emperor whose reign is
bequeathed to us as a series of gaudy *tableaux vivants*. A slave
steadied his hand as he plunged a dagger deep into his neck:
perhaps this understudy even made the fatal stroke for him.

Bulging in agony, in those final seconds Nero's goggle eyes were not accorded any clarity of vision. He went to his grave still in a state of self-delusion. 'What an artist the world loses in me!' he gasped. Thanks to the public nature of kingship, there were those on hand to record his dying fall. He knew better at any rate than to ask with Augustus if he had done well in his role in the comedy of life.

GALBA

(3 BC–AD 69)

'Equal to empire had he
never been emperor'

Galba was an old man, a childless widower. Inflexible and gouty, of middle height and stooping, skull-faced and hook-nosed, hands and feet distorted with age, bald as an egg, but still, rising seventy-three, in thrall to primitive lusts and evil counsellors, this aristocratic son of a dwarfish hunchback betrayed the weaknesses of age but none of the spirit of the age. His seven-month reign overlapped Nero's life by a single day in June 68: he was stern in his rejection of Nero's legacy.

In this year of tumult (Nero dead, Vespasian a distant prospect), a secret of empire was revealed. It was Tacitus who made this grandiloquent pronouncement. An emperor could be created elsewhere than at Rome (championed by legions and a groundswell of disaffection carefully exploited: bribes in the right places, the senate tactfully wooed — these conditions Tacitus omitted). There were other revelations, too, in the maelstrom of Nero's fall, namely that the principate was not an old man's game nor responsive to old-fashioned ideas of empire, though these would emerge only later. 'What mean you, fellow soldiers? I am yours and you are mine' is one version of Galba's dying words. But he was wrong. Galba did not belong to the soldiers nor they to him. Vigorous in mind he may have been, as Dio insists; also marked for greatness from childhood by none other than Augustus, as Suetonius offers; even an 'excellent prince': yet his political instincts were fallible. At the moment of acclamation he had disdained to pay the troops' accession donative: as a result, their loyalty clung to the memory of Augustus' open-handed progeny. Miserly and sour with rectitude, Galba remained a geriatric usurper.

As he sowed, so in time he reaped. No matter that his reign had been presaged in 200-year-old prophecies: omens were not breastplates and Galba's head would be hacked from his body by those with no interest in the numinous. Perhaps Galba's flaw was that, at a time for new departures, and in the light of Tacitus' 'secret', he remained in every important respect a quintessentially Roman creation: his mental landscape extended no further than the city of his birth. His were Republican qualities. His virtues were as austere and uncompromising as that Republican visual idiom he embraced in his portraiture, an imagery of patrician remoteness and heroic hauteur, sunken cheeks, furrowed brow, lips tight with disapproval: the clock turned back, an eschewal of populist deceits. But the Republic was dead – one of Galba's own family, opposed to Julius Caesar, had joined the conspiracy of Brutus and Cassius and died in its defence; and the idealized good looks of Augustus and his successors suited better the paternalism at the heart of the principate. Tacitus' summary is pithy: 'He was ruined by his old-fashioned inflexibility, and by an excessive sternness which we are no longer able to endure.'[1]

Not unusually, Suetonius' Galba is attended by portents throughout his long life. At the moment of greatest daring, forsaking the easy backwater of provincial governorship for fully armed conspiracy, he sees a foaling mule. And so his reign is foretold (as his grandfather had said it would be), bounty born of barrenness: impossible to turn back now or resist. It is the sort of logic-defying natural phenomenon the Romans loved as an alternative clairvoyance. In this, one of Suetonius' bleakest portraits, that miracle of the arid made fertile seems at odds with the aura of desiccation which emerges from Galba's rigid record. Suetonius suggests that we are wrong to regard him thus, wizened beyond any quickening of the blood, inhuman with age, though it is his own behaviour as emperor which compels this assessment. His appetite, he notes, foraging for examples, was impressive. In winter, his heavy eating began even before daybreak (for age did not prevent him from early rising and long days of endeavour in Rome's service). Impressive, too, in a man unable to endure the pressure of shoes on gout-swollen feet, were his intermittent sexual athletics. His homosexuality was of Rome's taboo-breaking variety: a preference for strong, full-grown men over the pert-arsed youths who were traditionally the older Roman's quarry. Suetonius offers a single, striking instance. News that the senate had ratified Galba's accession was delivered by his freedman and bedfellow (and former prisoner of Nero) Icelus. Overcome with the exhilaration of the moment, this dry-lipped old martinet took Icelus to one side and quickly fucked him. For his indignity, Icelus was rewarded with a leg-up to the knighthood.

Yet Galba's appetites, in contrast to those who had gone before, were neither omnivorous nor unrestrained. His response to Icelus was at variance with his reaction to Agrippina the Younger three decades earlier. That ambitious termagant set her cap at Galba during the latter's marriage to Aemilia Lepida (probably at the time Claudius made good a bequest to Galba of fifty million sesterces from the empress Livia, unpaid by Tiberius and Gaius).[2] Galba not only resisted the advances of the future empress, but failed to intervene when, at a gathering of Roman matrons, to considerable scandal his mother-in-law slapped her for her temerity. Given Agrippina's ability to cling to a grudge, this robust vignette may account for the relative quietness of Galba's career during the second half of Claudius' reign, as well as his later attitude towards Nero, Agrippina's son.

Indulgent only to his intimates, forbearing with friends and freedmen, forbidding in demeanour, Galba extolled the discipline of former times. If only he could have summoned to his cause an illusion of barrack-room camaraderie. But he was always the general and never the soldier. He took no pleasure in bloodshed, yet was liberal with the death sentence; without recourse to torture, still he killed. Once a soldier on an expedition sold his rations at an extortionate rate. Galba ordered that should the guilty man fall hungry, none must feed him. Hunger struck and the soldier starved to death. On another occasion, he cut off the hands of a dishonest money-lender and nailed them to his counter. The very chill of his authority is sinister. Even the lessons he had learned from Augustus' example misfired: a preference for simple living and lip-service to Republican nostalgia. In Galba's case, lack of ostentation compounded his reputation for meanness, his refusal to put on the raiment of magnificence which fitted the emperor's role; while the Republic he coveted was one of martial vigour in which the ordinary Roman was no more than a cog in a wheel, wooed with little bread and fewer circuses. He had no truck with Nero's sumptuous profligacy, those extravagant displays in the theatre, the nights of gaudy subversion when misrule torched the streets of Rome with blazing hedonism – though as a young man he had distinguished himself in the praetorship with a novel innovation at the Floralian Games: elephants walking a tightrope. The taste for whimsy was short-lived. Little wonder that, as Suetonius tells us, he 'incurred the hatred of almost all men of every class'. This rapid *dégringolade* took seven months, only five of which were spent in Rome.

———❦———

Like the protagonist in a work of literature, the Galba of the sources contains within himself seeds of his own downfall: character as plot. Historians traditionally ascribe to him a trio of mistakes: his brutal purges of the army; his refusal to pay the soldiers' donative; his misguided choice of successor. Each arises from discernible character traits: the love of discipline, money and noble birth. As a combination they failed to win adherents and cost Galba his reputation and his life. Compared with that of his predecessors, Galba's was a throne without foundations, built on a fragile consensus at a moment of crisis and unable, even at the outset, to unite all factions (the legions in Germany, as we shall see, offered support that was at best grudging). Nero had fallen despite every safeguard of the Julio-Claudian inheritance. How easily then might Galba, lacking those entitlements, fall too.

Did Galba understand that secret of empire revealed by Tacitus – or did he justify his elevation as the deserts of aristocratic birth? Certainly he failed to grasp the extent to which emperor-making powers belonged not to the would-be emperor (a mistake also made by Otho) but to those legions whose focus of loyalty was not Rome, the Empire or even a concept of Roman greatness but the present incumbent of the throne – a symbol. With Nero's death, the thread that bound Rome's scattered armies to the Palatine momentarily snapped. For Galba, loyalty was not a prize to be won but an enforceable aspect of military discipline. And so, recognizing its importance, he refused to fix the broken connection, prepared neither to bribe his soldiers with gifts of money nor to tender for their favour: 'I levy my soldiers, I do not buy them.' A comatose senate, accustomed now to fear and fawning, could no longer help him: there is evidence that eminent men, more aware than Galba of the direction the wind was blowing, hung back from supporting his ever-tottering regime. First in Germany, afterwards in the East, the thanes flew from him. His was assuredly not the spirit of the age.

It might have been different in the absence of a fourth mistake, namely the counsel he kept. Galba's *consilium* was effectively shrunk to a body of three. With certain irony Suetonius referred to these trusted, all-powerful attendants who never left his side as his 'tutors'. They were a curious trio, lambasted for corruption though none of the sources offers evidence. Successfully they held the world at bay for Galba. First, that burly bedfellow Icelus, who rewarded himself for pains in the discharge of duty by enriching himself at breakneck speed, the gains all his, the opprobrium for his misdeeds Galba's. Second, Titus Vinius and, third, Cornelius Laco, 'the one most worthless, the other most spiritless', according to Tacitus.[3] Vinius was a low-grade senator, 'a man of unbounded covetousness'. His claim to the emperor's ear rested on the sort of military experience and provincial governorship guaranteed to appeal to Galba; he had led Galba's army and his record as governor was a good one. The charms of Laco, 'intolerably haughty and indolent' in Suetonius' account, are less easily fathomed: his overriding characteristic was a knee-jerk need to oppose any plan not his own. Inexperience notwithstanding, Galba would appoint him Praetorian prefect. Perhaps he intended to retain effective control of the imperial guard himself, Laco no more than a cipher.

Stubborn and intractable, 'so weak and so credulous', as Tacitus dismissed him, the old man too often allowed himself to be guided by these gimcrack intimates, negligent of the odour of nefariousness that tainted each of them and compounded his own quickly acquired reputation for cruelty. Probably all three were more intelligent than contemporary sources are prepared to acknowledge: their success depended on successfully directing Galba and manipulating that intransigence which was one result of his age and outlook. If so, their intelligence was of a small-beer variety. At loggerheads with one another, 'being at variance and in smaller matters pursuing their own aims', Icelus, Vinius and Laco advised the emperor badly.[4] 'He so entrusted and handed himself over as their tool,' Suetonius writes, 'that his conduct was far from consistent: for now he was more exacting and niggardly, and now more extravagant and reckless, than became a prince chosen by the people and of his time of life.' In his downfall, they met their own day of reckoning.

On his death, the senate voted Galba a statue to be erected on a column where he was slain in the Forum. This commission was vetoed by Vespasian. Almost no physical record of Galba survives. His significance lies rather in the nature of his election to the principate and his symbolic role as an interim *princeps*. The Galba of the records is poised between the old world of the Augustan diarchy – accepting autocracy, hiding behind pious regret for the Republic, that deceit, 'good' and 'bad', Julio-Claudians had relished or reviled by turns – and a new world in which a ruler championed by the military worked for the good of the Empire and the support of his troops. It may be that, in unsettled times, Galba's disastrous record – his alienation of the troops and those fellow provincial governors who had made him Rome's seventh Caesar, added to his inability to win over the senate or the people of Rome – preserved the principate.

For as Otho would correctly discern, it was Galba's government which retrospectively lessened Nero's sting, Galba's stern misjudgements which contextualized the tyrannous folly of the last of Augustus' heirs, Galba's icy rectitude which glamorized Rome's first dynasty. It was not by accident that Vespasian and his sons, the second dynasty of Rome, made manifest in public as well as private their connections to their eccentric, imperious predecessors (albeit they assiduously gave Nero a wide berth).

———◦◦◦———

For his part, Galba was predisposed to look backwards. Born on 24 December 3 BC, in a house in the country near Tarracina southeast of Rome, Servius Sulpicius Galba was the younger son of a family whose distinction outclassed that of Augustus and his haughty clan (with notable exceptions: Livia and Domitius Ahenobarbus, for example). His family tree – in time prominently displayed in the emperor's atrium – traced lines of descent from Jupiter on his father's side and, on his mother's side, King Minos' wife Pasiphae, whose unnatural passion for Poseidon's white bull perhaps suggested to Galba's contemporaries his own invert's desire for thick-necked male lovers. In 68, such a parade of ancestral renown deliberately recalled the atria of Republican Rome, with their galleries of wax masks, as well as the Julian claim to descent from Venus. For the record of the Sulpicii Galbae was one of Republican eminence. The Servius Galba who, in 145 BC, became consul of Rome, was acclaimed by Suetonius as 'decidedly the most eloquent speaker of his time'. (Time would show that his descendant had inherited the name without the gifts.) Rome's seventh Caesar cherished, too, the legacy of his great-grandfather Quintus Catulus Capitolinus, consul in 78 BC, called 'Capitolinus' on account of his role in rebuilding the temple on the Capitoline, which he dedicated in 69 BC. We are told that Galba clung to Capitolinus' memory – he may have requested the inclusion of his name in his statue inscriptions – yet when his own turn came, he appeared uninterested in similar gestures of largesse. All his tastes were for retrenchment in the wake of Nero's extravagance. Such frugality, admirable in origin, was none of the emperor's part. It shows a muddle-headedness in reading the lessons of the past and the challenges of office. For all his preoccupation with pedigree – a blindness that would cost him dear – Galba overlooked the truth of the grandest families: that among the heroes and history-makers lurk numbskulls, nitwits, nonentities and the justly notorious. His own brother was among them: a petulant bankrupt who committed suicide when Tiberius found out his weakness. Enamoured of the past, Galba failed to respond to the changed circumstances of the present.

Up to a point, his career maintained the lustre of his forebears. A survivor of five reigns and immensely rich to boot, he had served as consul in 33 and governor successively of Upper Germany (an appointment by Gaius, following Gaetulicus' conspiracy), Africa (at Claudius' intervention) and, beginning in 60, Nearer Spain. (This last was a miscall on Nero's part. Suspicious of private citizens whose esteem soared too high, Nero nevertheless overlooked Galba's lofty reputation on the grounds, Plutarch tells us, 'that he was thought to be of a gentle nature, and his great age gave an added confidence that he would always act with caution'.[5]) It was more than a case of boxes ticked and trouble avoided. Under Tiberius, Galba advanced through the stages of the *cursus honorum* in orderly fashion (that canny old cynic of an emperor smiled at predictions of a glorious destiny for Galba in old age). He served Gaius, Claudius and Nero without mishap. Although the hallmarks of his governorships were his unrelenting military discipline, a legalistic frame of mind hardwired to inclemency and undoubted personal incorruptibility, Plutarch, in his role of Galba's apologist, records that he won golden words in Germany and Africa. Unenlightened, uncharismatic and solidly business-like as his approach appears with hindsight, the proconsulship brought him triumphal regalia and a trio of priesthoods. Family background increased his prestige: certainly he himself thought so. After three decades of public service, in the prominent display of his family tree he asserted his own superiority, trusting in the Roman belief in heredity; and aligned himself with the deified Julius (both invincibly patrician, both claiming descent from the firmament). It was a dangerous raising of the bar. Caesar had exploited family grandeur not primarily in a spirit of self-congratulation, but as part of a larger plan of legitimizing claims to pre-eminence based on solid achievement. A century after Caesar, in a world schooled to mistrust every claim of high birth bar the Julio-Claudians', Galba's family tree was intended of itself to guarantee his reign. Predictably it failed.

For Galba was indeed an old man. All the sources remark on his age: his body twisted with arthritis; the peculiar, unexplained growth of skin that hung from the left side of his torso, held in place by bandages; the hands unable to unroll documents; the gauntness of his face which accentuated the prominence of his nose (noble only in numismatic profile). Even the boy who attended him at public sacrifices in Spain had snow-white hair, its colour transformed from that of youth to age in an instant by way of omen. Galba's appearance, Tacitus and Dio agree, gave rise to ridicule – more than that, disgust. Tacitus blames widespread lack of judgement in degraded times, a childish and superficial outlook in which emperors were valued for 'the beauty and grace of their persons': we hear the historian's contempt.[6] But there was more to it than that. Galba's age was noteworthy since it marked him out as a survivor. In 68 he was one of a handful of scions of the great senatorial families of the Republic to have escaped imperial purges. His real distinction was not the cartography of grandeur revealed in his family tree, but his age, which in turn implied isolation. In his youth he had venerated customs of the past described by Suetonius as old and forgotten, including requiring his freedmen and slaves to appear before him twice a day, 'greeting him in the morning and bidding him farewell at evening, one by one'. Remote in outlook, mostly bereft of his peer group, this scrawny veteran represented a vanished moment. His challenge was to resist turning back the clock... the lure of anachronisms... an approach to the principate informed by unreliable memories of the Republic. 'As yet my strength is unimpaired,' he responded to a courtier who congratulated him on his appearance of vigour. It was a quotation from Homer and suitably heroic, but sycophant and emperor knew that both dissembled. Galba's appearance betrayed his age and physical condition. Self-deluded, too arrogant to concern himself with popular feeling, he failed to recognize that it was his age which shaped the instability of his regime, inspiring widespread and unsettling speculation about the identity of his successor – Suetonius claims this as the principal topic of conversation across Italy. It was a further weight on the emperor's shoulders. As we have seen, the burdens of empire weighed heavily on men far younger than Galba.

Last man standing is no basis for leadership choices. In 68, with Nero still on the throne, Galba could be presented as the obvious candidate to replace him (although this view was never universal). Distinguished by his record of service, his proximity to the imperial house through five reigns and his unimpeachable aristocracy, he ought to have lent his name to the gentlest of revolutions. The adrenaline of the great endeavour of toppling Nero may have prevented far-sightedness. 'The nobility of his birth and the perils of the times made what was really indolence pass for wisdom,' Tacitus claimed. 'He seemed greater than a subject while he was yet in a subject's rank, and by common consent would have been pronounced equal to empire had he never been emperor.'[7] It is among the historian's best-known epitaphs and acknowledges that, despite his mistakes, Galba, like emperors before him and after him, was a victim as much as a villain.

The creation of an emperor outside Rome began with a letter from Gaul. Its author was himself a romanized Gaul of royal descent. Gaius Julius Vindex was provincial governor of Gallia Lugdunensis. He would be dead within the year, killed for setting in motion a revolution. First steps included a rallying cry to fellow Gauls against conditions within the province and, looking further afield, Nero's inadequacies as emperor. To fellow governors, including Galba, Vindex dispatched overtures inviting support.

Encouraged by Vinius, Galba responded to Vindex' invitation on 2 April 68. (It is likely that tentative consultation among provincial governors had occupied him in the interim.) At Nova Carthago, he was acclaimed 'General of the Senate and People of Rome', a careful piece of equivocation which avoided such overtly imperial titles as 'Caesar' and 'Augustus'. The import of this inflammatory, deliberately Republican-sounding salutation was clear nonetheless and is said to have caused the histrionic Nero to faint. Suetonius justifies septuagenarian treachery on the grounds that Galba had intercepted instructions from Nero ordering his own assassination, an explanation which smacks of revisionism by Galban sympathizers at a later date. A more plausible catalyst is the death of Corbulo at Nero's hands the previous year in the aftermath of victory in Armenia. That vindictive and irrational murder may have suggested to Galba the extent of Nero's erratic misanthropy, the uncertain rewards of service and the precariousness of his own position.

Like Vindex before him, Galba requested local assistance. First to offer support was the governor of Lusitania, Marcus Salvius Otho, a disaffected former confidant of Nero and exhusband of Nero's wife Poppaea. Next Tiberius Julius Alexander, prefect of Egypt. Tardier was the commander of the legions in Upper Germany, Lucius Verginius Rufus, who may have been influenced in his protracted ambivalence by the overwhelming dislike of his troops for Galba.[8] His own legions' first choice to replace Nero, Rufus twice refused to be acclaimed emperor by his men. Instead, as he was bound to do, he put down Vindex' revolt, at the end of which Vindex was forced to commit suicide.*

Vindex' defeat briefly shook Galba's confidence. He withdrew to Clunia, a hill-town in the north of his province. There the course of Roman history was decided by timely discoveries in the Temple of Jupiter. A prophecy whose existence was revealed to the priest in a dream announced 'that one day there would

---

* Galba did not forget Rufus' tergiversation. Replaced by the ineffectual Hordeonius Flaccus, he was among a number of provincial governors to lose their posts during the new reign. Flaccus' weakness in turn passed the baton of revolt to Lower Germany, which Galba entrusted to the future emperor Vitellius. In an echo of the mistakes made by Nero in Galba's own case and that of another future emperor, Vespasian, Galba chose Vitellius for his apparent harmlessness, persuaded by his reputation for gluttony and his galloping bankruptcy.

come forth from Spain the ruler and lord of the world'. Galba responded energetically. From the province's leading nobles, he created an ersatz 'senate' intended to assist him. Appropriating the revenues of imperial property within the province, he had already set about increasing the armed forces at his disposal. Both courses of action – practical on the one hand, nodding towards Republican constitutional propriety on the other – steadied his resolve when he learned that Nero had dispatched troops under Petronius Turpilianus and Rubrius Gallus to quash his rebellion (in fact Gallus defected and Turpilianus' troops deserted).[9]

The defection which made Galba emperor of Rome, however, happened within the city itself. A low-born adventurer took it upon himself to turn king-maker. In the first instance his motives were probably self-preservation.

Nymphidius Sabinus was the son of an imperial freedwoman. Thanks to his slipshod approach to truthfulness, his father is unknown, but chief contenders include a gladiator called Marcianus and the emperor Gaius. By 65 prefect of the Praetorian Guard alongside Tigellinus, three years later Nymphidius had manoeuvred himself into a position of virtual control. It was a heady achievement for a man of unbridled ambition lacking scruples. Apparently more aware than Nero of the extent of the rebellion fomenting Empire-wide, Nymphidius embarked on a calculated gamble. He decided to transfer his allegiance to Galba. He would take with him the allegiance of the Praetorian Guard, that company of emperor-makers whose loyalty to Augustus' descendants had previously ranked high among the latter's trump cards.

It was a tall order but, as time would show, Nymphidius did not shrink from challenges. On the night of 8 June he announced to the Praetorians that Nero had abandoned the city and that they, the emperor's personal guard, were without an emperor.

Then, in Galba's name, making free with that immense fortune which he anticipated shortly having at his disposal, he promised them a donative bigger than any paid to date: 30,000 sesterces a man. On the same day the senate had declared Galba Rome's newest *princeps*; the following day, Nero committed suicide. But if Nymphidius had correctly judged the mood of the moment and the spirit of the men in his charge, he had misjudged his new master. Nymphidius' donatives would never be paid: too soon his broken promises contributed to Galba's death.

Galba set out for Rome, dressed, Suetonius tells us, in a cloak with a dagger hanging around his neck, the very model of military vigour had it not been for his physical decrepitude. At Narbo Martius in August, with every appearance of charm and consideration, he met representatives of the senate, entertaining them in a style of simple dignity that surely aped his earliest memories of Augustus. Conspicuously he disdained to make use of the palace furniture sent from Rome by Nymphidius (indeed, he pointedly omitted to acknowledge Nymphidius' gift): the power entrusted to him recognized a lifetime's service to the state, not at this stage a trumpery affair requiring stage-sets and elaborate costumes. In that spirit, early coin issues acclaimed an emperor of messianic qualities with no hint of personal grandeur. Considered and propagandist as with all imperial coinage, they were careful to temper Galba's attributes with proper acknowledgement of the role of the senate (which was virtually no role at all bar the maintenance of appearances in the face of considerable *force majeure*). They attested an emperor chosen 'by the Senate's decree for saving the citizens of Rome' no less,[10] and predictably celebrated peace, safety, liberty, harmony (a quality Galba's rule would do much to jeopardize) and, more controversially, Galba's equity (time would show that a vindictive emperor interpreted the term in the light of his own harsh requirements). Subsequent ironies notwithstanding, it was a dialect of selflessness and civic-mindedness at the outset of Galba's reign, old-fashioned duty before personal gain; and a whitewashing of those reservations about Galba's candidature which may have existed in many breasts that summer when legions and adventurers dictated the corollary to Nero's death.

In late October or early November, at the end of a progress described by Tacitus as 'slow and blood-stained', Galba arrived in Rome. That night the theatre staged Atellan farces, those runaround comedies of low humour and ribald buffoonery popular in the Republic (even Sulla was said to have turned his hand to writing an Atellan farce). It was an evening distinguished by laughter, most of it, according to Suetonius, at Galba's expense. For the Atellan farces, forerunners of pantomime and the *commedia dell'arte*, employed a small number of stock characters, among them a fat man, a clown and an old man on the brink of decrepitude. That night the old man was a skinflint bumpkin called 'Onesimus'. 'Here comes Onesimus from his farm,' began the actors. Like a ripple the laughter began. The audience joined in the song. When it finished, they began it again. And then again. Accompanying words with actions. Over and over that night they laughed at Onesimus-Galba. Their laughter was a complex emotion: born of relief certainly, but also of fear. For the crowd had heard a rumour of tidings outside the theatre, and what they had heard supplied grounds for apprehension.

It was, in its way, as much a public spectacle as any stage performance. Unlike slapstick comedy, it did not provoke laughter. According to Dio, more than 7,000 men were killed in an encounter with Galba's convoy at the Milvian Bridge on the outskirts of Rome (the real figure may be much smaller: the rumour itself is significant). The men were sailors whom Nero had recruited to form an impromptu legion. Greeting Galba noisily, they petitioned for formal acknowledgement of their altered status. The disciplinarian Galba had no truck with popular pressure and responded evasively. It was a tinderbox moment. Vociferously the would-be soldiers reiterated their protests; some even drew their swords. Goaded by fury, Galba gave orders to the troops under his command. They charged the protesters. Fatalities were widespread. With a semblance of calm restored, Galba thrust home his point. He ordered decimation, that obsolete Republican punishment by which errant soldiers themselves killed one in ten of their number by lot, while the nine randomly chosen survivors were compelled to watch. His orders were carried out. 'This shows that even if Galba was bowed down with age and disease,' Dio comments, pursuing a train of thought surely intended to echo Galba's own, 'yet his mind was vigorous and he did not believe that an emperor should submit to compulsion in anything.'[11]

Not only fellow soldiers watched that day, but those crowds of the public who had journeyed to greet the emperor. Even in a city habituated to bloodshed, currently overrun with soldiers and balanced in a precarious peace, their response is predictable. For they had witnessed a portent more powerful than foaling mules or white-haired sacristans or centuries-old predictions interred in temple precincts. Later the same month, as they had wished, Galba formed the remaining soldier-sailors into a regular unit, Legio I *Adiutrix*.

Nero's marines were not the only casualties of Galba's march
to Rome. By the time the winter emperor reached his capital,
his axe of retribution had swung widely. Petronius Turpillianus,
that general dispatched by Nero to quell Galba's rebellion, was
forced to commit suicide for his loyalty, despite the defection of
his troops which had prevented him from inflicting on Galba
any more than unease. Betuus Cilo had requested assistance in
quashing Vindex' rebellion: he died for his pains. Ditto Fonteius
Capito, governor of Lower Germany, killed by Fabius Valens
and Cornelius Aquinus with Galba's acquiescence, neither exact
motives nor circumstances of his murder easy to unravel. In
Africa, Galban loyalists destroyed the legionary legate Clodius
Macer, suspected of restricting the grain supply in order to
strengthen his attempt to seize the throne. By late autumn,
Nymphidius Sabinus had also breathed his last. His eminence
had been brief. Once frustration with Galba's refusal to co-opt
him as his principal adviser tipped the balance and encouraged
Nymphidius to canvas for the throne on his own behalf, his
days were numbered. Men of the Praetorian Guard killed him,
leaving the way open for Galba's preferred candidate, Laco, to
command their unit. Cingonius Varro, elected to the consulate
for 69, 'a corrupt and venal orator', according to Tacitus, was
killed for having written the speech Nymphidius proposed to
deliver to the Praetorians.

Luckier than most, in 68 Verginius Rufus escaped with his
life. Loyal to Nero in punishing Vindex, he was saved by verbal
pedantry: although he had renounced the throne for himself, he
had also resisted open opposition to Galba by repeatedly stating
that he would abide by the choice of the senate. His reward in
the short term was an existence of notable uncertainty. It was
mercy after a fashion. Not enough to convince any of those
who had witnessed the brutality of the Milvian Bridge. Popular

outrage focused in particular on the deaths of Cingonius Varro and Petronius Turpillianus, both of them senators of mature years.

———— ∞ ————

Galba 'considered that he had not seized the power but that it had been given to him (indeed he was constantly making this statement),' Dio writes.[12] As in his coinage, so in his public pronouncements: it was Galba's version of Augustus' illusion, himself called to serve, power a burden accepted with reluctance. The emperor may have intended more than lip-service by such posturing. Evidence for his relationship with the senate is scant but does not support the inference of Dio's statement, namely that Galba made steps towards forsaking autocracy in favour of government more in line with Republican precept: like all of his predecessors, he rated his own power more highly than that of the senate. Admittedly, Galba himself was of senatorial stock. Those quick-fire reprisals ordered on the journey to Rome unnerved both his own and Neronian supporters. In addition, Suetonius reports an unsubstantiated rumour that Galba had in mind a plan almost certain to win the senate's disapprobation. He contemplated restricting to two years the duration of those military commands, governorships and procuratorships which traditionally comprised elements of the careers of senators and equestrians. His targets were ambition and corruption. It was in part a continuation of Nero's policy of rewarding mediocrity. Since the outcome was to deny potential conspirators any platform for the purple, the only beneficiary would be Galba himself. It was also an incursion into the political sphere of the emperor's parade-ground discipline. As such it smacked of the sort of tyrannous high-handedness associated with the worst of Galba's predecessors. Suetonius is clear that in future appointments would only be made to those who 'did not wish them and declined them', perversity befitting Tiberius or Gaius. Dangerous, too, deliberately to engender a culture in which dissembling and dissimulation became essential.

Galba's seven-month reign was too short for such far-reaching reform. It did, however, permit a policy which demonstrates a similar willingness to deprive its victims of entitlements they considered rightfully their own. Nero's shadow lay long over Galba's reign – his profligacy and ill discipline, his un-Roman enfranchisement of elements of society which had no place on the Palatine: actors and artists, Greeks, freedmen, sexual exhibitionists, narcissists, gluttons and popinjays. Most of all, Nero's extravagance offended Galba. He estimated that Nero had squandered in presents 2,200 million sesterces, a sum sufficiently exorbitant in conjunction with the cost of recent civil disturbance to empty the imperial treasury. Galba's response was simple: the gifts must be returned. He devised a strategy which permitted recipients to keep a tenth part of their ill-gotten gains. The remainder would be collected by a new bureau of knights, thirty in Tacitus' account, fifty according to Suetonius. Where recipients were unable to satisfy these repayments (because the money had been spent or items sold or passed on), the recipients at one remove were also liable for restitution. Tacitus commends the plan's fairness. Its short-term effect was chaos and widespread insolvency. Across Rome auctions proliferated; a flooded market realized paltry prices. The treasury was not replenished. It is hard to see who benefited save those carpet-baggers with an eye to a bargain, Vinius chief among them if we believe Plutarch's version of events. 'The business had no limits but was far extended and affected many; it gave the emperor himself a bad name and brought envy and hatred upon Vinius as having made the emperor ungenerous and sordid with everybody else,' Dio comments.[13] This unpopular but high-profile policy did nothing to shore up Galba's ebbing support. Instead, to a disaffected soldiery were added those remaining adherents of Nero. In the senate house, an encroachment of doubts concerning the emperor's good sense and political acumen.

No equivalent of political correctness emasculated Roman humour. The Atellan farces exploited the old, the fat and the silly, each embraced in the open season of Roman ribaldry. Galba's age, we have seen, concerns the ancient sources. Their preoccupation was not with the comedy value of the emperor's advancing years nor an anxiety for his wellbeing. The significance of Galba becoming emperor at seventy-two, a greater age then than now, lies in the implications for Rome and the Empire of physical and mental infirmity and any diminishing of the faculties on the part of its supreme governor. Of questionable constitution and preoccupied with the transmission of his legacy, Augustus had spent much of his reign resolving the succession. In the case of Galba, at the beginning of his reign approaching Augustus' age at death, the question was doubly urgent. Although Augustus had a single daughter, Julia, his choice of successors potentially drew on a wide pool which included Julia's children, the children and grandchildren of Augustus' second wife Livia, and the grandchildren of his sister Octavia. The two sons born of Galba's marriage to Aemilia Lepida had died many years earlier, making his decision less straightforward. It was nevertheless a significant decision for Rome as well as for Galba – although events would prove that the emperor had failed to anticipate fully the nature of that significance to himself.

———————

Unfinished business set in train the final descent. In 68 the legions of the Rhine had made clear their support for Verginius Rufus. Galba's summary promotion to office did not inspire a volte-face. For obvious reasons, the new emperor did not make amends by rewarding the German troops for their part in suppressing Vindex' revolt. Yet whatever Galba's personal feelings, the reward for duty done was merited by custom and practice. It was one more offence with which to tar Galba's name.

Something of the degree of discontent among the provinces' seven legions was revealed to Vitellius on his arrival in Lower Germany in November. Within less than two months that discontent would manifest itself in aggressive action. Tacitus credits the procurator of Belgica, Pompeius Propinquus, with informing Galba's government that 'the legions of Upper Germany had broken through the obligations of their military oath and were demanding another emperor'.[14] At the beginning of January, soldiers responded to Flaccus' insistence that they renew the oath of loyalty to Galba, an annual requirement, with an oath to the senate. The Fourth Legion went further and toppled the emperor's statues. With a greater understanding than Galba of the source of ultimate power, they resolved, Suetonius relates, 'to send a deputation to the Praetorians with the following message: that the emperor created in Spain did not suit them and the Guard must choose one who would be acceptable to all the armies'. It would not be the first time the Praetorians had created an emperor. The circumstances surrounding Gaius' murder and Claudius' accession almost thirty years before had a surreptitious quality: in the case of Galba's replacement, the soldiers' message suggests that the time for circumspection is past. No one any longer doubted the army's power in emperor-making.

Except, at the eleventh hour, Galba himself. Ill winds from Germany convinced the emperor that the question of the succession must be settled at once. What is less clear is whether Galba realized the extent of feeling against him nurtured by these same Rhine legions. Certainly not in Suetonius' account, where Galba interprets dissent as originating from the soldiers' anxiety about his childlessness. He summoned a council to debate the matter. Predictably his 'tutors' pulled him in different directions, each swayed by his own ulterior motive. Galba overlooked the obvious candidate, Marcus Salvius Otho, that governor of Lusitania who had been first to support his bid for power. Given Otho's ambition and the pains he had taken to cultivate universal good opinion, Galba would pay heavily for this oversight. Fatal indeed was his choice of a humourless thirty-something aristocratic exile without *auctoritas*, renown or military experience. Lucius Calpurnius Piso Licinianus was distinguished by a stern moroseness and an exalted family tree, both akin to Galba's own. His character may have resembled that of the middle-aged Tiberius, adopted by Augustus. But Galba's adoption of Piso betrayed none of the half-heartedness and reservations of that earlier adoption. Unfortunately for Galba, nor did Piso possess Tiberius' undoubted qualifications for empire. The emperor first announced his decision to the Praetorians. Above the soldiers' camp, thunder and lightning tore a glowering sky. Rain gashed air heavy with forebodings. Galba's news was greeted with perfunctory cheering. Few present can have known that, even at this high-water mark in his fortunes, Piso stood not first in line to the throne but third. To the north, the legions of Lower Germany had not waited for Galba's deliberations but nominated a *princeps* of their own, their commander Aulus Vitellius. Nearer home, fired by jealousy, a one-time ally was hell-bent on revenge. Otho had no intention of abiding by the decision of Galba and his 'tutors'.

He grasped his chance on 15 January. That morning he was the only senator to attend the emperor at his sacrifice, for Galba suspected nothing. Not even when a soothsayer warned that danger was very close at hand did his thoughts turn to Otho. And so a second-rate coup, badly organized and limited in scope, removed that emperor who had been the provincial governors' riposte to the folly of the last of the Julio-Claudians. Galba was killed in the Forum, amid scenes of confusion and panic, toppled from his litter accidentally, slain where he fell. The shower of blades continued to rain down long after life had departed that twisted body. Piso died too, dragged from the Temple of Vesta and decapitated. Belatedly, as Otho's forces grabbed the upper hand, emperor and heir had announced payment of the donative Galba would not have paid under happier circumstances. It was too late. Abandoning their milch cow, Vinius, Laco and Icelus struggled to flee, as unworthy of Galba's trust now as at any point in his fleeting premiership. Vinius was cut down as he ran, stabbed from behind. Laco and Icelus perished later, the latter crucified.

Portents foretold this grizzly end (impossible that they should resist). As Galba made his autumn journey to Rome, a sacrificial ox, half-butchered and bleeding, furiously broke free of its bonds and charged the old man's carriage. Animated by agony, it stamped and kicked; it showered Galba with blood. The emperor dismounted his carriage and narrowly avoided being impaled on the lance of one of his own guards. Three months later, both pelting by blood and danger from his inner circle were realized in full. Galba's death possessed something of that nobility his politics had lacked. Humbled on the ground, he offered his neck without resistance or fear to the soldiers who surrounded him. His final command was curt and clear: that they strike him where he knelt, in keeping with their will.

OTHO

(AD 32–69)

'If I was worthy to be
Roman emperor...'

OTHO.

Otho is Suetonius' cursed Caesar, Plutarch's and Tacitus' too. The accounts agree: the omens were against him. (Plutarch labels them 'uncertain and of dubious origin'.[1]) Surrounded at intervals by soothsayers and an astrologer whom Suetonius calls Seleucus, Tacitus and Plutarch Ptolemaeus, Rome's eighth Caesar ignored every prophecy and portent bar one: that he would escape Nero's displeasure with his life and survive the last of the Julio-Claudians to rule as emperor of Rome.

His reign of three months did not outlast the spring. It ended in suicide. His death was noble, heroic, in the grand traditions of a warlike Republic. In the sources its manly rhetoric has the set-piece qualities of a scene from epic poetry or perhaps a history painting. Apparently a vigorous foil to the indolence of his life, Otho's death comes down to us as the sort of incident which once commended Roman history to British schoolrooms: lessons from one overweening empire appropriated in the service of another. 'If I was worthy to be Roman emperor, I ought to give my life freely for my country,' Plutarch's Otho tells his troops.[2] It is the spirit of Kitchener and Kipling and no parody is implied. Alone in the light of a new dawn, uncomplaining, with apparently no thought of personal suffering, he stabbed himself through the heart – like a sacrificial offering, blood spilt to prevent further bloodshed. Only a glass of water steadied his hand. He had first paid bequests to all his staff and destroyed correspondence incriminating to those he left behind.

Titian painted Otho in the guise of a Renaissance prince. In the copy of that painting which survives, a sword hangs at his side, his cloak surmounts shining armour. His hair is thick and curly (in fact he wore a wig), his arm strong and sinewy (his flesh was smooth from constant depilation); he appears heavily jowled, cheeks dark with a day's growth of stubble (throughout his life he used bread poultices to soften his skin and reduce facial hair). His expression is petulant, effete: so too the limpness of his pose, despite a stirring backdrop of mountains and penumbrous sky. His appearance confirms the rumour told to Suetonius by his father, that such was Otho's distaste for violence that the mere mention of the deaths of Brutus and Cassius made him shudder. He is unconvincingly martial. Were it not for the manner of his death, the majority of his contemporaries would have agreed. 'Believe me when I insist that I can die more honourably than I can reign,' he abjures his followers.[3] Ironically, his very death gave them reason to doubt him. For Otho, this tableau that is both intimate and universal represents a moment of apotheosis. It is a refutation of former waywardness, turning his back on erstwhile mediocrity – surely not the same bandy-legged, splay-footed devotee of Isis who, harried by grievances, had asked pettishly, 'What truck have I with impossible tasks?' Or, perhaps, just such a one, giving up when the going gets tough.

Plutarch described Otho as womanly and unaccustomed to command, a recipe for cowardice, misjudgement and vacillation. In time, in power struggles that were wholly opportunistic, Otho's luxury and licentiousness would be pitted against the stingy disciplinarianism of Galba and the gluttony and drunkenness of Vitellius: Hobson's choice. It was a measure of the depths to which Rome's throne had sunk by the beginning of 69. 'The most worthless of mortals had been selected… by some fatality to ruin the Empire,' Tacitus growls of Otho's conflict with Vitellius.[4] Less sceptical sources agree. 'For as regards prodigality, effeminacy, inexperience in war, and multiplicity of debts incurred in a previous state of poverty, it was hard to say which of them had the advantage.'[5] Pique had provoked Otho's coup; rashness undid him. Neither trait belonged in the arsenal of an emperor. In the first instance Otho was the choice neither of senators nor of soldiers. The decision to rule was his own, taken without consultation or popular pressure (despite the inevitable charade of the *recusatio imperii* offered to the senate): meagre and selfish in its ambitions. Of similar origin was the bolder decision to abrogate power through suicide. But he made a good death and there were signs that, with a carrying wind, Otho's principate might have offered a variant of Vespasian's middle way. Omens and the altar's bloody entrails decreed otherwise.

For in truth there was nothing shiftless about Marcus Salvius Otho, big-spending, high-living, loose-loving. By force of will he had maintained the upward trajectory of his recent family history. He did so not via the magistracies of the *cursus honorum*, as tradition demanded, but through close – some said very close – friendship with Nero, his near contemporary, whom he first met at one of Claudius' banquets. (Claudius had singled out for praise his father, Lucius Otho, after the latter foiled a conspiracy against the emperor's life. For the same reason a statue of Lucius decorated the palace, a rare mark of honour. Given the Romans' belief in the dependability of genetics, Otho cannot have failed to benefit from his father's high repute.) When the time came, he was also assiduous in courting the favour of all and any who could serve him, ruthless in pursuit of his goal. 'Altogether [he] acted the slave to make himself the master,' Tacitus records: the historian does not intend flattery.[6] Less laudable tactics included a flirtation with an influential freedwoman comfortably past her sell-by date. Shamelessly, without regard to honesty or kindliness, he pursued this ageing court jade as a conduit to Nero. Determined, though to outward appearance hell-bent on pleasure, Otho affected the courtier's insouciance. His model is the swan, paddling furiously beneath the water's smooth surface. His efforts succeeded, or he would not find himself included in our survey. But victory was short-lived in the extreme, the minutes of his reign recorded on a butterfly's wing-span. He died on 16 April 69, only days before his thirty-seventh birthday and less than a hundred days after being hailed as emperor. Suetonius records the beaten breasts and self-immolation of his supporters in the wake of that gloriously Roman death. His account comes closest to avoiding partisanship. For good measure he reports a claim that is substantiated by nothing in Otho's life: 'that he had put an end to Galba not so much for the sake of ruling, as of restoring the republic and liberty.'

In the sources Otho benefits from his opposition to Vitellius. The Flavians rewrote the history of this year of lawlessness, condemning Vitellius, repudiating Nero. Then as now, Otho occupies middle ground. With hindsight a man of straw, he was a secondary target in Flavian myth-making, the embodiment of the spirit of a misguided moment, no more – an aberrancy, when personal desire superseded claims of birth, prestige, experience or the appetite for public service... and none considered restoration of the Republic and liberty. As we shall see, it was an accusation Vespasian and his sons dare not countenance.

With civil war came innovation. If Galba was the emperor created outside Rome, Otho was the emperor created outside the ruling classes. We can reach our own conclusion on which was the more radical outcome for precedent-loving Romans. His pinchpenny coup was masterminded by a freedman called Onomastus, an officer of the imperial bodyguard, Barbius Proculus, and Veturius the subaltern. They were abetted in the first instance by a tiny handful of disaffected mercenaries. It was an act of daring which, questionable motives aside, ought not to have succeeded. That it did so indicates inherent weaknesses in the system. Otho's brief career did nothing to address those weaknesses. Like him, his successor was a man bent on personal gain, propelled by a section of the military beyond his natural ability, in Vitellius' case an emperor disposed only to the corruptibility of power. All that Vitellius had in his favour was a decent bloodline.

Granted, Otho's grandfather, also Marcus Salvius Otho, had been a senator. He was the first of his family to be so (his own mother, described as 'lowly', may have been a slave: he owed his advancement, according to Suetonius, to Livia's influence, a connection of sorts with the old regime). Originally the Othones came from Ferentium, descendants of Etruscan princes, a family of ancient lineage and illustrious reputation. There is an echo here of the long-dead Maecenas, whose easy backsliding into lubricious extravagance was also a feature of Otho's youth (indeed, Lucius Otho regularly flogged his second son for un-Roman frailties). Such 'distinction' could not be guaranteed to impress senatorial Rome.

The principate, however, as we have seen, looked kindly on provincials and those born outside Rome's aristocracy. Otho senior was evidently sufficiently wealthy to manage the senate's property qualification; his connection with Livia marks the

beginning of a relationship with the imperial court. In the next
generation, Lucius Otho endeared himself so successfully to
Tiberius (whom he resembled physically) that people believed
him to be the emperor's son. Coquettish freedwomen aside, it
would not have been difficult for the younger Marcus Salvius
Otho to gain admittance to palace life. But Otho did not stop
at winning Nero's friendship. Five years older than Agrippina's
son, he translated friendship into influence, affinity based on
shared interests and similarities (and any sexual liaison the
men embarked on); Suetonius claims on his behalf that Otho
'was privy to all the emperor's plans and secrets', including
Nero's plan to kill his mother. It would be wrong at this stage
to assume traitorous hankerings on Otho's part. The sources
are clear that he aspired to the throne only once the bonds of
friendship had been shattered, a process beginning in the late
50s. In the meantime, if his tastes inclined to power in the short
term, he pinned his hopes on a place in Nero's *consilium*.

Like Vespasian's association with Narcissus, a relationship
forged at the same time, Otho's connection with Nero would
become increasingly double-edged in the fluctuating political
climate of the period. As it happened, sexual jealousy destroyed
their friendship long before Nero forfeited mastery of Rome.
Following Nero's death, in the unsettled and uncertain new
world in which everything was to play for, the *novus homo* from
Ferentium maintained an accurate evaluation of his Neronian
credentials. As emperor he allowed the people to hail him
'Nero Otho'; it was their own innovation and arose, it seems,
spontaneously. Anticipating the outbreak of peace following
his own accession – Otho issued coins with the unambiguous
legend 'Peace throughout the world' (*pax orbis terrarum*)[7] – and
correctly judging that Galba's ham-fistedness had forced a
reassessment of Nero's true worth, he capitalized on this change

of heart in Rome by assigning fifty million sesterces to the task of completing the Golden House. Suetonius claims it as the first document Otho signed as emperor.* Co-architect of this monument to Julio-Claudian grandeur, Otho perhaps hoped to acquire by association an aura of legitimacy.

When it happened, Otho's route to power was anything but circuitous. It came about through a double jealousy, first of Nero, second of that honourable but unremarkable aristocratic exile Piso Licinianus. Otho's response in each case consisted of an act of revenge. Revenge twice taken, he found himself emperor of Rome.

The process began in 58 or 59. Nero dispatched Otho to Portugal as governor of Lusitania. It was a significant appointment for a man of twenty-six or twenty-seven yet to undertake the practorship (the usual stepping-stone to provincial governorship). But it was not a compliment. On the contrary, Nero intended the appointment as an act of banishment. It was an alternative to executing Otho and it owed its authorship to the tactful intervention of Seneca in what was an altogether unstatesmanlike squabble.

The circumstances of the falling-out of emperor and acolyte are characteristic of the dog days of Julio-Claudianism. The argument centred on one of those ambitious and imperious

---

* Funds for this extravagant act of homage may have been raised by confiscating the fortune so rapidly acquired by Vinius. Those ill-gotten gains were described by Otho on the day of his coup as evidence of greater rapacity and lawlessness than Vinius would have dared even had he been emperor.[8]

women who, beginning in the reign of Claudius, exploited high breeding and good looks to achieve access to a power which they were neither constitutionally entitled to nor temperamentally suited to. In this case Poppaea Sabina, sometimes called the Younger (her mother was that Poppaea Sabina the Elder whose beauty had earned even Tacitus' commendation and who had been forced in 47 to commit suicide by Claudius' third wife Messalina, another of the type). Although the sources tell a confusing story, it appears that Poppaea, as beautiful as her mother and ambitious to boot, was married to Otho. Frequently in the emperor's presence on account of the closeness of Otho and Nero's friendship, she attracted the latter's attention and the two embarked on a flirtation. (The alternative version has Otho marrying Poppaea specifically in order to make her available to Nero, then repenting too late of the pander's course for which he does not have the stomach.) As emperors will – as we have seen with Octavian and Gaius and will see again with Domitian – Nero exercised a form of *droit de seigneur* and took Poppaea from Otho. Events were not, however, as clean-cut as this suggests. Otho yielded one sexual partner to another with an ill grace and may have opposed the couple's marriage. For his part, Nero resented Otho's continuing affection for the woman both men now claimed as their wife. Only Seneca's solution of governorship of Lusitania served to remove the troublesome Otho from the equation still in possession of his life. The strength of feeling on all sides is attested by the length of Otho's sojourn in his westerly retreat and by Nero's failure to recall him in the aftermath of Poppaea's death in 65. Suetonius suggests that Nero contented himself with Otho's banishment as a form of damage limitation less likely to inspire gossip about palace bed-hopping than any course more obviously resembling retribution. Since Otho took the opportunity 'promotion' presented to fulfil the obligations of office with what the historian describes as 'remarkable moderation and integrity', his was the last laugh. As with Vespasian's later governorship of Judaea, Otho's Lusitanian banishment unexpectedly provided this louche and lackadaisical dandiprat with a springboard for empire.

If Nero had hoped to silence scurrilous whispers through Otho's removal, his success was only partial. Witty lines of doggerel circulated in smart salons. They were not quickly forgotten. On the brink of seizing power in 69, Otho found himself the victim of a smearing that resurrected with tabloid glee former habits of laxity and sexual indulgence. It formed the substance of Piso Licinianus' appeal to Galban troops on the day both Piso and Galba were killed. 'Already he is thinking of debaucheries, of revels, of tribes of mistresses,' he claimed of Otho. 'These things he holds the prizes of princely power, things in which the wanton enjoyment will be for him alone, the shame and the disgrace for all.'[9] As so often, the ancient mindset refused to countenance the possibility of change. Despite his record of service in Lusitania, Otho would not be permitted to escape his garishly perfumed youth at Nero's court. For Piso and Galba, that line was dictated by expediency. But it accounts too for the impact of Otho's 'noble' death – the artificial oppositionalism of selfish youth and selfless demise invoked by ancient authors not in pursuit of veracity but in the interests of vigorous rhetorical contrast.

In the event, Piso's oratory was powerless to avert the consequences of Galba's poor judgement. Otho became emperor of Rome with an 'army' whose core consisted of fifteen soldiers, the principate his for the price of a stewardship at court. (The bankrupt Otho funded purchase of the loyalty of his tiny band of fighting men with the million sesterces which Suetonius tells us he had extorted from one of Galba's slaves in return for securing him a steward's position.) Tacitus' contempt, predictably, is boundless. But Tacitus, like Piso, would see only half the story.

Suetonius pulls no punches: while it lasted, Otho's support for Galba was nothing concerned with Galba, everything about Otho. It represented to the younger man a belated opportunity for revenge against Nero. A decade had passed since Otho's banishment in the wake of Poppaea's infidelity. Poppaea was dead, kicked out of this world by Nero, who now himself hovered on the brink of losing all. When, on 2 April 68, Servius Sulpicius Galba, governor of Nearer Spain, declared himself representative of the senate and people of Rome, Otho was first among provincial governors to join his cause. He gave Galba gold and silver goblets and even tables to be melted down for currency. Sharing Galba's carriage, he set out on the journey to Rome. The older man, invincibly snobbish, nevertheless considered his comrade-in-arms 'inferior to none as a man of affairs'.[10] Already the tide was turning. The erstwhile drunkard, extravagant and foppish, in debt to the tune of anything between 5 and 200 million sesterces depending on the source consulted, had governed Lusitania with credit. Now, by dint of good behaviour and careful benefactions to Galba's associates and inspired by Seleucus' prophecy, which Suetonius dates to this point, we see the emergence of a different Otho, the man who in time would die with honour, lamented by his troops. Only the length of his memory offers pause for thought, a doubt about the princely qualities revealed in this slow-fermenting vengeance.

Otho interpreted Seleucus' presentiment as an indication that Galba would adopt him as his successor. We know that it was not to be. Otho's response to disappointment which verged on shock appears to have been instinctive. He glimpsed the principate within his grasp: neither Galba nor Piso could withhold the prize that was rightfully his. (In addition, Suetonius and Tacitus claim that Otho's debts denied him freedom of choice: only the throne could save him. Recklessness born of despair as much as anger shaped his course: he would rather die defying Galba than at the hands of his creditors.) On 15 January, nine months into Galba's reign, Otho attended the emperor in his sacrifice in the temple. But Otho stayed only to hear the soothsayer's prophecy of doom. Complacent with portents, he left the temple mid-service to meet, he claimed, architects and surveyors: racked by debts as all Rome knew, he could afford only the most derelict of houses. By the Temple of Saturn in the Forum, he joined the risible band of helpmeets won over to his cause. Together they embarked on a coup – small in scale, short in duration, disorderly and ill-disciplined – which eventually won the day.

As evening's shadows lengthened, Otho was received by the senate at a meeting he himself had convened. The senators' unedifying response to a revolution in which they had played no part survives in the written record as a syrupy cocktail of congratulation, flattery and adulation. 'The more insincere their demonstrations, the more they multiplied them,' Tacitus reports.[11] Little matter. Those insincerities encompassed the title 'Augustus', the grant of tribunician power and a full roster of imperial honours. They also sanctioned implicitly a development of far-reaching implications: that the principate could fall to an opportunistic outsider through crime. It was no longer a catalyst for unity but the inspiration for conflict motivated neither by ideal nor by principle. Given Otho's *fait accompli*, and the air of sinister menace which had blackened Rome since morning, the senate was in no position to debate the changing complexion of the purple. Shamefaced, it took its place among the losers of Otho's coup, its power to direct the tide in Rome's affairs cruelly exposed once again as a nostalgic illusion.

After a decade's absence from Rome, Otho asked for no more. Nero, Galba, Piso, even Poppaea – all who had opposed him were dead. The victory was his own and only his, since no point had been at stake: Otho's argument with Galba was not dynastic, ideological, philosophical or even political, it was simply a struggle between a man who wanted to be *princeps* and believed himself portent-bound to be so and the man who threatened to thwart that aspiration, 'his rage against Galba... his envy of Piso', as Tacitus has it.[12] There would be no benefit to Rome or Romans from Otho's victory (save to those troops denied a donative by Galba, recompensed by his spendthrift successor). The swift-approaching contest between Otho and Vitellius would replicate this selfish emptiness. Before that, in the aftermath of Galba's murder, soldiers attached to poles his severed head and that of his nominated heir and paraded them among the standards of the cohorts. Otho himself witnessed this carnival of the macabre at the end of a day of bloodshed and folly. (The sources report his particular pleasure at the sight of Piso's bleeding head, which 'he felt to be a right and lawful subject of rejoicing'.[13]) Vanished now was that distaste for violence which once had made him shudder at the mention of Brutus and Cassius' fates. The spectacle on Rome's streets was no more degraded than Otho's own suspension of finer feelings.

Driven by ambition and the pettiness of revenge, Rome's newest emperor had nevertheless not forfeited good sense. On early coin issues Otho embraced the language of conciliation and reassurance: 'SECURITAS P R', the safety and freedom from care of the Roman people.[14] We have no reason to assume irony. It is one of Dio's 'many temperate acts intended to conciliate the people'.[15]

———

Following success, equanimity. 'He did not remember his own private grievances against any man soever,' Plutarch tells us.[16] It was an attitude in stark contrast to Galba's stony vindictiveness. Instead, apprised at his accession of Vitellius' counter-bid for power (which, we have seen, can be traced at least to the beginning of the year and the German soldiery's failure to swear the New Year oath of loyalty), Otho apparently set out to achieve a consensus in Rome and, looking further afield, support among the legions of the Empire. He invoked the auspices of Augustus, Livia and Claudius to endow his regime with divine protection as well as to confer that legitimacy which, even now, remained the exclusive possession of the Julio-Claudians.[17] With an eye to the armies of the East, he reappointed Vespasian's brother Flavius Sabinus to the post of city prefect from which Galba had removed him. Looking north, he confirmed a March consulship for Verginius Rufus, former commander of the Rhine legions. (This careful piece of flattery does not appear to have adherents in Germany.) In Rome itself, with greater success, he applied himself to increasing his power base by winning over supporters of his murdered predecessor. Among high-profile defections to his cause was the distinguished general and Galban loyalist Marius Celsus. Sparing Celsus won Otho not only a first-rate military commander but an Empire-wide reputation for mercifulness, a quality prized highly by successive emperors. In a gesture guaranteed to contrast with Galba's meanness, Otho restored confiscated property to Neronian victims in cases where restitution was possible.

Politically astute, this programme of inclusion wore an appropriately 'imperial' aspect. Unlike Gaius, Otho required no lessons in the dignity of the purple. 'To the surprise of all,' Tacitus recorded, Otho 'was not sinking down into luxury and sloth. He deferred his pleasure, concealed his profligacy.'[18] For Tacitus, there is always a pickle in the pie. Such behaviour, far from reassuring Rome's upper classes, served only to increase their misgivings: 'men dreaded all the more virtues so false, and vices so certain to return.' It may be true. Given the speed at which Otho's reign was overtaken by calamity, former vices had no opportunity to return.

To outward appearances Otho's conduct at the beginning of his principate offered a direct refutation of the Tacitean assurance that power acquired by crime could not be retained by a sudden assumption of moderation.[19] By decree of the senate, Otho laid at least one ghost of the past. He ordained the restoration of surviving statues of Poppaea.* Unrepentant regarding his connection with Nero's regime, Otho's loyalty was above all things pragmatic. The letter he wrote to Tigellinus demanding his suicide sacrificed Nero's hated ex-Praetorian prefect to expediency and a notable groundswell of popular pressure.

---

* This also served to confirm belief in Otho's love for Poppaea and that version of earlier events in which Nero's appropriation of his wife, far from being planned by Otho, arose unforeseen and unwelcome. Such an explanation had the added benefit of appearing to justify Otho's anger against his former friend and lessen the culpability of his revenge.

Having achieved power unconstitutionally, Otho cultivated punctiliousness in relation to Roman procedural propriety. Although in company with his brother Salvius Titianus he replaced Galba and Vinius as consuls for the first two months of the year, in his arrangements for the consulship thereafter he largely respected appointments already made by Nero and Galba. The result, according to Plutarch, was to convince Rome's noblest and most influential citizens that, far from being 'some genius of retribution or avenging spirit that had suddenly fallen upon the state', Otho would preside over a government of smiling countenance.[20] Such was the nature of Vitellius' threat that it would not be enough. Nor was it sufficient to grant the emperor quiet rest. While anxieties about Vitellius and the German legions filled his days, his nights were disturbed by dreams of Galba. In Otho's dream, Galba returned to life to oust his youthful usurper. Awake, he struggled with expiatory rites, acts of propitiation whose outcome he could not predict. His dream prevented him from sleeping. In the morning, dizzy with tiredness, he stumbled in the palace or the temple. Taking the auspices, a storm blew up. With relish, Suetonius recounts this concatenation of portents. To author as to reader the writing is on the wall.

Otho's war record fails to impress. On balance the arena of war was not the ideal environment for this emperor preoccupied with the softness of his skin and the sleek alignment of a toupee which, commended for its verisimilitude by Suetonius, in surviving portraiture resembles nothing so much as a crocheted tea-cosy. Emperor in the interests of self-fulfilment, Otho possessed neither experience of military campaigning nor any connection with the troops beyond his ability to pay their wages.

In this, too, he represents a departure for the principate to date. Unfortunately for Otho, inexperience and unsuitability were not enough to stem the tides of war. For his efforts on the campaign trail, he would afterwards be rewarded in Juvenal's *Satires* with unflattering comparisons with Cleopatra.[21]

At first, it seems, Otho had doubted war's inevitability. His initial response to news of Vitellius' revolt had been a deputation from the senate instructed to inform the insurgents that a new emperor had already been chosen and that peaceable acquiescence represented the wiser course. Predictably it fell flat. Otho then opened a correspondence with Vitellius, in which emperor offered to buy off would-be emperor and, in Suetonius' version, enter into a tentative power-sharing arrangement. Vitellius' reply made a similar offer to Otho, at which point their communication degenerated into an undignified exchange of insults – 'foolish and ridiculous', as Plutarch points out, since one stormed the other with reproaches applicable to both, chief among them their common unsuitability to reign.[22] In March, with no alternative in sight and, in Tacitus' account, mindful that delay had hastened Nero's downfall, Otho left Rome for a head-on collision with Vitellius' men in northern Italy.

Suetonius devotes less space to the brief campaign in which Otho was defeated (although this constitutes the major event of his principate) than to the consequences of that defeat. There is a workaday quality to his report, as if the portents which attended Otho's departure render further explanation superfluous. The emperor's leave-taking was double-damned: he embarked when the sacred shields had been removed from the Temple of Mars, during the days of mourning which commenced the festival of Cybele, both alike inauspicious. Added to religious proscriptions was the meteorological glitch of the Tiber in flood.

Otho's route out of Rome, which took him across the Campus Martius and eventually along the Via Flaminia, was blocked by fallen buildings: risen to unprecedented heights, the river had broken its banks, engulfing not only the city's poorer, low-lying districts but areas usually reckoned safe from flooding. Tacitus and Plutarch add to this potent mix a statue of Julius Caesar revolving on its pedestal on an island in the Tiber so that it pointed not west but east, and the sudden, spine-chilling phenomenon, in the porch of the Temple of Jupiter, of Victory, mounted in a chariot, dropping the chariot's reins 'as if she had not power to hold them'.[23] In Etruria, ancestral homeland of the Othones, an ox spoke aloud, its unexpected utterance undoubtedly a litany of peril.

Aided by a clutch of generals – some said too many – Otho had not been entirely lax in his preparations. Assistance was promised in the form of the seven legions of Dalmatia, Pannonia and Moesia: these troops had already embarked on the long journey west. In Rome, sketchy training programmes sought belatedly to ready that rag-tag agglomeration of fighting men which was Otho's inheritance from the war-shunning Nero, men more used to 'spectacles and festivals and plays' than military manoeuvres, according to Plutarch.[24] In addition, 2,000 gladiators had been conscripted in the emperor's cause. Vitellius remained in Germany awaiting further recruits. Active leadership of his campaign belonged to Valens and Caecina. Too late now for Otho's men to close the Alpine passes: the horse had already bolted. Instead, the Othonians decided to create a defensive frontier along the line of the river Po. It was here, heedless of omens, flushed with victory in a clutch of minor skirmishes and too hasty to await the arrival of first reinforcements from the East, that Otho gave the order for engagement. On 14 April, dizzy with the conflicting advice of his generals, he urged immediate battle. We know for ourselves the outcome.

Plutarch attributes this tactical failure on Otho's part to a crisis of nerves, and quotes the emperor's secretary, a rhetorician called Secundus:

> Otho himself could not longer bear up against the uncertainty of the issue, nor endure (so effeminate was he and so unused to command) his own thoughts of the dire peril confronting him; but worn out by his anxieties, he veiled his eyes, like one about to leap from a precipice, and hastened to commit his cause to fortune.[25]

It was the same instinct which prompts men to stake everything on the fall of a card, that fecklessness and daring which, so recently, had won for Otho an empire.

———— ⚬⚬⚬ ————

Nothing in that first defeat gave grounds for hopelessness, but Otho's mind was made up. In Suetonius' account, his decision to commit suicide rather than further endanger Roman lives was immediate. He did not despair of success in the long run, nor did he mistrust his forces soon to be augmented with the legions of the East. Unusually among Rome's emperors he had no appetite for blood or the loss of life. 'Wanton Otho still could win the day,' Martial wrote afterwards. 'But cursing war with all its price of blood, He pierced his heart and perished as he stood.'[26] He had not led his troops at Bedriacum. Earlier he had won golden words by his presence among his men on the march north: acerbic commentators observed his eleventh-hour disdain for his usually stringent grooming regime. But at the crucial battle he had remained safely to the rear in his camp at Brixellum (modern Brescello). Sound tactics, it was a miscall in terms of morale-boosting and leadership. He would make no such mistakes in death.

Perhaps it was the troops which were the problem. A principate without military support was untenable. But a principate whose only justification was its thraldom to its troops was equally so. For events in Rome had already exposed the hollowness of the charade even before campaigning began. They took the form of an incident interpreted by Suetonius as proof of the affection and loyalty of the Praetorian Guard towards their Caesar. Suetonius glosses over the extent to which that affection and loyalty, in this case spurs to lawlessness, made Otho their puppet and their victim.

A plan to transport troops from their station at Ostia to Rome also involved transportation of military equipment. Unexpectedly, the decision of the commanding officer to begin the process at night, under cover of partial darkness, led to a misapprehension that the real plan was not the safe carriage of arms and armour to the capital but a full-scale coup orchestrated by the senate for Otho's overthrow. At a gallop, outraged Praetorians made for the imperial palace where Otho was hosting a banquet for eighty leading senators and their wives. The result was temporary anarchy.

For the Praetorians the emperor's banquet provided an ideal opportunity to eliminate all Otho's enemies at a sitting. For the senate, the emperor's perfidy in bringing them together only to kill them exceeded the worst affronts of recent history. For Otho, confused, uncertain and dashed by twin loyalties, it was a graphic illustration of the true nature of the balance of power in his relationship with his personal fighting force. He hastened the senators out of the palace by unfrequented passages. Then, as soldiers stormed the palace, he begged their cooperation with arguments, entreaties and, at last, when no other course prevailed, tears.

Like so much in this year of upheavals and bogus emperors, it was a night of hair-raising indignity. Ill discipline came close to destroying the senate and the emperor's authority was exposed as non-existent. Otho's recourse had been the woman's part of crying. It surely unnerved him. It may too have sickened him. It was an ominous preliminary to civil war.

———————

On the eve of death, a leave-taking. Otho's brother, his nephew and his friends, Suetonius tells us. Plutarch awards the honours to his nephew Cocceius, 'who was still a youth', and whom Otho had intended to adopt as his heir following victory over Vitellius. From uncle to nephew a final imprecation: 'Do not altogether forget, and do not too well remember, that you had a Caesar for an uncle.'[27] At one level a statement of that moderation which had characterized Otho's brief supremacy, it was also by way of apology. An admission that Otho's was a principate without legitimacy, justified neither by birth nor even by merit: no grounds for revenge. It had been an exercise in opportunism. A grand, inglorious gamble – reason in the future for family pride – it appeared in the light of defeat too flimsy and unfounded to inspire further bloodshed of the sort Otho meant to avert through his death.

Cocceius dispatched, Otho sought out a quiet, private place in which to write letters. He wrote only two. The first addressed his sister, intended to lessen her sorrow. Otho's second letter was directed to Statilia Messalina, the noblewoman whom Nero had chosen as his third wife after the death of Poppaea and a long-standing affair. Curly-haired, pale-cheeked, with an overwhelming appearance of resignation both in the Capitoline Museums' contemporary bust and in a sixteenth-century image by the Mantuan painter Teodoro Ghisi, Messalina had been chosen by Otho to be entrusted with his corpse. More than that, his memory. For it was Nero's widow Messalina, Suetonius tells us, whom this ambitious one-time coxcomb and former husband of Poppaea had chosen to marry had he lived.

VITELLIUS

(AD 15–69)

'A series of carousals and revels'

In place of pride, envy, covetousness, wrath and even lust (a weakness he put behind him in manhood), the emperor Vitellius espoused gluttony and sloth. This career flatterer, through whose veins coursed the blood of artisans, shopkeepers and ne'er-do-wells (a cobbler, a baker, an informer and a carpet-bagger), was of 'an easygoing and lavish disposition', 'a kindly disposition', 'his nature... marked by simplicity and liberality' – on this point conflicting sources agree.

His besetting sins, Suetonius tells us, 'were luxury and cruelty', a delight 'in inflicting death and torture on anyone whatsoever and for any cause whatever'. The author provides examples but no names and few details, testimony that cannot be verified. Aside from the unedifying suggestion that Vitellius starved his mother to death in order to fulfil a trumpery prediction (not even the utterance of an oracle) 'that he would rule securely and for a long time, but only if he should survive his parent', there is more evidence of the former weakness than the latter. Undoubtedly he possessed a gift for tactlessness and blunt speaking, cruelty after a fashion. His dismissal of Otho's unpretentious tomb – a small mausoleum for a small man – did not impress his contemporaries and continues to alienate modern readers. Ditto his tasteless statement on the battlefield of Otho's defeat, rancid with forty-day-old unburied corpses, 'that the odour of a dead enemy was sweet and that of a fellow citizen sweeter still'. Such lapses probably occupied him less than that addiction enumerated by Dio: luxury and licentiousness. His fecklessness took the form of prodigality, heedless of the economic depredations to Rome's treasury of a year of civil war.

For reasons that do not survive, Vitellius was the first of Rome's emperors to reject the senate's award both of the title 'Augustus' and of the name 'Caesar'.* Instead, describing himself as *'imperator'*, he had assumed already the surname 'Germanicus', itself formerly in the gift of the senate. It was awarded by the army which had made him emperor – the legions of Upper and Lower Germany – and labelled him as surely as any brand applied to criminal or cattle.

Consistently denigrated by Flavian propaganda, Vitellius nevertheless does not rank high among the villains of imperial Rome: his indolence saw to that. Tacitus claims that 'he was more than content to enjoy the present hour with no thought beyond'.[1] It was a harmless inclination save in one entrusted with the direction of the world's mightiest empire at a moment of danger and irresolution which demanded a second Augustus or at least a bureaucrat of Tiberius' cool stamp. He was 'naturally without energy',[2] politically moderate and entirely ignorant of military affairs – so far, remarkably like Otho. Most of all, he was consumed by the diktats of what Suetonius labels his 'bottomless gullet': more assiduous in pursuit of a full belly than in restoring Rome's solvency, army discipline or senatorial

---

* His rejection extended to titles only and did not compromise his power. Indeed, almost in the same breath, this bloated gourmand conferred upon himself perpetual consulship. Neither 'Augustus' nor 'Caesar', he accepted no less a settlement than Augustus had devised.

morale; and too sluggish in his efforts to create a broad support base for his rule. Dio insists that he drained the treasury of 900 million sesterces, a suggestively exaggerated figure: in a period of civil unrest, all of it was spent on dinners. (A silver serving dish so large that a special furnace was built in open fields for its manufacture reportedly cost a million sesterces.)

By Roman standards he was tall. It was his sole eminence. His face was red with overindulgence, his body a bulging, bulbous excrescence. He walked with a limp, not on account of the burdens of obesity but thanks to a shattered thigh received in a chariot-race alongside the emperor Gaius. Hard to discern in the balloon-faced torpor of his portrait corpus the delicious young boy who had so tempted and delighted the ageing Tiberius that he earned the moniker 'Sphinctria', 'sphincter artist', a name that speaks for itself. It cannot have been an enviable youth, stained, as Suetonius describes it, 'by every sort of baseness'. Perhaps an ambitious father put him up to it: certainly it was the career of Vitellius senior, called Lucius, which benefited in the first instance from his son's hard submission on Capri. (Lucius Vitellius held three consulships under Claudius, with whom, like Otho's father, he was closely associated. Such was the intimacy of emperor and senator that it was Lucius Vitellius who, alongside Narcissus, accompanied Claudius' return to Rome after news emerged of Messalina's 'marriage' to Silius.) Dio dismisses the seven months of Vitellius' premiership as 'nothing but a series of carousals and revels'.[3] It is an echo of Tacitus' taunt of living in the moment and suggests too something of that instinct for escapism which, discarding Nero, Romans had already decided did not fit the *princeps'* part. We ought not to wonder that, after such a youth, Vitellius preferred to indulge different appetites: that he did so to the detriment of efficiency and clear-sightedness was a prescription for failure.

Vitellius' violent death has a pathos absent from much of our chronicle. Like Galba and Otho before him, he achieved in death a fleeting greatness that was never his in life. At the eleventh hour, a fickle people deserted and derided this emperor who, when the going was good, possessed all the attributes of an affable *bon viveur* bar the mechanism that separates amiable indulgence from sickening excess. The people's errant faithlessness was a repeating pattern in this year of conflict and armed uncertainty as Rome struggled to move forward in the vacuum following Nero's suicide. Dragged through the city's streets by soldiers, shabbily disguised and unwilling, Vitellius was exposed to the taunts and jeers of the mob. Their complaints were not political (hardly factional), not even economic. They reserved their scorn for his bodily defects. In this interlude when gamblers tossed for the highest stakes, the ordinary Roman did not revisit the protests of his forefathers, angered, for example, at Mark Antony's offer to Caesar of a royal crown at the Festival of the Lupercalia: schoolboy derision replaced convictions. They pelted him with dung and shit. They called him 'incendiary' and 'glutton'. They laughed at the wreckage of his huge physique. In vain this man who had made few claims for himself, attributing with injudicious candour the gift of empire to his troops, besought them, 'And yet I was your emperor.' They hacked his head from his body, severing for ever that supercharged alimentary canal. Then they hurled his body into the Tiber on a hook, much as butchers and fishmongers handle their wares, its cumbersome passage undoubtedly accompanied by further ribald laughter. The goddess Minerva, whom Vitellius had invoked as his protectress – and in whose name he once created a gastronomic extravaganza of stomach-churning 'delicacy', a 'Shield of Minerva' consisting of pheasant and peacock brains, pike livers, flamingoes' tongues and lamprey milt, each

ingredient shipped from the furthest frontiers of the Empire –
declined to intervene either with omens or with obstacles.

In 1882 the unedifying spectacle of Vitellius' last hours
inspired the debut at the Paris Salon of a French history painter
who would afterwards specialize in grandly scaled canvases of
ancient brutality or classical titillation. So successful was Georges
Rochegrosse's horrible painting *Vitellius Dragged through the Streets
of Rome by the People* that he reprised the composition two years
later and won the prestigious Priz du Salon with his *Andromaque*,
complete with severed heads, exposed breasts and lashings of
blood. The action of both paintings centres on a staircase, down
which protagonists tumble in angry cascade, faces taut, garbed
in acrid shadows. Bound and captive, Andromache is locked
in impassioned struggle. She gestures towards a baby, perhaps
Astyanax, her son by Hector: she will never see the child again.
In Vitellius' case, all struggle is past. It is life itself which is being
torn from him, but he musters no defiance. The huge emperor
is tied with rope, trussed and criss-crossed with cords like an
unwieldy sacrifice. His toga has fallen from his shoulders, his
neck and face are flecked with blood. Passive and unprotesting,
he awaits certain death with fear in his eyes and a blade
rudely thrust beneath his chin. In its dark-hued viciousness,
Rochegrosse's unlovely image of vanished hope and mob misrule
replicates the horror of the sources. 'You blocks, you stones, you
worse than senseless things! O you hard hearts, you cruel men of
Rome,' Marullus admonishes the crowd in Shakespeare's *Julius
Caesar* for their abandonment of Pompey. So it was with Vitellius.
Perhaps in the emperor's unseeing eyes is a glimmer of regret that
troops once faithful to him had prevented his abdication, one of
the sounder policies of his short, pointless principate.

It may have been an inevitable end for this good-time
Roman who had been buggered by Tiberius, raced chariots

with Gaius, gambled with Claudius and encouraged Nero in theatrical indignity, and whose popularity as *princeps* rested on his assiduous attendance at the theatre. No matter that he declined at first the title 'Caesar': Julio-Claudian credentials raised him up and dashed him down. The extravagance of his self-abandonment perpetuated into the next chapter of Rome's imperial history the excess and extravagance of Augustus' heirs. According to Dio, 'He was insatiate in gorging himself, and was constantly vomiting up what he ate, being nourished by the mere passage of the food',[4] a process repeated three or four times every day with emetics and purges as necessary, each bowel-busting banquet billed at more than 400,000 sesterces. In 69, as Vespasian would show he had realized, prodigality was no longer the *princeps'* proudest perquisite. Times had changed. Not Vitellius.

He was not, as we have seen, Rome's first irresponsible emperor: Gaius and Nero were both fatigued by duty. Yet this ninth Caesar was the first to behave with consistent irresponsibility from a position of weakness. 'He was never so absorbed in serious business that he forgot his pleasures,' Tacitus tells us.[5] The record of his reign suggests that he was seldom absorbed in serious business at all, devoted instead to a parody of good living, befuddled and queasy while his troops, encamped on the banks of the Tiber, succumbed either to excess like his own or to dysentery, and distant armies mobilized in the name of Vespasian. A puppet of his legions, he may never have craved the throne. It was won for him in a single battle at which Vitellius himself was not present. But Otho's surrender did not amount to conclusive military defeat: support remained for the three-month emperor among the population and military alike. 'The soldiers of the Fourteenth legion were particularly bold,' Tacitus records, 'declaring that they had never been defeated.'[6]

Vitellius responded by ordering XIV *Gemina Martia Victrix* to Britain, a posting sufficiently remote to keep them from rabble-rousing in Rome; he also dispatched another troublesome legion, I *Adiutrix*, to Spain. In other instances he appeared unaware of that sense of irresolution which characterized the year's third rapid-fire change of regime. The threat of the armies of the East left him apparently unconcerned – Dio describes him as going on 'with his luxurious living';[7] so too stirrings of dissent on the Rhine, which in time increased in clamorousness. His focus was closer to home: the whirl of banquets and a new imperial guard which he formed after disbanding the Praetorians, elevating in their place 20,000 doughty German legionaries – too many soldiers in the city, badly disciplined and rapacious. When disaster threatened, he invoked the assistance of his cook and his pastry chef to smuggle him in a litter out of his besieged palace to safety.

As they survive in the sources, his actions confuse us: for all his seeming recklessness, Vitellius evidently meant to found a dynasty. Although he refused for himself the title 'Augustus', he created his mother Sestilia 'Augusta' on his arrival in Rome in July 69. Earlier, at a victory celebration at Lugdunum, he had paraded in front of the troops his son by his second wife, Galeria Fundana, dressed in the accoutrements of imperial rank. It was a sign of dynastic intent undermined only by the boy's status as a six-year-old virtual mute suffering from a chronic stammer. In addition, Vitellius issued gold and silver coins featuring images not only of his son but also of his daughter; other coins celebrated his father, who had added to his tally of consulships the censorship too. Vitellius was only the second generation of his recent family to attain prominence. Nothing daunted, he asserted through his coinage claims to a stake in Rome's past and future. As far as it went, it was shrewd policy:

among Vitellius' few distinctions was his possession of an heir of his own blood, a claim unmatched by Galba, Otho or any of his predecessors (since the sons of Tiberius and Claudius had not survived); while given Romans' belief in heredity, such a father added lustre to his son's imperial candidacy. The tide of events would jeer at Vitellius' numismatic hubris, his own reign quickly over, his son (youth notwithstanding) killed by an associate of Vespasian's. By Dio's time his memory survived only in a name given to expensive cakes.[8]

Like the Divine Julius and Otho before him, Vitellius was a spendthrift restored to solvency by the premiership. Such were the constraints on his purse previously that, leaving Rome for governorship of Lower Germany in the autumn of 68, he had funded his journey by pawning a pearl earring belonging to his mother and extorting 50,000 sesterces from an unwisely importunate freedman on a trumped-up action for damages. (His wife and children he was forced to rehouse in a rented garret.) Afterwards, invested with power by the senate, he was unable to pay the troops' accession donative. A principate which began in straitened circumstances quickly revealed the larger, more pressing bankruptcy at its heart.

Vitellius was the emperor defeated by Rome. A proactive governor of Lower Germany, he won over to his cause the disaffected legions of two provinces within less than two months; Suetonius describes them as welcoming him with hands upraised as if in thanks to heaven. Invested with ultimate power in the capital, he was unable to maintain either momentum or resolve. Earlier, in 60, he had served as proconsul of Africa with 'exceptional integrity for two successive years'; in the discharge of the Roman priesthoods awarded to him by Nero in the same period, he stooped to theft and deceit. We may never know if those generals who placed Vitellius on the throne subsequently wondered at their choice. Examination of the emperor's former record would have removed their grounds for surprise. As it happened, it hardly mattered. Awaiting Vespasian's victory, no serious alternative candidate for the purple suggested himself. In the two months that elapsed between Vitellius' confirmation as emperor by the senate at Ticinum (modern Pavia) and his arrival in Rome, the city had no leader and no real government. That no ambitious adventurer snatched the opportunity to step into the breach and usurp Vitellius' unclaimed throne tells us much about the crisis in Rome's affairs.

In a technique with which we are now familiar, Suetonius offers us alternative accounts of Vitellius' family history: on the one hand, ancient nobility gilded by association with a goddess of the countryside; hard-nosed, low-level self-seeking on the other. Whatever the truth, Vitellius' own career combined both impulses. His history, particularly at Nero's court, was one of grasping sycophancy, but as emperor he was capable of clemency and modesty towards his opponents and he had earlier shown himself a gifted provincial administrator able to assess and respond to the needs of situations outside his ken. Prior to Vespasian, one lesson of this tumultuous year was the inadequacy of imperial proconsulships as an apprenticeship for the throne: like Vitellius, Galba and Otho had both served with distinction abroad.

If Suetonius is reliable, Aulus Vitellius, born in AD 15, inherited as much from the uncle whose name he shared as from his father. That Aulus Vitellius, one of four sons of the equestrian Publius Vitellius of Nuceria – 'whether of ancient stock or of parents and forefathers in whom he could take no pride, unquestionably... a steward of Augustus' – inclined to luxury and died during his consulship in 32, when his impressionable nephew was seventeen. This uncle was 'especially notorious for the magnificence of his feasts'. Of his three brothers, only Lucius Vitellius, father of the future emperor, maintained a course approaching credit, though Suetonius darkens his memory with accusations of overweening obsequiousness towards Gaius – whom he worshipped openly as a living god, the first in Rome to do so – and Claudius, whose wives and freedmen he cultivated with shameless fawning. (He resorted to carrying about with him like a talisman a shoe belonging to the empress Messalina, which he concealed beneath his toga and occasionally, when observed, withdrew and kissed.) Such cloying fulsomeness earned dividends. A notably successful governor of Syria, Lucius Vitellius added to the triple consulship and censorship stewardship of the Empire while Claudius was absent from Rome on his expedition to Britain in 43 – access to power that was unusual during this period for a senator outside the imperial family. It exposed his two sons, both of them future consuls, to the innermost workings of the state. We cannot know to what extent, if any, that experience inspired future ambitions, nor do we read of the reaction of Vitellius' mother Sestilia to her husband's proximity to Claudius' government. Tacitus casts Sestilia as an old-fashioned matron worthy of the Republic, serious and righteous. (Her reaction to her son's principate is one of despondency rather than delight.) Perhaps those were the very qualities which drove her husband into the arms of that freedwoman whose spittle, Suetonius tells us, Lucius Vitellius mixed with honey and rubbed on his throat and his jaws as medicine.

Such a close association with the former regime may explain why Vitellius felt able to rule without adopting 'Augustus' or

'Caesar' as elements of his official nomenclature: under the circumstances, such verbal links were superfluous. It may also account for the apparently limited efforts he would ultimately make to justify his position as *princeps*. In instituting sacrifices to Nero's memory at an altar on the Campus Martius, he both reiterated his Julio-Claudian credentials and sought to enfranchise remaining Neronian sympathizers (among whom he counted himself and could certainly have numbered those German legions who, responsible for his own premiership, had hailed Galba only under duress and never acclaimed Otho); he also retained Nero's coinage (and that of Galba and Otho) and resisted confiscating gifts bestowed by his predecessors. Deliberately or otherwise, Vitellius played a double game, simultaneously declaring his own loyalties and placing himself in a continuum of imperial rulers of Rome that did not distinguish between Julio-Claudians and more recent incumbents. Over the course of the following decade, Vespasian's and Titus' efforts to capitalize on their connections with Claudius and Britannicus respectively show that the political climate in Rome had not changed to the extent that Augustus' family could be lightly overlooked. What appeared like moderation may have been a miscall on Vitellius' part.

For an audience which accepted the view that character was immutable and fixed from earliest infancy, Suetonius' portrait of Vitellius includes speaking details. Such were the (unspecified) predictions of the horoscope produced by astrologers at his birth that his father determined to prevent any award of a province to his son, while his mother apparently 'mourned over him as lost' after his dispatch by Galba to Lower Germany and subsequent acclamation as emperor. Those predictions presumably touched upon that 'cruelty' later asserted by the sources, which Suetonius instances in the period before Vitellius' elevation in an unpleasant anecdote concerning his first marriage. Vitellius had a son by his wife Petronia. Blind in one eye, Petronianus was rumoured to have been poisoned by his father, possibly to prevent him from inheriting Petronia's fortune (which, we assume, Vitellius wanted for himself). Suetonius reports this crime as hearsay. The future *princeps'* own explanation was that, discovered in a plan to kill Vitellius and seized by guilt, Petronianus himself swallowed the poison he had mixed. We must make up our own minds. It is true that Vitellius would later express concern about the fates of his wife and children in the event of his abdication. But it is also true, as we have seen, that the sources preserve accusations of matricide and attest to a prodigal's need for money matched by a lack of scruple in obtaining it: he is reported as embezzling the public revenues of Sinuessa and Formiae and instituting wholly deceitful legal proceedings when a creditor pressed him too hard for repayment.

On 1 January 69 the legions of Lower Germany refused to swear loyalty to Galba. One day later, German legionary commander and Neronian loyalist Fabius Valens hailed Vitellius as *princeps*. On 3 January, the legions mutinied in Upper Germany too, making cause with their neighbours. It was the first of two legionary revolutions that month. The second, which took place in Rome on 15 January and won the senate's acknowledgement, made Otho emperor. To the latter's colours rallied the legions of the Danube and Illyricum and those in the East; Vitellius was the unanimous choice of Western armies, including Britain. In Tacitus' account, the craving for empire lay not with Vitellius but with Valens, who 'stirred [Vitellius'] sluggish nature to covetousness rather than to hope'.[9] It may also have been Valens, in partnership with his Upper German counterpart Aulus Caecina Alienus, 'a handsome young man of towering stature and boundless ambition' with whom he was otherwise out of sympathy, who strengthened Vitellius' resolve against that barrage of missives dispatched from Rome by Otho, offering the former payment and sweet words in return for renouncing his claim to the throne. Whatever Vitellius' frame of mind, neither Valens nor Caecina was predisposed to compromise. Both smarted under supposed slights from Galba – the former because of Galba's failure to recognize in any concrete form his role in killing Fonteius Capito, the latter thanks to a prosecution brought by Galba against his embezzlement of public money during a quaestorship in Baetica. Like opportunists before and since, Caecina '[concealed] his private wounds among the misfortunes of the state' and departed the Rhine for Rome at the head of his legion.[10] Valens mobilized at the same time: his route, through Gaul, was longer and slower. This disposition of troops left Vitellius himself with the task of recruiting additional men for his rump army, at the head of which he also in time departed the legionary camps bent on combat with the Othonians. Valens' and Caecina's men regrouped in northern Italy outside Bedriacum, where Otho made his fateful decision to engage in premature battle. We know already the outcome. It was over long before Vitellius arrived.

Victory, however, was qualified, at one level no more than defeatism on Otho's part. Suetonius presents Vitellius' emergence as Rome's ruler with ambivalence, recording those portents which decreed from the outset a short span for his principate: equestrian statues of the new emperor which, not yet complete, 'on a sudden all collapsed with broken legs', and Vitellius' own laurel crown which tumbled into a gully. As with Otho, the omens were against the ninth Caesar. Undeterred, he ordered the execution of a number of soldiers who had assisted Otho's murder of Galba, but resisted large-scale reprisals.

Those he spared included Otho's brother Salvius Titianus, a high-profile instance of clemency. His advance through Gaul took on the festal aspect of a triumphal progress, an affair of civic banquets, elegant boat trips, public spectacles and soldiers behaving badly. Private hosts were bankrupted in their attempts to satiate his jaded and intemperate appetite, and Tacitus recalls the Adriatic and Tyrrhenian Seas humming with vehicles hurrying to supply his every whim.[11] The governor of Lugdunensis, a rich man of good family called Junius Blaesus, even lent the threadbare Vitellius clothes fitting his new station. It may have been a high point of this swinish reign. In Rome, news of Otho's defeat and Vitellius' victory, announced in the theatre, was greeted with applause but no outbreaks of disorder. Afraid any longer to express partisanship, a fear shared by the senate, the people responded to this latest change of regime with a passionless demonstration of what was expected of them. In time, they would learn something of that contempt which Tacitus attributes to Vitellius' own troops, inspired by the emperor's flabbiness of mind and body, his lethargy and indolence, and his slovenliness in the matter of military as well as personal discipline.

All that lay in the future on the hot July day when Vitellius made his entry into the capital. If the omens foretold disaster and wiser counsellors harboured misgivings, Vitellius himself exulted in a moment of personal glory. At the head of 60,000 troops, attended in Tacitus' version by a damning collection of 'actors, flocks of eunuchs and every other characteristic feature of Nero's court', he had planned his arrival in the garb of a conquering general, mounted, sword-toting, driving before him senators and people alike. Sounder minds prevailed: the emperor was made aware of the injudiciousness of presenting himself to the people of Rome as the conqueror of his fellow

Romans. He wore civilian clothes and processed on foot. Those members of the senate who had travelled with him since the accession audience at Ticinum followed in his wake. None was under any illusion. Tacitus claims that the senate had already 'passed votes of praise and gratitude to the troops from Germany' for their role in Vitellius' victory, a powerful statement of its own debasement;[12] while Vitellius, in accepting the name Germanicus, which he in turn conferred upon his son, announced himself not as conqueror of the Rhine, the name's former meaning, but as the appointee of the German legions. It was an invitation to factionalism and short-sighted at a moment when the government of Rome desperately needed consensus and strong guidance independent of the demands of any single self-interest.[13] In the evening, celebration took the only form Vitellius understood: a dinner organized by his brother at which 2,000 of the choicest fishes and a colossal 7,000 birds were served. Suetonius condemned such excess as 'notorious'.

With hindsight the biographer's censoriousness adds little to our understanding. Even as Vitellius enjoyed that orgy of fin and feather, enemy forces were mobilizing. In Judaea, Vespasian had withheld the oath of loyalty. It was a sign. On 1 July, as the Vitellian convoy carved its uproarious passage through the country north of Rome, Tiberius Julius Alexander, prefect of Egypt, declared his legions' support not for Vitellius but for Vespasian. Two days later, Syria and Judaea followed suit. The armies of the East, once loyal to Otho, disdained his successor, preferring instead a commander of their own. Such, at any rate, is the argument afterwards propounded by Flavian propaganda, in which Vespasian is borne aloft on wings of popular support. It would be naïve to overlook the probability of top-level coordination. Vitellius retained as city prefect Vespasian's brother Flavius Sabinus. It was a gesture from which he failed to benefit. Once Flavian victory was assured, Sabinus would attempt to negotiate for Vitellius a peaceful handover of power.

But Vitellius' was not a regime of negotiation and consensus. He owed his throne to force: the will of the German legions. In August, in Moesia, another legion felt similarly moved. 'So great was the soldiers' anger at Vitellius and their eagerness for plunder,' Dio reports, that they marched on Italy under their commander Antonius Primus, heedless of alternative Flavian plans formulated at a higher level. On 24 October, they engaged with Vitellian troops on almost exactly the same spot at which the latter had so recently defeated troops loyal to Otho. On that occasion, Caecina and Valens had shared the victory. Six months later, Vitellius' men were virtually leaderless. Apprised of the threat from the East, Caecina had moved first to the Empire's defence. But his loyalty proved of a flexuous quality, corrupted, according to Tacitus, by Sabinus' agents. Predictably he defected. Less predictably, he failed to convince his soldiers to join him. Enervated by the months of illness, indolence and ill discipline in Rome, perturbed by the ominous symbolism of a blood-red eclipse of the moon, but determined and surprisingly strong in spirit, the Vitellians fought at Bedriacum in the name of an emperor who, as with earlier victory, was himself far away.

Vitellius remained in Rome, making occasional sorties to his villa at Aricia south of the city. In September he had sent Valens to the north. In Suetonius' account, the emperor's days are numbered and every course of action equally futile; Tacitus scorns his 'hiding away in the shady arbour of his suburban estate, as if he were one of those slothful animals that lie around in a torpor, so long as you keep on feeding them'.[14] In the short term, with no news of defeat and both commanders busy in the field, Vitellius had grounds for maintaining a semblance of normality. With Cremona sacked and Primus' troops en route for Rome, all certainty vanished. Vitellius responded by sending troops to block the Apennine passes in an attempt to halt the enemy's advance. Afterwards he joined the soldiers there himself. But the portents had defected as surely as Caecina. Vitellius offered sacrifice and prepared to address the army. A crowd of vultures targeted the altar, scattering the offerings and threatening to knock over the emperor. It was not a challenge to which Vitellius was capable of rising. Dio describes him as harried by indecision, erratic in his mood swings, oscillating between defiance and despair; unable to fix on a single course, to decide even on what clothes to wear, befuddled by fear or panic or simply the occlusions of good living. In place of leadership, he invoked the people's pity, appearing before them clinging to the infant Germanicus. His speeches were contrary and confusing, advocating by turns war and defiance or an instant surrender and his own withdrawal into private life. It was the only period in his reign when Vitellius was required to act decisively: he failed. Dio describes the effect of his bewilderment as 'chill[ing] the enthusiasm of almost everybody else, for when they saw him rushing hither and thither in such a frenzy, they ceased to carry out their orders with their usual diligence and began to consider their own interests as well as his'.[15] Vitellius succeeded only in inspiring contempt; in that way, he lost the other half of the war.

A plan that he should abdicate, the first in our story, came to nothing. It was spearheaded by Sabinus and promised the emperor 100 million sesterces and a country estate in return for a peaceful handover of power. It failed, in Tacitus' account, thanks to a spectacular *coup de théâtre* inadvertently engineered by none other than Vitellius himself. On 18 December, surrounded by his family, his household and his soldiers and himself dressed in mourning, Vitellius appeared in the Forum. He explained the course he had decided upon,

> saying that he withdrew for the sake of peace and his country; he asked the people simply to remember him and to have pity on his brother, his wife, and his innocent young children. As he spoke, he held out his young son in his arms, commending him now to one or another, again to the whole assembly; finally, when tears choked his voice, taking his dagger from his side he offered it to the consul who stood beside him, as if surrendering his power of life and death over the citizens.[16]

Neither consul nor citizens would accept his symbolic surrender. When Vitellius moved away to return the insignia of office to the Temple of Concord, his path was blocked. Only the road to the palace remained open. In a state of bewilderment, Vitellius returned to his gilded cage. It was the opposite of what he had intended. Once, in a province of the north, soldiers had made him emperor. Now they forced him to keep faith with that pact.

With Vitellian forces defeated everywhere bar Rome, it represented a moment of crisis. Sabinus pressed the emperor to honour their agreement. But Vitellius was powerless. Action belonged to the soldiers and they seized the initiative in startling fashion, besieging the Capitoline Hill where Sabinus had taken refuge and burning to the ground the Temple of Jupiter Optimus Maximus. Sabinus himself was taken prisoner and killed; Vespasian's younger son Domitian escaped. Reprisals were swift once Primus' men reached Rome. Vitellius fled the palace in a litter carried by kitchen slaves, his destination a house belonging to his wife on the Aventine. Too late he changed his mind. He returned to the palace, which everyone else had now deserted. The price of vacillation was his life.

———— ∽◦◦◦ ————

Through the corridors of the empty palace limped this bulky man with the crushed upper leg, his chariot-racing injury and the first wound dealt him by the principate. As in the case of Gaius before him, in whose company he had sustained that injury, the ancient biographer's image of the emperor of Rome haunting the corridors of his own palace in search of peace and succour is a disturbing one. It will end badly for Vitellius, we know.

He has chosen to put on a ragged and filthy tunic by way of disguise. Concealed around his waist is a belt filled with gold pieces. Now he hides in the only place he can find safe enough to conceal him till darkness falls. The room is small and foul-smelling: here palace guard dogs take their rest. Vitellius lies down with them, barricading the door against intruders with a couch and a mattress. His thoughts are not of sleep but of his escape under cover of night to Tarracina, where his brother has promised him safety. It is not to be. When, inevitably, he is discovered by enemy soldiers who have stormed the palace, the foul-smelling tunic is gashed with blood. For the dogs have bitten him, those denizens of his own house. He attempts to dissemble, pretending that he is not Vitellius, not the emperor. The soldiers are not deceived. They tie a noose around his neck and bind his hands behind his back. Like a dog they lead him away from the palace and through the streets of Rome towards the Staircase of Wailing, where he is tortured and beheaded. 'And yet I was your emperor,' he offers, the same claim which minutes earlier he had denied. In truth, Vitellius was and was not emperor of Rome, a stopgap figurehead briefly exalted by conflict, afterwards consumed by the dogs of war.

VESPASIAN

(AD 9–79)

'The fox changes his fur,
but not his nature'

It began in the cauldron of civil war and ended in the cold douches of a provincial watering hole. In between, the reign of Vespasian of the Flavii, Suetonius' 'unexpected' emperor, eschewed both fire and ice. Level-headed and continent, disinclined to rashness, alert to cheats and jocular in the face of his own well-publicized miserliness, this tenth Caesar – acclaimed only on the cusp of his sixtieth birthday – restrained extravagance and licentiousness where he found it. He did so without personal compromise. These details alone, assuming that they are true, distinguish him from his immoderate predecessors and account for his success where Galba, Otho and Vitellius had spectacularly failed.

'The fox changes his fur, but not his nature,' an irate yokel taunted him. And so, to Vespasian's credit, it proved to be. Under the Julio-Claudian heirs of Augustus and those would-be emperors of 69, that tag applied to the principate itself, emperor succeeding emperor, a shift in iconography, overweening fallibility consistently a hallmark. The decade of Vespasian's rule marks a watershed. Rome changed: luxury was checked, aristocratic grandeur replaced by circumspection and, on the Palatine, a culture more prosaic. This affable, strong-limbed soldier, piously devoted to the memory of his grandmother, observed a monthly fast day and, with equal assiduousness, the state of Rome's coffers, and remained for the most part apparently impervious to the corruptions of office. The nameless concubines with whom at intervals he shared his bed were rewarded with bulging purses of sesterces – payments the emperor could well afford – but denied the influence of former imperial women. (Save in the matter of Vespasian's mistress Caenis selling offices and imperial decisions, a rumour recorded by Cassius Dio,[1] who added that Vespasian himself happily profited from such a trade, the majesty of Flavian women was circumscribed. Confined to hairdressing, it survives in the ziggurat arrangements of stiff, liquorice-allsorts curls which decorate the sculpted busts of first-century princesses.) The army's emperor – like Galba, Otho and Vitellius before him, as Suetonius takes care to point out – Vespasian reconstituted the senate and wooed its members with courtesy, on the surface punctilious and attentive, but never lost sight of first loyalties. Effectively omnipotent, this provincial-knight-made-good massacred Latin vowels but spared the majority of Romans. Such mildness is remarkable in our chronicle. Equally remarkable in Suetonius' reckoning, it emerged from a house of no distinction – without the loftiness of that patrician sense of entitlement which, in Augustus' successors, had valued at naught suffering, iniquity or even workaday diligence; different even from the families of Otho and Vitellius. Fine words have been expended in Vespasian's name. Not least, that in ending civil war, he cleansed the entire world of its madness. Like all victories – and few can have inspired such a paean – it came with a price tag: according to Cassius Dio, some 50,000 casualties.

Marked covetousness notwithstanding, history – including Suetonius' *Life* – celebrates the deified Vespasian as a 'good' emperor. So too did the majority of his contemporaries. He restored Rome to order and sought to make good the inviolability of the *princeps'* place, prizing regard over ostentation; like Augustus, he cultivated a semblance of concern for Republican sensibilities, and paraded his respect for Rome's ancient ceremonies in a widespread programme of temple restoration. He lost no chance of celebrating that peace of which he himself claimed authorship. Between the Basilica Aemilia and the Argiletum, on the site of a former meat market,[2] he built a Temple of Peace eulogized by Pliny the Elder as one of the wonders of the world. A veritable open-air museum, it displayed for Roman edification golden vessels from the Temple of Jerusalem, alongside ancient masterpieces of painting and sculpture.[3] In a city battered by civil war, he raised taxes, including the *fiscus Judaicus* paid by Jews, to fund an immediate Rome-wide rebuilding initiative: among its objects was restoration of the Claudian aqueduct and a reliable water-supply, and a network of roads and bridges including the Appian and Flaminian Ways. At an age when many Roman magistrates confined themselves to carping and overeating, he appeared at the restoration of the Temple of Jupiter on the Capitoline ready to remove debris in a basket carried on his head. Into that basket he piled broken remnants of the most important temple in the Roman world, the same building which, months earlier, as fear and misery gripped the city, had given fleeting refuge to his son Domitian and, once before, sheltered Brutus and the tyrannicides in the aftermath of Caesar's murder. The figure of the toiling Vespasian, vigorous if bulky, symbolized a city on the brink of rebirth. It is not an image we can apply to Nero, whose building of the Golden House took account only of private pleasures and threatened to force ordinary Romans beyond the city boundaries; to Galba, patrician and geriatric; to Vitellius, fat and fuddled with good living. Happy to hoist hods,

Vespasian embraced a kingship grounded in service; he avoided the tyrannical, sadistic, insane and megalomaniac tendencies of recent incumbents. Little surprise, then, that popular feeling, as Dio claims, was strong in his favour, swayed by his prudence and good nature.[4] As rationales go, posthumous acclaim for this 'good' Caesar seems starkly black and white.

Look again and the truth is more complex, multi-tissued as an onion. It must include that Flavian revisionism which insisted that Vespasian's seizing the throne arose not from personal avidity but from civic-mindedness at a moment when breakdown of order threatened and the rule of law and of the senate appeared perilously challenged. What are we to think? Incurably superstitious, Suetonius fudges the issue with portents. Presumably, as Tacitus suggests, he took his cue from Flavian spin.[5] Suetonius' Vespasian is a man in thrall to the numinous, beset by omens and supernatural signs of coming greatness. With circumspection – perhaps a suggestion of a raised eyebrow – Cassius Dio accepted a similar explanation.[6] We have learned to be wary of those who feign innocence or reluctance in the face of glittering prizes. It was a convention, a necessary apologia for having succeeded where others had so recently failed. Suetonius' compendium of portents – from an ox prostrate in obeisance before Vespasian to a remarkable, storm-proof cypress tree, a revolving statue of Julius Caesar and the spectre of a rheumatic freedman restored to mobility and able to walk through temple walls – served the purpose of whitewash: propaganda, no more or less. It was a denial of the bloody hell of Vitellius' downfall and of the gruesome and unconstitutional inauguration of a reforming dynasty born out of lawlessness and hatred in the year of Suetonius' own birth. It was the best possible gloss on a moment when only deeds counted, when the last mechanisms of Republican routes to power were seen to bow to the harsher truths of military might; when tradition – inadequate before the menace of anarchy – fell trampled under the feet of too many ruleless soldiers bent on slaughter. It invested Vespasian's victory with the vindication of inevitability, where there could be no inevitability: accidents, opportunism and a carrying wind played as great a role in the Flavian settlement as any messianic predeterminism on Vespasian's part. Like Julian descent from the goddess Venus Genetrix, and Numerius Atticus' lucrative vision of Augustus' ascent to heaven, it was the stuff of myth and legend, impossible to verify or gainsay. All-important, it exempted Vespasian from blame: he was not responsible for what had happened to him. It was an alternative, highly convenient rhetoric of ambition. For good measure, as we have seen, Suetonius employed similar portents to imbue Vitellius' downfall with the same irresistibility.

Ancient sources invoke every nebulous presentiment to underscore the legitimacy of Vespasian's rule. Archaeology and soothsaying combined in the find of ancient vases reportedly unearthed in a consecrated spot at Tegea in Greek Arcadia: the vases featured images that bore a striking resemblance to Vespasian. Suetonius and Dio go a step further, with recourse to Christ-like powers. They portray the new-made emperor curing blindness and a withered hand with spit and a healing kick. It is not a cynical account (we read, for example, that the Alexandrians witnessed these feats unimpressed and heartily detested Vespasian the cure-all). But in ancient Rome, those who lacked prestige benefited from intimations of divinity. Vespasian himself, consistently unassuming, dreams in Greece of good fortune for himself and his family – imaginings we are right to trust whether or not we guess at the extent of that good fortune. Even if we suspect hyperbole, his record as it survives solidly reiterates his fitness for power. The portents, we assume, backed the right man. The chronicle is one of plain dealing and plain speaking; in Suetonius' words, of an empire 'unsettled and, as it were, drifting... at last taken in hand and given stability'; bankruptcy to the tune of 40,000 million sesterces righted; a sensible head on strong shoulders, after eighteen months in which no fewer than four emperors had met grizzly and untimely deaths. Respected by the legions, exercising tight control over the Praetorian Guard and rationalizing membership of the senate, Vespasian bore the imprint of the survivor. Buffeted by civil war, the Empire needed an emperor, restoration of the Republic the dream of a fond minority. A vacancy existed. Scattered legions chose Vespasian to fill it. The seasoned soldier with a characteristic facial grimace described as that of one straining to defecate did not demur. All that was wanting were the will to grandeur – at best an ambiguous attribute – and something of that *dignitas* which the Romans held dear.

———◦◦◦———

He was an unlikely dreamer, this down-to-earth soldier-king with a genius for military discipline and a taste for mess-room bawdy. Amused by the huge cock of a giant, he quoted Homer, poetry in the service of puerility. Even in the bedroom, his was a business-like approach. When a woman protested that she was dying with love for him, he promptly fucked her. For her pains he reimbursed her generously and entered in the ledger of his accounts the simple mnemonic: 'To a passion for Vespasian.' He revoked an army commission when the new officer arrived to thank him reeking of unguents and pomades. His explanation was curt. 'I should have preferred you to smell of garlic' – the scents of the wayside and the kitchen more appealing to this hill-born Sabine than all the perfumes of Arabia. Heedless of advancing age, his days were consumed by industry, beginning, like those of Galba, before daybreak when the sky was still thick with shadows. For here was a man defined by the practical, decisive and quick to action. He understood, too, how to play precept-loving Romans at their own game. He cherished a vision of dynastic immortality, his own reign the prelude to that of his sons, and legitimized this un-Republican aspiration in another dream which again found its way into the written accounts. In the middle of the palace vestibule, the sleeping Vespasian saw a balance. At one end stood Vespasian and his grown-up sons, Titus and Domitian; at the other, Claudius and Nero. To the Roman mind the import was clear: the Flavian trio would reign supreme for the same time-span as the last of the Julio-Claudians, a total of twenty-seven years. And so it came to pass, sanctioned by clairvoyance. (Else Suetonius would hardly have seen fit to mention it.) Vespasian dreamed when it suited him. For the most part he had no need for fantasy, despite the personal astrologer Tacitus places in his retinue.

Once, Vespasian had been goaded into public office only by the contempt of his ambitious mother, Vespasia Polla. She teased him with the success of his elder brother Sabinus, consul in 47 and later twice created city prefect of Rome. Polla harried Vespasian towards the senate not with the encouragement of affection but with that maternal determination which threads a course through Roman history like marbling in a side of beef – an upstart Livia, Volumnia of the Sabine Hills, Vitellius' Sextilia all over again. Later, championed by legions, Vespasian displaced Vitellius and hoisted himself to ultimate glory. Then there was no mother's bittersweet cajoling; instead, the enthusiastic support of army chiefs, fellow provincial governors and client kings – Sohaemus of Sophene, Herod Agrippa II of Peraea, Antiochus of Commagene (wealthy and magnificent) and Vologaesus the Parthian, who contributed 40,000 bowmen to the cause. It was an unlikely, unpredictable journey. Along its course Vespasian narrowly avoided death and skirted bankruptcy. He embraced voluntary banishment (hiding in obscurity from Nero's displeasure) and weathered ridicule. At Gaius' command, he had faced humiliation in the streets of Rome, pelted with mud for his failure as aedile to keep the thoroughfares clean. Afterwards, perhaps through his own fault, he suffered a similar fate in a marketplace in modern-day Tunisia, mud on this occasion giving way to turnips.

For many, the most striking aspect of Vespasian's remarkable ascent, as with Augustus' hegemony a century earlier, was the insignificance of his origins. His was a family of equestrian rank tarnished by associations of tax-gathering and labour-contracting (the latter denied by Suetonius). Its atrium stood empty of those wax ancestor masks which, on festival days, in aristocratic households mimetically restored to life the great and the good of Roman public service. Among the achievements of this non-patrician emperor was his very insistence on his humble, decidedly unaristocratic background. Behind that smokescreen he might plan and plot unobserved. His aid was not vaunting descent but those omens which the historians insist officially shaped his ends. Omens, yes; divine offshoots in the Flavian family tree, no. Vespasian had no interest in the misguided toadies who struggled to unearth connections between the Flavii and a companion of Jupiter's son Hercules. In his attempt to reassert the personal authority of the *princeps* – and to do so with broad support – he was hamstrung rather than uplifted by godly DNA. His Everyman posturing was no deceit. He was a stranger to snobbery and too canny to allow himself to be rebranded in the Julio-Claudian mould. Even in his portraiture he eschewed their model, a bull-necked, bald-headed, warts-and-all imagery of age and its imperfections replacing the classicized perfection of those god-like Augustans: its sober verisimilitude was the nearest Vespasian came to flirting with the Republic. In his public life he required the freedom of ordinariness; in his private life he evidently preferred it. A widower at the time of his accession, he had been married to the daughter of a quaestor's clerk, Flavius Liberalis. Probably a kinswoman of sorts, her free-born status was nevertheless in doubt – hardly a glittering match. His long-term mistress Caenis was associated with Claudius' mother Antonia. The queen-mother's friend, she was also her former slave,[7] and as such, despite a love which lasted a lifetime, ineligible to marry Vespasian under that Augustan legislation which criminalized marriage between an equestrian and a freedwoman.[8]

Like his wife and his daughter, Vespasian's forceful, socially aspirant mother did not live to witness the triumph of his seventh decade. Perhaps he would not have wished it. Suetonius ascribes his upbringing chiefly to his paternal grandmother, Tertulla, whose small estate at Cosa lay in mountainous farming country northeast of Rome. It was Tertulla, not Polla, who remained an object of veneration for Vespasian, hers the house he revisited as emperor over and over again. Its furnishings and condition were preserved as a tribute to her memory – and, surely, the memory of childhood happiness uncoloured by a mother's harsh taunts. Of the home of his father, Titus Flavius Sabinus, which Suetonius sites in a small village beyond Reate (modern Rieti) called Falacrina, even the precise location has been lost. The region's fame was confined to its mules.

———————

Yet neither Vespasia Polla, nor the character of Sabinus'
antecedents, can be erased from the record. Despite the
provincial accent to which he clung until his death, Vespasian
belonged to a family already on the move – ironically, given
his ultimate usurpation of their throne, their progress a Julio-
Claudian success story. Three times his maternal grandfather
had served as military tribune; his mother's brother was
senator and praetor. Polla was not wrong to cherish hopes
of more to come. Hers was the family from which the future
emperor took his surname. Her family's was the trajectory his
life would follow, outstripping the small-town distinction of
those sepulchral monuments which Suetonius tells us crowded
a steep spot on the road from Nursia to Spoletium, itself known
as 'Vespasiae'. For his part, Sabinus was acclaimed for the
honesty of his tax-gathering in Asia. Before his death, he had
amassed a fortune from banking. That fortune, more than the
habit of honesty, would accelerate the social mobility of his
sons, the younger Sabinus and Vespasian, sufficient in the short
term for the senatorial property qualification and rapacious
Roman electioneering. Its recent origins – the memory of leaner
times – underpinned Vespasian's excessive meanness, ridiculed
throughout the sources, acknowledged by the emperor without
remorse.

Vespasian's garb of provincialism, then, was almost certainly
considered. Prior to his principate, it served a protective purpose.
In the eyes of the Julio-Claudians and their associates, it
disqualified Vespasian from any but insignificant office-holding,
a curtailment to reasonable ambition – 'a man... in no wise to
be feared because of the obscurity of his family and his name'.

It, as much as military prowess, encouraged Nero to appoint Vespasian to the Judaean command in 67. Suetonius relishes the irony. So fateful a miscalculation recalls Galba's appointment of Vitellius to Lower Germany, that proud fool's egregious equation of corruption with ineptitude. Later, emblematic, the throne his own, Vespasian's rustic middlingness seemed to Romans a guarantee of Neronian elitism quashed... perhaps a mark of family piety... of stubbornness... of the arrogance of the successful outsider. Perhaps, more pertinently, it provided a further means of associating Vespasian with Augustus, both 'new men' whose conspicuous talents seemed to sidestep the courtier's fandangles. By the summer of 69, when the legions hailed him as emperor, Vespasian had a lifetime behind him: too late for the leopard to change his spots or, in his case, the fox his fur. More than forty years had passed since, aged sixteen, he put on the *toga virilis* in 25 or 26, more than thirty years since he was elected to the aedileship on his second attempt and subsequently the praetorship. (The lacklustre attainments of the intervening decade – tribune of the soldiers in Thrace, quaestorship in Crete and Cyrene – were the under-achievements which goaded Vespasia Polla into tartness.) If Vespasian's career encompassed setbacks, it was also, of course, marked by notable successes, particularly during Claudius' reign (as emperor, Vespasian would commemorate his early sponsor by building a temple to the Deified Claudius on the Caelian Hill). Experience furnished an accurate assessment of the value in all this of the mellifluousness of his speech – and the limited damage accruing from frankness concerning his family's obscurity.

As in the Republic, so too under the principate. Vote-winning was a costly business only loosely caught up with popular favour. Where family history failed to supply the *novus homo* with a ready-made political profile, the void could be filled by patrons and prominent protectors – best of all, by friends in high places: courtiers, freedmen, even the emperor's smile. For all his country boy's vowels and his determination as *princeps* to distance himself from the court politics of past regimes, Vespasian did not lack worldly wisdom. Gaius had heaped mud upon the hapless aedile of 38: as praetor, his erstwhile victim importuned the senate for special games to celebrate the emperor's victory in Germany. In the same space, he thanked the emperor for honouring him with an invitation to dinner. Following Gaius' death, Claudius' freedman Narcissus was among those who championed Vespasian's cause.

Such nuggets of sycophancy and self-serving trouble us. Indicative of a degree of hard-headedness, they fly in the face of that Flavian propaganda which insists on a no-nonsense nature impatient of machinations, disdaining the place-seeker's insincerity. They refute that denial of ambition Suetonius invokes portents to express. And they suggest, too, the extent to which, equestrian rank and mangled diphthongs notwithstanding, Vespasian the Sabine newcomer operated from within the system, the insider's outsider. A mother's ambition… a father's new-made fortune… personal opportunism: Vespasian's advance through the magistracies of the *cursus honorum* was anything but revolutionary.

In the final months of 51, he reached the consulship. It was a reward for military achievements. In Germany, thanks to Narcissus' influence, he had commanded a legion stationed near modern-day Strasbourg;[9] in Britain, a focus of Claudius' own imperial ambitions, the tally of his successes included more than twenty towns reduced to subjection and the Isle of Wight peaceful under Roman rule. That last 'victory' – clearly over-egged in Rome, where neither the island's tiny size nor its nugatory strategic importance can have been accurately understood – earned Vespasian triumphal regalia in 47. He had fought more than thirty battles. Impressive in his tirelessness, with a head for tactics, strategies and the organized disposal of troops, as well as a hands-on approach, rapport with his men and crowd-pleasing carelessness in the matter of his own comforts, the Vespasian of the sources is a natural soldier, the equal (bar his money-grubbing) of the generals of antiquity, according to Tacitus.[10] A brace of priesthoods followed the awards of 47, then finally the consulship. Vespasian was forty-two.

In ascending the highest rung of the ladder, he had equalled the record of his maternal uncle and satisfied the yearnings of a mother who may or may not have survived to bear witness. His own feelings are unknown. Briefly eminent, he would discover that, in the short term, there was no more to come, a surprise to those readers who extrapolate from Suetonius a narrative of inevitability. In 51 his wife Domitilla gave birth to a second son, Domitian, a brother for Titus, born in 39, and the couple's daughter, the younger Domitilla. Claudius divorced Messalina. On the Palatine a new wind was blowing. The emperor, as we have seen, took as his fourth wife his niece Agrippina the Younger. A tang of fear coloured the air. There were accusations, recriminations, careers abruptly shattered; Claudius' grip on government was loosening. In palace precincts, hunger for power replaced lust as the prevailing appetite. As a dynamic, it was simultaneously more determined and deadlier. In Rome at large, imperial politics toppled to the politics of the imperial family, a high-risk confrontationalism in which there could be only one winner – as Agrippina herself would learn to her cost. Claudius' bride Agrippina had ambitions. Agrippina had a venomous capacity for hatred. Agrippina had a son and, from the outset, a court party of her own. Vespasian was not among its number, with the result that he held no court appointment during Claudius' final years or the beginning of Nero's principate. Other losers in the fallout included Narcissus. Once Agrippina's enemy, Claudius' puffed-up freedman could not escape her loathing. We can assume that the same brush tarred Vespasian. In his case the empress's enmity was not personal or he could scarcely have escaped with his life. Sabinus continued as city prefect; Titus – for a spell fortune's favourite – continued to take his lessons alongside Britannicus, Claudius' son by Messalina. For Vespasian, a hiatus had been reached – appropriately a caesura. Father of three, soldier, senator and priest, he found himself for the moment less well placed than either his brother or his elder son, estranged from the machinery of power.

———

Beginning in 63, two appointments recalled Vespasian to life. The first was a proconsulship of limited lustre. Far from enriching Vespasian, short-term overlordship in the Roman province of Africa – today a slice of North Africa centred on Tunisia – brought him to the brink of financial collapse and earned him, while it lasted, a degree of personal unpopularity, the source of which is unclear, buoyantly expressed in a pelting with vegetables in the port of Hadrumetum. The second was a command which, we have seen, he won precisely on account of his indifferent social status. First in Africa, afterwards in Judaea, Vespasian embarked on the journey which led him out of the shadows towards the purple.

His route was necessarily unorthodox. He had no right to the throne, no grounds for covetousness or hope, no reason to contemplate his own preferment: like Otho, in principle barred by caste from imperial aspirations, but unlike Otho, able to reflect on the unhappy history of the latter's fleeting prominence. Vespasian's position echoed that of Verginius Rufus, the knight chosen as emperor by German legions following Nero's suicide. Rufus, who would be offered the throne on two occasions, declined on grounds of birth. Eventually, as we have seen, after a significant, voluble interval of silence, he pledged his support for the unimpeachably aristocratic Galba, that veteran of the empress Livia's court. On his tombstone he ordered the inscription, 'Here lies Rufus, who, after defeating Vindex, did not take power but gave it to the fatherland.'

Until Vitellius' victory over Otho, a Flavian principate was not even a probability. Haemorrhaging money in Rome's best interests under a cruel African sun in 63, Vespasian can have had no inkling of his final destination. He may have resented that roll of fortune's dice which had allotted him an obscure appointment offering such threadbare recompense. Indeed, for Vespasian there were *no* pecuniary rewards in Africa. His duties cost him dear. The proconsulship over, he was forced to mortgage his estates to his brother, poor again in Rome's name as he had been in the aftermath of the aedileship and quaestorship, reduced then to living in a tenement building in an unfashionable district. On this occasion, to support his family and maintain repayments, he set himself up as a dealer in mules. As an indignity, it pinpoints the precariousness of his position as *novus homo* and Neronian outsider. Evidently he was unable to take for granted either the emperor's lucrative favour or the comfortable safety net of unearned family sesterces, his father's fortune dissipated in the service of two sons' senatorial ambitions. Suetonius' use of language in describing Vespasian's latest calling affirms the exigency of his position. Does the author imply dishonesty, the second-hand car salesman's trick of talking up the second rate, in Vespasian's equine dealings? Certainly he presents the enterprise without indulgence. Vespasian's chosen entrepreneurship returned him to the land of his forefathers and the jobbing status of the non-aristocrat. Even in one who would afterwards rule with honour, it constituted anything but grounds for praise.

The proconsulship had been awarded by lot, no particular gift from Nero. But Nero it was who, all unwitting, came to Vespasian's rescue in the donkey-dealing doldrums of the mid-sixties. The emperor placed Vespasian at the head of three legions in rebellious Judaea. In time, Nero was among those whose downfall would prove as essential to Vespasian's ascent as the support of the legions with which he endowed him. The appointment, which suited Nero, was not intended as a compliment to its recipient. Less than a year before his departure for the East, Vespasian had played Russian roulette with *lèse-majesté*. Travelling through Greece in the emperor's suite, the tradesman ex-consul disgraced himself at an imperial song recital. Exact circumstances are unclear. Did Vespasian, as the sources indicate, really fall asleep, or was he simply unwise enough to leave early? It hardly matters. Enough to note Suetonius' assertion that Draconian strictures sought to prevent the disturbance of Nero's performances. Women gave birth on the spot, uncomfortable and unassisted in the theatre, rather than court displeasure by departing, while those goaded beyond endurance feigned death as the only fail-safe grounds for certain removal. Vespasian's transgression cut short his Hellenic holiday and sent him scuttling out of reach of imperial ire. Happily, within the space of half a year, Nero's mood had changed. Proven military prowess and a lack of aristocratic distinction emphasized by his current indebtedness outweighed Vespasian's faulty etiquette and his flawed connoisseurship.

In February 67, Jewish rebellion in Judaea gave Vespasian a purpose. It also endowed him with position – a return to public service – and in the long term, unconsidered by Nero, the foundations of a power base. Without the First Jewish Revolt (prosaically described by the Jewish historian Josephus as an upheaval of the greatest magnitude),[11] the support of the governor of neighbouring Syria, Gaius Licinius Mucianus, and renewed military command, Titus Flavius Vespasianus would not have become Rome's tenth Caesar and progenitor of the Empire's second dynasty. That fabled destiny, like the Flavian advance from Reate to the senate house, was a Julio-Claudian bequest.

In Vespasian's historiography, the Judaean command proved a gift to Suetonius, too. 'There had spread over all the Orient', we read, 'an old and established belief that it was fated at that time for men coming from Judaea to rule the world.' Suetonius' relief is almost palpable. Here, at the moment when a man since deified stands on the brink of treason, poised to seize the Empire for himself, the *numina* again come to the historian's rescue. Vespasian's path is foretold, preordained, his promotion the spoils of fortune: gift-wrapped in omens, there can be no question of personal ambition or cupidity. An emperor-made-god finds exoneration in portents. Suetonius, of course, adopted his own interpretation of that 'old and established belief' in Judaean-sent world-rulers. He awarded the honours to Vespasian and Titus, their acquaintance with the region prior to 67 less than a stamp in a passport – the elder born in a farmhouse fifty miles from Rome, the younger the creature of a dismal city tenement block. Yet at one level both were indeed 'born' in Judaea, Roman mettle proven in the crucible of war. Modern readers will furnish their own interpretations.

But that is to jump ahead. Nero for one had not troubled himself with Eastern prophecies. He did not baulk at the supplementary legions placed at Vespasian's disposal, the cavalry and auxiliaries, a mighty force extending to some 50,000 fighting men, sufficient surely for the task of revolution.[12] Nero's concept of the East championed Greece alone; his conquests were won with lyres. He left Judaea to the Sabine rough diamond who, lacking musicality, had once won victories for Claudius and since governed Africa with honesty but no gain.

Unlike Vespasian's principate, Roman victory in Judaea was certain, even once events in Rome had forced Vespasian to entrust command to his elder son Titus, who was twenty-eight at the time, with little of his father's experience. Supreme in numbers, training and technology, the Romans overpowered the insurgents. They advanced roughshod over Jewish fighters and Jewish sensibilities: consistently they offered every possible affront to the insurrectionists. In the face of siege tactics and bandit warfare, Vespasian's approach was dogged and methodical. Energetic, tough, occasionally inspired and able to conjure reserves of courage like rabbits from a trickster's hat, he plotted a course from town to town as his opponents sought to establish their stronghold first in one location, then the next. Mackerel on a fisherman's line, he seized each rebel encampment in turn, beginning in Galilee, Jerusalem his goal. Even the fitful nature of his campaign did not seriously endanger its outcome. He paused in his offensive following Nero's suicide in 68; in 69, fighting was temporarily suspended when Vespasian left Judaea for Egypt and a bigger battle, in which more than a province was at stake.

As it happened, it was Titus, not Vespasian, who conquered Jerusalem, in August 70, after a siege of epic proportions lasting 140 days. By then, the older man could afford to share both laurels and limelight, and laughed at his own pretensions in coveting the grandeur of a triumph in Rome as acknowledgement of his generalship. For by 70 the world had turned upside down. There would be no more trading in mules or mortgages between brothers, no hiding in obscurity from a prima-donna sovereign smarting under imaginary sleights. The dynasty of Julius and Augustus, born out of genius, had ended in something resembling the chaos of farce, Augustus' great-great-grandson virtually alone on the Palatine in lamenting his own inglorious demise. On 1 July in Egypt, and two days later in Judaea, Vespasian was acclaimed as *imperator*. It was more than Vespasia Polla had conceived, this eleventh-hour equality with Gaius, Claudius and Nero. The men who raised their voices in his cause were, like him, soldiers. It would be naïve to assume surprise on Vespasian's part. Suetonius admits that his 'hope of imperial dignity', kindled by those convenient portents, was then of long duration.

In Rome itself, the senate dragged its heels. Not until 22 December did it officially grant Vespasian full imperial honours and privileges, including the award of *imperium*. Suetonius neglects even to mention the senate's role, an instance of rubber-stamping, the prize of empire no longer in its gift. The tenth Caesar remained absent from Rome, although the city – numb after too many interludes of butchery – was now his, administered in his name by a former provincial governor, Mucianus, and his eighteen-year-old younger son Domitian. A stranger to self-delusion, the new emperor estimated senatorial

blandishments at their true worth. Setting the tone for his
ten-year premiership, he resisted dissimulation. He dated his
accession not by any decree or award of the senate's, nor
by his own arrival on the Capitol, but by those first Eastern
acclamations made by men familiar with his deeds (although
not privy to any full disclosure of his motives). In the Temple
of Serapis in Alexandria, eulogized in the fourth century by
Ammianus Marcellinus as 'splendid to a point that words
would only diminish its beauty',[13] Vespasian had consulted the
auspices for guidance at the most critical moment of his life. His
focus was not the temple's beauty. The memory of loyal shouts
ringing in his ears, he made sacrifices again and again. Blood,
smoke and charred offerings – burnt flesh, singed skin – tincted
air dense as incense, and Vespasian experienced a vision: he saw
the figure of his freedman Basilides, arms outstretched, offering
him garlands, sacred branches and loaves, though Basilides
was far away and physically infirm. Like every incursion of the
supernatural into Vespasian's historical record, it was a sign, of
course. Next dispatches brought news of Vitellius' death.

How had it come about, this revolution for which there were
no constitutional precedents, this 'happy' ending which Dio
estimated at a cost of 50,000 deaths? Certainly not in any way
that is likely to be revealed to us completely. Victors have a
habit of kicking over the traces, chucking out the account
books and starting afresh. So it was with the Flavians. One
explanation lies in that hotchpotch of signs and signifiers listed
by Suetonius, tokens of the good fortune attendant on Vespasian
(as well as of Vitellius' certain demise). This constituted
Vespasian's own explanation, as early coin issues celebrating

the emperor's fortune attest. An affectation of easygoing modesty notwithstanding, Rome's tenth *princeps* was nothing if not thorough. He made public the substance of his dreams and portents and, in the everyday currency of Rome's taverns and marketplaces, reiterated their message of divine intervention. In addition, Suetonius (like Tacitus) highlights the role of legions clamorous in support of the new man from Judaea, a soldiery trigger-happy in the knowledge that, a century after Actium, the choice of emperor lay within its own grasp. Both suggestions leave gaps and raise questions. Persuasive as it must have been to Roman minds that Nero had dreamed he was commanded to take from its shrine the sacred chariot of Jupiter Optimus Maximus and deliver it to Vespasian's house, the visions of a doomed man, reported in the time of his disgrace and preserved in the written accounts of his successors, do not invite blind trust. As it survives in *The Twelve Caesars*, the Flavian settlement takes little account of Vespasian himself. Prior to his accession, he is a magnet for presentiments, a cardboard cutout of the physical attributes of Roman manhood: a portrait of unassumingness distinct from the common run only in his martial arts. We glimpse his strengths and weaknesses through a prism of impending glory.

How different he appears from his partner in crime, Gaius Licinius Mucianus, and his sons Titus and Domitian. His sons will succeed him as emperors – Titus like him a model of the 'good' ruler, Domitian a study in all that is most disgraceful, victim of the ancients' weakness for vigorous contrast. For the moment, both younger men display flashes of selfishness and self-importance at odds with our portrait of their father. Their loyalty is a fragile, shifting thing, in thrall to their own desires and devices. Neither shares Vespasian's military genius, although Titus has gained experience of warfare in Britain and Germany and Judaean victory is imminent. At this stage, their undisciplined appetites embrace wide-ranging depravity – the chronicler's taste for tittle-tattle perhaps. In power, Vespasian's outlook will reveal itself as explicitly dynastic. His hopes then centre on his sons, acclaimed like the heirs of Augustus as *principes iuventutis*, 'Princes of Youth' – Flavian self-regard a feature of both his own and Titus' principates: in Vespasian's reign, senatorial offices, imperial titles and numismatic acclamations are all enlisted in the service of the family trio. In the struggle for power, the contributions of Titus and Domitian counted less than the efforts of Mucianus, Tiberius Julius Alexander (the same Jewish equestrian prefect of Egypt who later served alongside Titus in Judaea), and the unlooked-for support of an opportunistic Pannonian legionary commander of questionable renown, Marcus Antonius Primus.

Suetonius underplays Mucianus' role. He is unable to reconcile his own theory of omens and portents with Mucianus' untenable claim that it was he who single-handedly made Vespasian emperor. The Neronian ex-consul and lordly governor of Syria, who in his youth had run through a fortune in pursuit of high placement, and afterwards, for unspecified reasons, earned the disapproval of Claudius, emerges more forcefully from Tacitus' *Histories*. There he is a study in contradictions, as much a vehicle for rhetorical dexterity on the writer's part as a credible biographical portrait: evil and good, arrogant and courteous, vigorous and self-indulgent, a construct of pithy polarities. He is a raffish, boldly disreputable figure, whose dissipated prodigality and opulent hauteur – the dark side of Julio-Claudian grandeur – will jar in the new reign of moderation. Catamites follow him in flotilla. But his private life does not besmirch his position. He appears the very model of a Roman major general. Eminent in his magnificence, his wealth and that personal greatness which generated the prestige Romans celebrated as *dignitas*, he possessed the added gift of conferring the best possible gloss on his own words and deeds. He is, it seems, a would-be emperor. Princely, he lacks humility and the attributes of a subject. Prior to the intervention of Titus, whose charm and good looks effect a rapprochement between the neighbouring governors, he regards Vespasian with jealous contempt, even hostility, unwilling to acknowledge parity either of office or of person. That haughtiness is the prerogative of high birth and never wholly gives way to amity. In time, Mucianus would fail to treat the emperor Vespasian with the deference due to his elevation. He may not have had the stomach or the humility for such an inversion of the natural order. Enough that, conscious of his childlessness and age, and wooed by Titus, he forswears personal hopes of the purple.

Writer and historian, Mucianus compiled a natural history of the East. It was remembered by Pliny the Elder as rich in reports of miraculous happenings, Roman belief in natural phenomena one connection between these two men of widely differing backgrounds and outlook. Literary endeavours aside, his contribution to Vespasian's cause was the three Roman legions stationed in Syria. But he was not the Flavian's Svengali, save in the luridness of his sexual proclivities, nor was he Vespasian's Maecenas. The one-time governors' association was pragmatic, a considered and tactical decision on both their parts. (If Tacitus can be trusted, Mucianus' habitual priority was neither equity nor truth but the depth of a man's purse, and he may simply have relished the prospect of influencing Rome's next emperor to his own benefit.) Whatever his motives, the Syrian legions doubled the number of troops at Vespasian's disposal.

Those same troops had acclaimed Vespasian as *imperator* by the middle of July 69. Vitellius had been emperor of Rome for three months. At the beginning of July, as we have seen, similar acclamations had already been made in Egypt and in Vespasian's own province of Judaea. At a council of war, Mucianus chose for himself the role of Rome's conqueror, setting out on the long march westwards at the head of his sixth legion and 13,000 veterans.[14] Vespasian journeyed to Egypt. In Alexandria, where his arrival inspired the Nile to overflow, and Pelusium, a border fortress on the easternmost banks of the Nile, he intended to restrict the supply of grain to Italy, as a means if necessary of starving Vitellius' Rome into surrender. It was a plan of which his brother Sabinus, reappointed to the office of city prefect by Otho, was already apprised, the brothers complicit despite the potentially contentious nature of Sabinus' recent 'assistance' in the matter of Vespasian's finances. As it happened, the plan would not be necessary.

We do not know whether sight of that portent recorded by Suetonius before the battle of Bedriacum was reported to the hapless Otho. Two eagles fought in full view of the assembled troops. One defeated, a third approached from the East – 'direction of the rising sun'... of Egypt, Syria and Judaea – and drove away the victor. There were pressing, more concrete reasons for Otho's suicide. But soldiers present that day were impressed by the evident symbolism of this airy puppetry.

Among them was the Danubian legionary commander and determined rabble-rouser Marcus Antonius Primus. A convicted forger disgraced in the reign of Nero, at fifty Antonius was the sort of restless thrill-seeker who finds his métier in the theatre of war. He declared his support for Vespasian in a spectacular gesture which nullified Mucianus' proposed march on the capital and Vespasian's war of attrition. Unsanctioned by authority, in October Antonius engaged Vitellian troops at the battle of Cremona in north-central Italy. He inflicted an overwhelming defeat. So ferocious and unforgiving was the encounter at Cremona that, in Tacitus' account, it represents the very end of that city, 286 years after its foundation. Afterwards, puffed with victory but clearly not sated, Antonius led his men south towards Rome. There, entering the city via a quiet district of the northeast, they again routed Vitellian forces. It was the feast of the Saturnalia and easy in the free-for-all holiday atmosphere to initiate what quickly developed into full-scale rioting in surrounding streets – a bloody spectacle, according to Tacitus, watched by cheering, jeering Romans as if the Empire's future governance were just another gladiatorial combat. Legionary banners acclaimed Vespasian. It was victory for the cause after a fashion. On this occasion neither Vespasian nor Suetonius had recourse to portents to establish blamelessness.

Surely Vespasian entertained the highest hopes on his arrival in Rome more than a year later. The oracle of the god of Carmel, whom he had consulted in Judaea, had promised that whatever he planned or wished, however great, would come to pass. It was an unequivocal response – possibly, dangerously, *carte blanche*. As throughout his public life, Vespasian interpreted the green light responsibly. He assumed the consulship – shared with Titus, a suffect appointment granted to Mucianus – and addressed himself clear-sightedly to the task in hand as he saw it.

It was as if, from the outset, he had dedicated himself to winning that good opinion with which posterity continues to furnish him. 'He considered nothing more essential than first to strengthen the state, which was tottering and almost overthrown,' Suetonius tells us, 'and then to embellish it as well.' Did he hope to vindicate his legitimacy through a surfeit of civic-mindedness? Was good behaviour the surest means of self-preservation, new building on Rome's streets as much a metaphor for order restored as that review of membership of the senate he pursued following his revival of the censorship in 73? The ancient author, habitually impartial, comes close to panegyric. In truth, the new man at the top was prepared to undertake almost any measure to shore up his position, understandably reluctant to replicate the swift downward spirals of Galba, Otho or Vitellius, and to stabilize the 'tottering' state.

The regime needed adherents. Veteran of that pelting in Hadrumetum, Vespasian understood with no prompting from Juvenal that the commons of Rome would cheer anyone who fed and entertained them, too poor for the luxury of political discernment. Roman senators were lured less readily. They could as easily cherish the memory of the affable, well-born Vitellius, like Vespasian popular with his troops and distinguished by a reputation for integrity during his provincial governorship in Africa. On the streets of Rome, Vespasian cultivated a jocular buffoonery. He was quick to jest, apparently without self-importance, his humour unrarefied, blokeish and winning, laughter at his own expense. Behind palace doors, he entertained a continuous stream of senate members and himself accepted invitations to dinner. He transferred his principal residence from the Palatine – superior eyrie of the Julio-Claudians – to the Gardens of Sallust, a bequest to Tiberius from Sallustius Crispus in AD 20. There his doors stood open to all callers. It was an arrangement reminiscent of senatorial practice under the Republic. In the Flavian charm offensive, accessibility and openness were to be the keynotes. At the same time, in an irreconcilable (and unpublicized) impulse, he controlled the principal appointments of state with a tight grasp, avoiding those distinguished by family history – an untenable policy on his part – in favour of men who had demonstrated loyalty and friendship to him personally. In 71, for example, he may have appointed Tiberius Julius Alexander to share prefectship of the Praetorian Guard with Titus.[15] He himself shared the consulship with Titus seven times – in 70, 72, 74, 75, 76, 77 and 79 – exploiting the office for personal and dynastic gain. Family monopoly was deliberate and more than simply a security measure. His revival of the censorship in 73 enabled him to re-examine the make-up of the senate and fill vacancies with his own nominees – some sixty-nine senators, including Romans, Italians and provincials.[16] Suetonius casts what may as easily have been self-serving as a moral crusade, Vespasian's criteria for senatorial rank merit, worthiness and respectability. As under the Republic, so under the first Flavian: the great magistracies of state were the means of conferring that personal prestige or *auctoritas* which, municipal bourgeois that he was, Vespasian could not take for granted.

The Rome in which Vespasian found himself – received rapturously in the months following the Flavian sack of Jerusalem – was a city partly purged. The murderous hell of Antonius' conquest had passed. Vitellius' ugly death, an unedifying example of mass viciousness and the fickleness of mob rule, had inspired rabid atrocities on the part of Flavian troops and even civilians: looting, slaughter and rampaging bloodlust like that of foxes released into a chicken coop. Prior to Antonius' arrival in Rome, Vespasian's mortgage-broking brother Sabinus had perished in the torching of the Temple of Jupiter Capitolinus as order buckled before misrule. More fortunate than his uncle, Domitian – left behind for the duration of the Judaean campaign – managed to escape from the same hiding-place. It was an event on which Domitian would later pleasurably dwell, as if, like Vespasian's nimbus of portents, escape invested him with quasi-divinity. In years to come, he built a temple on the spot of his delivery. In it he placed a statue of himself borne aloft by Jupiter Custos ('Jupiter the Guardian'). Portraiture is never neutral in imperial Rome: that Domitian should present himself in such a light, cradled by a god, is a vainglorious gesture at odds with Flavian understatement, not to mention Vespasian's ability to laugh at himself. In the short term, while terror gripped the streets, Domitian the survivor, saved by the intervention of Jupiter Custos or otherwise, had savoured his freedom in an orgy of partying. Immature, headstrong, dizzy with the splendid destiny suddenly revealed to him and insensitive to niceties in the relief of remaining alive, he had accepted as his father's representative the soldier's acclamation of 'Caesar'. But he was not Caesar. 'There was no emperor and there were no laws,' Tacitus records. The integration into the Flavian narrative of Domitian's miraculous escape from fire and perfervid Vitellians would remain temporarily unresolved. Later it formed a cornerstone of that unhappy emperor's personal mythology.

Arriving in early 70, it was Mucianus who in fact played the Caesar's part, the language of command instinctively within his lexicon. He expelled Antonius' lawless troops from the city and sidelined their light-fingered commander, who was even then rewarding himself with plunder from the imperial household. (His history of pliant loyalties offered limited grounds for trust.) Antonius left Rome first to plead his cause before Vespasian in Alexandria, afterwards – Vespasian having smoothed his ruffled feathers with admirable diplomacy – for retirement in his native Tolosa (modern Toulouse). Mucianus' thoughts turned then to Domitian. Amiably or otherwise, he set about curbing the young man's pretensions and herding him back within the fold. Together he and Domitian began that reconstituting of the Roman machinery which Vespasian would continue, appointing governors and prefects. Mucianus executed Vitellius' son. It was a necessary precaution perhaps, but one Vespasian himself could not have taken without forfeiting the garb of good-naturedness he had chosen as an alternative to lofty birth or that 'great renown' with which Suetonius endows him at this point.

For the better part of a year Mucianus oversaw the business of government, preparing for Vespasian's autumn arrival and the less explosive, more challenging task of restoration. In Dio's account, it is Mucianus who embarked on the programme of tax increases which, in time, overcame Rome's staggering post-Nero, post-civil war deficit, estimated by Vespasian in Suetonius' account at 40,000 million sesterces at a time when the annual tax revenue was only 800 million sesterces.[17] He 'gather[ed] countless sums into the public treasury with the greatest eagerness from every possible quarter, thereby relieving Vespasian of the censure which such a proceeding entailed';[18] as the year drew to its close, he encouraged Vespasian to pursue a similar policy. Briefly, the self-proclaimed king-maker enjoyed absolute power. He was authorized, he claimed, by a ring bearing the imprint of the imperial seal, given to him by Vespasian. Only Domitian, appointed urban praetor with consular powers, shared Mucianus' temporary majesty. In the fortunes of this loose-living libertine with a talent for intrigue but neither the ambition nor the courage to aim for ultimate honours, it represented a high-water mark. In the years that followed, despite a position of esteem and influence at Vespasian's court, he would never again wield such unqualified power.

Vespasian banished the astrologers from Rome. No need for them
and their ilk now: the portents' work was done. Did he set up in
that house at the Gardens of Sallust those antique vases whose
iconography proclaimed his supremacy? We will probably never
know. In place of soldiers' boots and breastplates, the streets of
Rome rang with the sound of the emperor's task of rebuilding. A
year later, the route of Vespasian and Titus' triumph of Jerusalem
bore witness to the speedy eradication of civil-war scars. In the
interval, Vespasian had addressed himself to the backlog of legal
cases unheard in eighteen months of fighting and confusion;
declared an amnesty for Neronian informers; examined the
composition of various legions in order to diffuse lingering
Vitellian loyalty; and evolved a model of working alongside the
senate in which, while every courtesy was observed, an emperor
of non-senatorial background maintained full decision-making
powers over that body which had procrastinated for half a year
before investing him with *imperium*. His focus, like that of every
new-made *princeps* before him, was the maintenance of his own
position. Although Vespasian's power had been formalized in
December 69 in the so-called *lex de imperio Vespasiani*, which
conferred on the new emperor either by law or by decree of the
senate all of those powers enjoyed formally and informally by
his Julio-Claudian predecessors, as well as the authority to do
'whatsoever he may deem to serve the interests of the State and
the dignity of all things divine and human, public and private',[19]
for fullest success this ubiquitous remit demanded both popular
and senatorial consensus. Vespasian broadcast the policies he
intended to adopt to that end numismatically. The legends of his
coinage lulled Romans with sound-bites: ROMA RESURGENS,

LIBERTAS RESTITUTA. As it happened, in both short and long terms his gifts to Rome were peace and solvency. He enshrined the first in that glittering temple acclaimed by Pliny; the latter survives in a wealth of anecdotes which animate the sources.

The Alexandrians called Vespasian 'Cybiosactes'. It was the surname of an Alexandrian king of notorious penny-pinching and scarcely a compliment since the attributes of kingship, particularly in the East, embraced munificence. In Suetonius' *Life*, Vespasian's reputation for covetousness pre-dates his principate. Perhaps it accounts for his turnip-pelting in Hadrumetum – a boisterous response to a problem with the city's food supply brought about by the proconsul's meanness. The same shortcoming may also have contributed to Vespasian's poor election performances at the outset of his career (he achieved the aedileship only on his second attempt, in sixth place by a whisker). If so, Rome's new emperor would feign no false remorse. Parsimony quickly became a watchword of his policy making, celebrated by Vespasian as a Flavian virtue. It was the right approach at the right time, sole means of reversing the depredations of civil war and generations of Julio-Claudian folly. Like Mucianus, Vespasian amassed revenues with lip smacking delight. The process even inspired in this down-to-earth burgomaster uncharacteristically creative thinking. He placed a tax on the use of public urinals. The initiative offended Titus, whose concept of imperial dignity had been shaped by his childhood at Claudius' court. Beneath Titus' wrinkled nose, Vespasian held out coins gathered in the first levy. Tersely the son agreed with the father's assessment that the money did not smell. And yet, Vespasian smiled, it came from piss.

But parsimony, the emperor knew, must be balanced: that was the lesson to be learned from Galba's mistakes. There must

be largesse, a talent for the sweeping gesture. Vespasian's purse
targeted the arts. A restorer of statues, a tragedian called Apelles
or Apellaris, lyre-players Terpnus and Diodorus, and a successful
but impecunious poet called Saleius Bassus – all received
payments from Vespasian of up to half a million sesterces.[20] At
the same time the emperor endowed chairs of rhetoric in Rome
and Athens, each with a salary of 100,000 sesterces. Perhaps the
policy was Titus' in inspiration. Educated to the highest level,
Titus wrote poetry in Latin and Greek and even turned his hand
to Greek tragedy. Vespasian's own accomplishments can hardly
have soared so high. His understanding was born of insight, not
letters. He recognized the role of spectacle, visual propaganda
like his coin slogans writ large or that token hefting of temple
debris from the Capitoline. Although building work remained
unfinished at the time of his death, the Flavian amphitheatre,
known since the Middle Ages as the Colosseum, was Vespasian's
gift to the Roman people. On the site of the pool at the centre of
Nero's Golden House complex, it was funded with Jewish spoils
and first planned, Vespasian claimed, by Augustus. As Titus
would demonstrate, it allowed tens of thousands of spectators at
a single sitting to witness visual extravaganzas of eye-watering
excess. From its steeply tiered seats, the Roman mob absorbed
the thrilling narcotic of mass bloodshed.

———

For the majority in Rome, gladiatorial combat was as close
as they would come to bloodshed during Vespasian's reign.
So too, for the most part, it proved for the emperor himself.
The man who rose early and devoted his day to work, pausing
from the business of empire only to drive through the rebuilt
city, take a siesta or indulge in perfunctory sex with the

succession of unnamed concubines who consoled him after Caenis' death, did not scruple to conceal in the interests of security his whereabouts or timetable. He ended Claudius' habit of searching his guests – ended too that culture of fear and uncertainty in which opposition, not daring to speak out, corkscrewed underground into labyrinthine conspiracy. In Suetonius' account, 'He bore the frank language of his friends, the quips of pleaders and the impudence of the philosophers with the greatest patience.' That last group continued its opposition to the principate and the nature of imperial power within it, consistent in its carping and criticism. Vespasian responded with understatement. He dismissed a banished Cynic called Demetrius as no more than a cur: 'Though you do your best to persuade me to kill you, I don't kill dogs for barking.' To a former friend, Helvidius Priscus, praetor in 70, he showed less leniency. In this instance, the sources attribute blame to Helvidius himself, over-zealous in his impertinence, determined to give offence, in Dio's account the linch-pin of a large-scale revolutionary plot. Vespasian ordered his exile and execution in 75. His hasty countermanding of that decision came too late: Helvidius, whom Dio's Vespasian had grown to hate, died too soon for imperial clemency. In the last year of his reign, two further former friends were detected in a conspiracy to kill Vespasian: at Titus' instigation, Titus Clodius Eprius Marcellus and Aulus Caecina Alienus were dealt with in summary fashion. The former preferred to cut his throat with a razor than face the senate's sentence, the latter met death in a palace corridor. He was probably taken unawares. Neither could have known that for Vespasian too the sands of time were running out.

In the end there could be no resisting death. Like so much in Vespasian's life, it was foretold in portents. 'The Heavens themselves blaze[d] forth the death of princes,' as Calpurnia tells Shakespeare's Julius Caesar on the brink of tragedy.[21] A comet appeared in the heavens and the doors of the Mausoleum of Augustus opened of their own volition. A joker still, Vespasian interpreted the former as boding ill to the king of Parthia, long-haired as any shooting star; the latter to Junia Calvina, a great-great-granddaughter of Augustus through Julia the Younger as well as Vitellius' sister-in-law. Suetonius records the affable emperor's humorous impulse. Apparently dispassionate, his version of events does not lack pathos. Approaching his seventieth birthday and the tenth anniversary of his accession, Vespasian may simply have clung to life, drawing death's teeth through jests. Perhaps he was afraid. All was in vain. After a lifetime's exploitation of the numinous – and scant attention to the state of his health bar occasional massaging at the baths complex – it was impossible to repudiate the supernatural now.

Fever had struck during a tour of Campania. Doubly afflicted, the gouty emperor cut short his peregrinations, returned to Rome and promptly departed for Aquae Cutiliae. This bathing resort noted for its natural springs, where Vespasian had continued to spend his summers, lay in the Flavian homeland near Reate. There, uncharacteristically overindulgent, the emperor drank excessive quantities of cold spring-water. As his fever intensified, that guiltless bibulousness further irritated his intestines.

He retreated to a house which may have been that of his grandmother at Cosa, that repository of happy memories which he had never allowed himself to abandon or outgrow. Assiduously – against the advice of his physicians, according to Dio – he continued to play the emperor's part.[22] From his sickbed he struggled to manage as much as possible of the business of government, like Augustus and Claudius at a loss how to beguile these dog days save in the customary public service. Did he really say 'I think I am becoming a god'? As the shadows closed in, that instinct for the practical did not desert him. It was no more than a recognition that his sons, either from gratitude or, like the Julio-Claudians, making capital from kinship with the heavens, would actively promote his deification. The statement may have been an instruction to Titus, the dying man shrewd enough to see that, though his own reign represented a revolution on the Palatine, Rome had not changed so much that an emperor at the outset of his reign would not benefit from a father who was also a god. Or perhaps it was less considered. Dragged in and out of consciousness by fever, the clarity of his thoughts blurred, Vespasian gave vent to subconscious aspirations he may otherwise have chosen to keep hidden. If instead he meant to joke, it was one last splendid riposte to the grandiose self-delusions of his Augustan predecessors with their twopence-halfpenny approach to pantheism.

Or was Vespasian writing his own epitaph, a summation of his pilgrim's progress, that long, previously untrodden path from provincial obscurity to the loftiness of the purple on which he had acquitted himself with shrewdness, consistency and honour? Impossible to tell. Those who record the statement – Suetonius and Cassius Dio – do so without levity. By contrast, a recent commentator characterizes it as a hostile sneer on the part of Vespasian's contemporaries, a deliberate echo of Claudius' 'Oh! I think I've messed myself' in Seneca's satirical *Apocolocyntosis*.[23] If so, Vespasian, not his detractors, has the last laugh. Thanks to Titus, he did indeed become a god.

Before that, the last trump – a vicious attack of diarrhoea which overwhelmed the failing man and thwarted his ambition to die standing. It was an ironic, explosive, unlooked-for end for one whose facial expression had so often been likened to that of a man battling costiveness and who had replaced former imperial cruelty and caprice with a harmless taste for lavatorial humour and coarse ribaldry. That Vespasian's death provided grounds for the rumour (believed by the future emperor Hadrian) that Titus had poisoned him at a banquet confirms that unexpectedness which is implicit in Alienus' and Marcellus' last-minute conspiracy. Gout aside, and despite a life which had encompassed both physical hardships and emotional strain, Vespasian, unlike the majority of his predecessors, was a virtual stranger to bodily frailty.

For almost ten years he had paved the way for his sons' succession, the right to nominate the eleventh Caesar arguably encompassed by those catch-all provisions of the *lex de imperio Vespasiani*. 'My sons shall succeed me or no one shall,' he had asserted, a red rag to the bullish Helvidius. None doubted the earnestness of his intent. And now he stood on the brink of godhead, gilding at a stroke both Titus and Domitian with the lustre of his own self-proclaimed divinity. His remains were interred in the Mausoleum of Augustus. In death as in life were associated Rome's two great founders of dynasties destined to deteriorate.

───◦◦◦───

There was a theatrical, occasionally irreverent quality to imperial and aristocratic Roman funerals.[24] Paid mourners feigned operatic grief – female professionals who wept, tugged their hair, beat their breasts. Musicians and dancers swelled the processions. Dressed in clothing that indicated the highest attainments of the deceased, an actor impersonated the object of mourning in words and gestures deemed characteristic. In a celebration which embraced every emotion from patriotism to genuine sorrow, no lip-pursing concept of deathbed respect curtailed the actor's behaviour.[25]

At Vespasian's funeral, the emperor's wax death-mask was worn by a leading mime-player called Favor. Favor assailed the procurators: 'How much will this funeral cost me?' The answer – an impressively large sum – provoked a ready reply: 'Give me a fraction of that and be done with the body: hurl it into the Tiber.'

TITUS

(AD 39–81)

‘The delight and darling of
the human race’

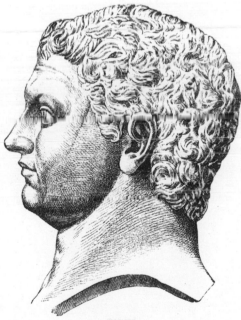

TITUS

Hardly anyone ever came to the throne with so evil a reputation as Titus. Like iron filings to a magnet, accusations adhered to him: he was arrogant, cruel, unchaste, greedy and tyrannical. His passage to the purple in June 79, so doggedly plotted by Vespasian, was ultimately cleared by an explosion of shit – his father's fatal diarrhoea. His brief reign would be marked by emissions, eruptions and explosions on a mighty scale. That first dark stain – notoriety more fitting the Julio-Claudians than the Flavians – was swiftly erased, history rewritten, misgivings dispelled. He became, in Suetonius' account, 'most kindly by nature', indulgent, the scourge of informers, a patient and forgiving brother. Not for the first time, the historian has his cake and eats it. Perhaps Titus did too. For more than rumour was confounded by the apparent volte-face of Suetonius' Titus: like Otho first Hyde, then Jekyll, he exploded the ancient biographical convention that character, unsusceptible to circumstance, was fully formed from infancy – the fox who changed his nature with his fur. As Dio has it, 'Titus after becoming ruler committed no act of murder or of amatory passion, but showed himself upright... and self-controlled.'[1]

At the outset, unsurprisingly, there was no sign of popular rejoicing – indeed, there *was* no rejoicing. Vespasian dead was

305

grounds for regret. Far from degenerating, his reign had improved over time, civil strife banished, the treasury replenished, an alternative to the spent dregs of Augustus' gene pool lordly on the Palatine. Why welcome his demise? During Titus' principate, the very elements trumpeted disdain and disappointment. Rome burned; plague raged; in the south Pompeii, Herculaneum, Oplontis and Stabiae perished under nineteen hours of volcanic lava – and Titus (of middling height and pot-bellied but laying claim, in retrospect, to exceptional talents) transformed himself from villain to victor, and vanquisher of Roman hearts to boot. All within the space of two years, two months and twenty days.

At his own reckoning, this slum-born emperor was destined to earn his coronet in shadier regions than the Forum. He might, he said, have been a prince among forgers, such was his skill at imitating handwriting. Happily as it turned out, petty crime was not his vocation, nor his only talent.

Posterity mocks the meagreness of Titus' self-appraisal. He survives today in different garb – a tragic lover, celebrated in seventeenth-century verse by Racine, Corneille and Thomas Otway; and, from ancient times, unlover-like, in the stone erection that bears his name, souvenir of a mighty general. Today the Arch of Titus – elegantly albeit triumphantly bombastic – frames glimpses of another, more famous Flavian monument, the Colosseum (begun by Vespasian, completed by Titus). Do not be distracted. The Arch's carved panels record the conquest of Jerusalem, the Temple sacked, its treasures stolen, the same episode which afterwards inspired artists from Poussin to David Roberts; a triumph in Rome complete with prisoners and plunder including the seven-branched candelabrum snatched from the Holy of Holies – Rome's disgrace or one of her finest hours, depending on the point of view. The glory and the spoils of that bloody impiety are claimed for Titus alone. The Arch presents a vision of Titus' career that is compressed like snapshots in a magic-lantern show into a narrative of highlights, all martial, all victorious, culminating in his deification. It is the story of a life filtered teleologically through the prism of a single incident, debated now and even then. Surviving portraiture is in every way more rounded. Titus' is a comparatively bland iconography, unromanticized but resisting ghoulishness. Its middle way skirts popular loathing and victorious carnage. Statues and busts of Titus – brow furrowed in imitation of Vespasian – deny the calculation of the small-beer criminal, the dash of the romantic hero, the conqueror's swagger or even warrior-like prowess; avuncular, heavily jowled and running to fat, mostly benign-seeming. Given this eleventh Caesar's subsequent election to the gods, anything else would be surprising.

Suetonius cocks a snook at Titus' image of himself as forger *manqué*, which may anyway have been a throw-away comment not intended for the ears of history. For Titus' destiny was to rule: as in Vespasian's case, oracles and clairvoyants agreed. In the event his reign was short. Its very brevity may account for its success: certainly Cassius Dio and the poet Ausonius thought so.[2] Or perhaps, as Suetonius intimates, it was the misprision that he would prove a second Nero, unexpectedly but consistently parried, which provided the happy outcome to this tale of the unexpected.

Parrying Nero, we know, was a central tenet of Flavian policy. Not for Vespasian and his sons Otho's celebration of a lost friend nor the grandeur of Julio-Claudian descent with its weighty baggage of attitudes and assumptions. Not for them an arrogant kingship revelling in personal distinction nor, at Vespasian's death, a court culture of extravagance, sadism and murderous family mistrust. They had experienced this at first hand and witnessed too the turmoil of its collapse. Theirs was a new way. Vespasian's was an earthy, amiable, spade-calling-spade, farting-and-belching, barrack-room Italianness. Unlike Nero, he had not succumbed to cultural effeteness and pursued a vision of Greece, any more than he had emptied Rome's coffers chasing pleasure, sung for his subjects or paraded his contempt for Roman sensibilities by dressing as a bride and offering both arse and troth to a former slave. Nothing in Vespasian's policy-making or public behaviour had suggested a craving for golden statues. He laughed to scorn attempts to relate him to Rome's pantheon and cheerfully broadcast the inferiority of his connections. Admitted, the Flavians accepted autocracy. Willingly and without complaint, they accepted those generous provisions of the *lex de imperio Vespasiani* by which the Republic died another death. But they insisted on a gulf of clear blue water – flexible and delineated to serve their own purposes – between themselves and their predecessors, theirs a duty-focused, merit-based principate with no stake in the divinity of Augustus or his haughty progeny. New emperors flaunted new clothes. As an alternative approach to absolutism and a means of bringing stability and a semblance of unity in the wake of civil war, it spoke of Vespasian's shrewdness.

Titus was shrewd too. He perpetuated the same illusion. As with his portraiture, so apparently with his policy: a careful assimilation of father and son, toeing the line, a sense of continuity and dynastic coherence, the Flavian way; only in Titus' case, marked not by Vespasian's piss-taxing parsimony but by an oft-repeated show of largesse – generosity and forebearance the autocrat's prerogatives. To his enemies he described his pre-eminence as destiny's gift, his throne neither an accident of birth nor, crucially, a prize within other men's grasp. Happy with his lot – and which emperor, bar the protesting Tiberius of the early years, was ever not? – he repaid destiny by offering mainland Italians a father's love. He understood the power of a speaking gesture, as generous with words as with deeds, in the historical record as accomplished a public-relations supremo as Augustus. Puppet-master of this Titus who emerges from darkness into light, Suetonius offers us implicitly the possibility that his beneficence, concealed till his accession, was mummery: pragmatism, nothing less. It was certainly unexpected by those who anticipated a return to the bad old days of Agrippina's brat – rightly so, given Titus' track record?

***

Titus Flavius Vespasianus had enjoyed a childhood of sunshine and shadows. He was born at the midpoint in Gaius' short principate, AD 39. The place was a tenement building – its name suggests seven storeys – probably on the Quirinal,³ that hill once associated with the ancient Sabines, in Titus' youth remote from Rome's aristocratic epicentre of the Palatine. There his mother Domitilla laboured in a cramped, dark room to give him life. Later, in accordance with Flavian posturing about humble birth, the room became a tourist attraction, lowly linen sanitized by a history of good behaviour. At the time, family circumstances were straitened. Elections to the aedileship and the praetorship had drained Vespasian's purse. There was no one at hand to provide a bailout. In marrying a kinswoman of uncertain status, Titus' father had even forsaken the safety net of a dowry.

At Gaius' command, as we have seen, Vespasian the aedile had been pelted with mud, an irksome punishment for his failure to keep clean the streets of Rome. At no point can Titus have been encouraged to regret this mud-slinger's gruesome demise occurring in his third year, nor to regard the family that spawned him with anything but circumspection. Childish prejudice notwithstanding, Vespasian's first-born shared his own fast-rising fortunes under Gaius' successor Claudius. Indeed, promoted beyond his father's rank, the Quirinal behind him, Titus was brought up as a child courtier. He became the devoted companion of Claudius' son Britannicus, whose lessons and tutors he shared. This detail, which Titus would later emphasize, exploiting his association with a 'good' Julio-Claudian as evidence of imperial legitimacy, lends his early years (of which little is known otherwise) a fable-like quality. In Flavian propaganda, he is the supporting actor of pantomime and fairytale, the prince's friend familiar with palace ways: one foot in the door, associated but not implicated, sufficiently obscure to survive skullduggery and evil plots... the lamb who escapes sacrifice. As indeed proved to be the case. If that good nature which afterwards characterized his reputation as emperor was indeed an affectation, assumed in the interests of popularity and security, Titus learned the value of dissimulation young, at Britannicus' side. He was next to Britannicus when the latter drank the fatal draught prepared for him by his wicked stepbrother Nero. Foremost among Titus' childhood ailments in Suetonius' account was the lingering illness he sustained after draining dregs of poison from his friend's cup.[4] In 55, only sixteen years old, Titus was forced to acknowledge that the good need not end happily, nor the bad unhappily. It was a recipe for cynicism which, with hindsight, offers grounds for exoneration.

For Suetonius, Titus' willingness to share his friend's misfortune is a symbolic act, a show of sympathy, and surely intended by an earnest young man as a demonstration of loyalty. Perhaps it is more, too – the baton of kingship assumed by the low-born friend of whom a physiognomist summoned by Narcissus had claimed that he and not Britannicus would inherit his father's greatness. If so, that act of usurpation was unconscious on Titus' part. A quarter of a century later, he commissioned a golden statue of Britannicus for his palace; he appeared behind an ivory statue of Britannicus at the opening of the Colosseum. By then a lifetime had passed since the two men – both now sons of emperors, one laurel-wreathed, the other invested with garlands by tragedy – had shared the anointing of that same poisoned chalice. Suetonius does not invite us to query the depth of Titus' friendship for the dead boy or his motives in perpetuating before Roman crowds that distant amity.

When Titus was twelve, his mother gave birth to a brother, Domitian, and his father attained the consulship, a neat example of Roman gender roles satisfactorily fulfilled. Domitian's birth cannot have impacted greatly on Titus' life, Vespasian's ascent more so. Yet this token of worldly success – the highest appointment of the *cursus honorum*, the result, as we have seen, of military service and high standing at the Claudian court – proved illusory. Lacking office in the wake of the consulship, Vespasian withdrew from public life for a dozen years. His return to prominence as proconsul of Africa led to renewed imperial contact, this time with Nero. His father's fluctuating career caused Titus greater concern than the squalls of an infant brother: Vespasian was pelted with vegetables in the marketplace in Hadrumetum and afterwards, when best behaviour was the order of the day, yawned his way through an imperial song recital. In the intervening wilderness years, of which little is known, Domitilla died and the family fortunes suffered an abrupt decline. His mother's death scarred Domitian more than Titus, the loss of family prestige ditto. Not for Domitian a childhood at court, sharing Rome's best teachers, an education in imperial politics and the nuances of the colour purple; nor that sense of entitlement characteristic of Titus' behaviour prior to his accession, acquired perhaps from proximity to Britannicus and Vespasian's good odour. If Domitian chafed at blessings withheld, Titus learned the whimsicality of fate, its perils and setbacks. In time those different responses became factors which shaped the brothers' divergent interpretations of ultimate power.

There were lessons to be learned at the court of the emperor Nero. As under Gaius, life was cheap, favour capricious. Unwittingly, Vespasian had demonstrated indifference to his master's performance skills – under the circumstances Titus could not depend on this least predictable *princeps*, nor would Vespasian have encouraged such reliance. Instead, former benefits under Claudius offered Titus the wherewithal for a career of his own outside palace confines. That education which he had shared with Britannicus had created a young man of gifts, sophisticated, even a belle-lettrist in his parts, the author of Latin poetry as well as tragedies and poems in Greek – like Julius Caesar, Tiberius and Claudius, one capable of containing the world in words and thus, surely one day, of shaping the written record. For good measure Suetonius throws into the mix good looks, horsemanship, musicality and – all-important – a talent for arms, though this can scarcely have been visible in the beginning. Roman electioneering, of course, begged more than ability. Like his father, Titus had not been Agrippina's man, nor was he now an acolyte of Nero's. The former Flavian patrons Narcissus and Lucius Vitellius were no longer on hand to expedite his progress. He embarked on political life unspectacularly, offices of the vigintivirate and military service abroad followed by a period practising law in Rome – the latter perhaps no more than a divertissement, channelling his facility with words; in time he attained the quaestorship.[5] It was the beginning of a textbook senatorial career. It was also nothing special.

But Titus was his father's son. As Nero, touring Greece, sang his way out of a job, Vespasian was moving closer to that position from which, before the decade was out, he would revolutionize Rome's concept of its leading citizen. The fortunes of father and son were inextricably entwined. In time commentators would attribute to Titus' support the success of Vespasian's later years, unique in the history of the principate to date. In the first place – and more often – the advantage worked in the opposite direction, father to son. It was the Roman way and should not concern us unduly, for Romans believed in heredity, the transmission of skills and attributes through successive generations, paternity a blueprint for the future, the mark of the father indelible: a guarantee. 'Brave noble men father brave noble children,' the poet Horace had written in Augustus' reign. 'In bulls and horses likewise the male's stamp shows clearly: we never find fear bred from fierceness, eagles hatching doves.'[6] In Titus' case, Vespasian's were mighty coat tails, capable of offering both flight and protection. From a distance, there are grounds for believing that the success of Titus' short rule was attributable to measured continuance of the policies of the previous reign; it could not have continued so indefinitely. The new emperor's most striking innovation was his affectation of open-handedness where Vespasian had revelled in stinginess. But all that lay in the future. In 67, for father *and* son, Judaea, not Rome, was the challenge.

Titus' role was legionary commander. He was twenty-eight years old, a veteran of military postings in Germany and Britain. He was also twice married, both widower and divorcee. He had divorced his second wife, the well-connected Marcia Furnilla, in the aftermath of the Pisonian conspiracy for motives of political expediency, Furnilla's family having forfeited Nero's favour. Shortly before, Furnilla gave birth to Titus' only child. At this stage the sources indicate no particular fondness for the child, a daughter called Julia (after 71, she was brought up not in Titus' house but in that of her married uncle Domitian). Nor, in the case of either marriage, do they reveal emotional involvement with his spouses, an oversight suggestive of unsusceptibility or, at best, self-containment. In Judaea over the course of the next three years Titus would achieve military glory and an independent profile, emerging from his father's shadow; he also won the love of an ambitious, attentive mistress eleven years his senior. In his own lifetime he earned plaudits for the former, while the latter, thanks to the mistress in question, gave rise to deep mistrust. History has preferred to reverse that order. The desecration of Judaism's inner sanctum remains an angry blot. Meanwhile in theatres and opera houses around the world Titus still lays claim to immortality. His heroism, Suetonius insisted, consists of an act of renunciation made unwillingly to a yet more unwilling lover. As Racine has it, 'Oh Rome!… Wretched me! Must I be emperor and love?'[7]

In truth, when it came, it was (or should have been) Vespasian's victory. Vespasian, we know, was the commander of 50,000 troops in Judaea, he the military mastermind, experienced, accomplished. But Vespasian had embarked on a bigger campaign. With his father poised to become Rome's new ruler, a promotion Tacitus claims as Titus' in inspiration,[8] Titus was left to finish the job of conquest, annexing for himself spoils and renown. In August 69, Mucianus set off for Rome at the head of pro-Flavian troops. He had thrown in his lot with Vespasian, erstwhile jealousy forgotten, the hard knot of his resentment softened, as we have seen, by Titus' charm and the younger man's good looks. His purpose was the overthrow of Vitellius. At the same time, Vespasian and Titus journeyed to Alexandria. If necessary, Vespasian meant to seize control of Egypt's grain shipments, his means of starving Vitellian Italy into submission.[9] Titus continued on to Palestine. There, aided at Vespasian's direction by the Jewish former procurator of Judaea, Tiberius Julius Alexander, a man of proven military ability, he embarked on the siege of the fortified city of Jerusalem.

It was 10 August 70 when a Roman soldier hurled the flaming torch which destroyed the Temple and facilitated the theft of its treasures. According to Jewish historian Josephus, Titus' apologist, that over-zealous soldier acted in direct contravention of his master's wishes.[10] The later classical account of Sulpicius Severus, perhaps inspired by passages of Tacitus' *Histories* which have since been lost, argues the flip side of the coin.[11] If the truth is unreclaimable, the sources appear to voice no regret on Titus' part – unless the origin of that single stab of conscience, which Suetonius records on his deathbed, was his sanction of the defilement of the Holy of Holies and, later the same day, sacrifices to Roman standards made in the temple precincts, a double heresy of blood and flame. The evidence of the Arch of Titus, albeit a commission instigated by Domitian after Titus' death, is discouraging. In 70, the temple burned. Its precincts glistened with the blood of the faithful. The Table of the Shewbread and all its golden furniture, dragged into the daylight, were dispatched to Rome. Jerusalem, besieged through a long period of attrition, struggled no more. Its defences had been breached for the last time and the temple would never be rebuilt.

In October and November, at Caesarea Maritima and Berytus respectively, Titus celebrated the birthdays of his brother and his father. On both occasions, Josephus unflinchingly records, the celebrations included the slaughter of several thousand Jewish prisoners, 'who perished in combats with wild beasts or in fighting each another or by being burnt alive'.[12] To modern ears, these sound unedifying spectacles: Roman opinion baulked only at the modesty of the death toll. Impresario-like, in ashes and gore Titus shared his glory with Vespasian and Domitian. It was Flavian *égoïsme à trois*, a pact sealed in the public suffering of the vanquished – oblations made to the family's household gods writ large. Vespasian surely approved the policy. Josephus notwithstanding, the manner of Titus' birthday tributes suggests a singular lack of remorse. It is what we should expect from a conquering hero.

The following year Titus shared with Vespasian the grandest triumph in Rome's history. Tableaux charting four years of conflict wound their way through the capital, followed by Simon ben Giora, architect of the revolt, dragged by a halter, humbled and scourged.[13] For all its vaunting symbolism, this vainglorious street parade was insufficient to settle the Judaean account (closure would only be achieved once another kinsman, Flavius Silva, stormed Masada in 73, forcing the mass suicide of the last rebel group). Foremost for Titus among the campaign's loose ends in 71 was the Jewish queen who had sided with Rome against her co-religionists. Her name was Berenice.

A statue in Athens describes Julia Berenice as a 'great' queen.[14] Surviving sources make it clear that her name was coupled with many less flattering adjectives besides. She was rich, foreign, Jewish, powerful, libidinous... and female – impossible not to fall victim to the long arm of Augustan propaganda. Berenice became Titus' Cleopatra. In his treatment of his Eastern queen, the second of the Flavians would prove himself a greater and a lesser man than Mark Antony. As with his winning demeanour as *princeps*, and like his earlier jettisoning of Marcia Furnilla, the instinct for political survival sidelined more complex truths; Titus escaped with his life and Rome's throne. Or perhaps Suetonius was mistaken and, when the time came, renunciation was easy, appetites slaked, all passion spent.

A great-granddaughter of Herod the Great, Berenice had been married three times when, in 66, the high-handedness and brutality of procurator Gessus Florius provoked the First Jewish Revolt in Judaea and a large-scale Roman military presence under Vespasian's command. Her spouses included a connection of Titus' associate Tiberius Julius Alexander, chosen on account of his wealth, and her uncle, another Herod, whom Claudius had created king of Chalcis; but the longest relationship in her life was with her brother, Agrippa II, one of several client kings educated at the imperial court in Rome. According to Josephus, whose enmity towards Berenice still taints her posterity, her final marriage – to King Polemo of Cilicia (a match she both made and unmade herself) – arose from her desire to curtail rumours of an incestuous relationship between the royal siblings. If this were the case, Josephus made sure that Berenice failed. The 'inappropriate sexual desire' he cited as her grounds for divorcing Polemo, who had converted to Judaism at her request, was for Agrippa. It was not, of course, the whole story. The sources omit mention of the first meeting of Titus and Berenice, which probably took place in Ptolemais or, with greater ceremony, at Agrippa's splendid palace at his administrative capital of Caesarea Philippi:[15] all agree on its long-term success. The relationship of the Roman quaestorian legionary legate and the Jewish princess branded by history a siren would survive for more than a decade, despite lengthy separations and at least one preliminary breaking-off. Thanks to a rich literary tradition – inspired by a single line in Suetonius' account – it has endured two millennia.

Titus' own feelings, however, are frequently unclear, attested only in Tacitean insinuation.[16] His sexual tastes, like those of many of his contemporaries, ranged widely. He had a weakness for dancing boys and male prostitutes and shared his contemporaries' bath-house fascination with eunuchs. These were the associates – source of his reputation for lewdness – whom he forswore on his accession to the purple. As love objects go, Berenice was more highly charged than any shimmying catamite and shared their fate, discarded in order to silence those who quibbled and carped. For she, Cleopatra in miniature, more than any teenage cock-tease inspired fear and loathing in Roman minds, damned in equal measure by her religion and her sexual independence. Loving Berenice would become for Titus a matter of high politics. When crunch-time came, he preferred duty... or the dictates of *romanitas*... or fidelity to Vespasian's model of an imperial court free from petticoats government... or perhaps simply self-interest.

―――

The triumph of Jerusalem, celebrated within days of Titus' arrival in Rome in 71, served useful purposes for Titus and Vespasian. It quashed reports of a rift between father and son. It invested the fledgling regime with military élan and, in doing so, something of that prestige which the equestrian Flavii lacked. It underlined the imperial nature of Flavian rule, since under the Julio-Claudians triumphs had become the exclusive prerogative of the imperial family. It exploited visual symbolism to assert from the outset Vespasian's dynastic intent and his choice of Titus as successor.[17]

Vespasian and Titus wore identical clothes, each dressed as the god Jupiter; they offered identical prayers and sacrifices. Quadriga-drawn, they appeared before the people of Rome as *princeps* and helpmeet.[18] Thereafter, Suetonius claims, Titus abandoned any personal agenda, partner in government to his sexagenarian father. As we have seen, the two men shared the consulship in 70, 72, 74, 75, 76, 77 and 79. In tandem with Vespasian, Titus exercised tribunician power and that of the censorship; father and son shared priesthoods. Coins minted in 71 acclaimed Titus as DESIGNATUS IMPERATOR, *princeps*-elect.[19] It did not amount to becoming Vespasian's equal, but it laid down a strategy for the future. In Josephus' account, Romans flocked to support the self-aggrandizing aspirations of this family of equestrian provincials who had succeeded where Galba, Otho and Vitellius had failed: they prayed 'that Vespasian, his sons and all their posterity might continue in the Roman government for a very long time'. Vespasian's dream was of a stable and secure Rome. But it was not compounded of altruism alone. It was also a vision of enduring power for his own line. The family from nowhere had taken a one-way ticket and Titus was his father's nominated heir. Business-like, Suetonius tells us, Titus took upon himself 'the discharge of almost all duties': he 'personally dictated letters and wrote edicts in his father's name, and even read his speeches in the senate in lieu of a quaestor',[20] experience which doubtless contributed to his ability as emperor to compete with his secretaries in the matter of shorthand dictation.

More surprising is that the beneficiary of Vespasian's dynastic imperative took no steps himself to assure through remarriage the succession which, throughout his decade-long principate, was among his father's principal concerns.

———◦◦◦———

Instead, Titus led what on the surface appears a double life: by day a diligent bureaucrat vigilant in the maintenance of Vespasian's security and wellbeing, after nightfall a hardened carouser, lover of a foreign queen, anathema to Rome. Since neither drunkenness nor wantonness impacted on his conduct of public duties, the distinction is misleading – unless we agree that a faculty for compartmentalization is a signifier of emotional detachment, perhaps an approach to cruelty. Titus' prominence under Vespasian, nurtured by the latter in coin inscriptions and the language of Roman pageantry, inspired, we are told, overwhelmingly negative responses among his contemporaries. Only an apparent change of character, coinciding with his father's death, finally brought about recognition of his fulfilment of his official role. Vespasian had sought to banish the spectre of the Julio-Claudians, in particular that aspect of their insistence on the principate as a family affair which had resulted under Augustus' heirs in the politicization of imperial private life. Time would prove that the inheritance was unshirkable. Can it be construed as a challenge to the rowdy, roistering Titus of the seventies? Emperor-in-waiting, he scarcely seems to have cared.

———◦◦◦———

As it happened, Titus' assessment of the leeway available to him was correct. History showed that revolution in Rome was a rarefied business, confined to the city's political classes: his behaviour was his own affair so long as it failed to incite conspiracies. His accession to the throne in June 79 passed unopposed. Little matter that his cruelty, catamites and, it was rumoured, corruption in accepting bribes for court sentences – all, as we have seen, standard behaviour under the principate – poisoned his reputation. Tiberius was proof that ill repute alone did not topple thrones, while even the 'good' Vespasian had taken a cut of the fees extorted by his mistress Caenis for expediting imperial decision-making. The support of the Praetorian Guards, known to be crucial, had been guaranteed since 71 when Titus was appointed Praetorian prefect. This was the first time this important post had been filled by so close a relative of the emperor's: in addition to giving Titus responsibility for his father's security, it also placed him at the head of the largest military force in Italy.[21] Titus' assiduity in exploiting his position to eliminate dissent, though flattering to the Guard itself and within the letter (if not the spirit) of the Guard's purpose, offended strict legalities and suggested a nature inclined to tyranny. Winning hearts and minds does not appear to have recommended itself as an aim. Mucianus had reduced the numbers of Guards from Vitellius' swollen tally. Into Rome's public gathering places, so the story goes, Titus sent the remnants of this virtual private police force. At his instruction, they denounced suspected conspirators. Those who were named as often died. In Suetonius' reckoning, it was a provision for Titus' own future safety; in the short term, it added further dark coruscations to his notoriety. His murder of the ex-consul Aulus Caecina Alienus, a noted opportunist whose turncoat support had nevertheless contributed to Vespasian's successful bid for power in 69, shocked even unsentimental Romans: Caecina was stabbed as he left Titus' dinner-party on the eve of delivering a harangue to the troops. That would-be conspiracy, in the dog days of Vespasian's reign, was probably genuine. Caecina's track record of oscillating loyalties offers limited scope for exculpation. As a response to a perceived threat, Titus' behaviour was ruthless and ruthlessly successful. Caecina's revolt died with him.

———◦◦◦◦———

Revolution when it came was not the work of disaffected senators but of Titus himself. It did not emerge, like Jerusalem's surrender, in conflagration. There was no conspiracy, no exchange of contumely in the senate house, no convulsions in Rome's smooth running. Rather, with the power and the glory his, the emperor Titus, Rome's eleventh *princeps* and the first non-Julio-Claudian to succeed through the hereditary principle,[22] embraced benignity. In the ancient sources it appears a change quite as significant as any plotted by Caecina or his ilk; it may just as easily have been a case of smoke and mirrors, another instance of pragmatism. As one of the shortest reigning of the twelve Caesars, his principate beset by unprecedented natural disasters, Titus had few opportunities to review or discard his father's interpretation of imperial government: his task was repeatedly immediate, its concerns those which in succeeding millennia would be associated with the concept of 'welfare monarchy'. Embracing paternalism, he maintained Vespasian's golden mean. His reaction to large-scale setbacks was effective, considered, balanced: legacy perhaps of that early exposure to fate's unpredictability which had robbed him, for example, of Britannicus' friendship. If vigorous appetites had enlivened his youth, duty would characterize his reign, an unremarkable day-by-day diligence which he was nevertheless at pains to make public. Tacitus responds with understatement: Titus 'practised more self-restraint in his own than in his father's reign'.[23] That self-restraint exchanged love of pleasure for a 'father'-like love for each and every one of Rome's children. So startling a metamorphosis glossed autocracy with benignity.

There were inevitably exceptions to his kindliness. Among them were informers, whom Titus renounced as a group, subjecting them to public punishment before selling them as slaves; and Berenice.

Berenice had not remained in Agrippa's palace at Caesarea Philippi. In 75 she is recorded as resident in Rome, her brother with her, the forty-seven-year-old matron married to Titus in all but name. Such, at any rate, was evidently Berenice's own interpretation. It was an arrangement strikingly suggestive of that earlier Tiber-side residency of Cleopatra in her role as Caesar's mistress and co-parent. In time, unlike Cleopatra, Berenice would be rewarded with neither golden statues in the temple nor the forced sacrifice of her life and her kingdom. Presumably on account of her age, she does not appear to have borne Titus any children to inspire Roman apprehension: her very presence in Rome was enough. In Cassius Dio's account, philosophers spoke out publicly against the couple;[24] at least one paid for his protest with his life. But one Cynic silenced was not enough to win for Berenice a ring and a crown. She, too, paid the price of their denunciation, banished by her lover. Like Caesar's Egyptian queen, in loving Rome she surrendered happiness and pride.

Berenice, however, returned to Rome. Her reappearance followed close on the heels of Vespasian's death. Was she propelled across slow expanses of the ancient world by that image of herself as Titus' wife? If so, she was to be disappointed. No warm welcome awaited her in Rome's hills. It is that disappointment, product of a love sufficient to allow hope to triumph over reason, experience and even certainty, which underscores her tragedy.

As for Titus, the only surviving record of his feelings on Berenice's final departure in 79 is Suetonius' assessment of mutual regret. This is the evidence we must balance against an overhasty assumption that, like his divorce from Marcia Furnilla and his overthrow of those former sex objects, the dancing boys, whose public performances he never again allowed himself to witness, Titus permitted his feelings to be directed by expediency and opportunism. Suetonius' Titus is the most sincere of all imperial holders of the office of *pontifex maximus*, determined that the high-priesthood act as guarantee of his pure intentions. On Vespasian's death, did the instinct for power overmaster earthier appetites? Or did Titus sacrifice Berenice in Rome's favour with a heavy heart? Driven by duty, determination or indifference, in the two years, two months and twenty days that remained to him, Titus kept faith with that apparent spirit of self-denial which, the tragedians would have us believe, shaped his treatment of his Eastern queen. That he confined lustful impulses thereafter to cuckolding his brother Domitian remains unsubstantiated rumour and is possibly an instance of confused chronology. Perhaps, as Alma-Tadema's painting *The Triumph of Titus* (1885) suggests, the period of Titus' ascendancy in Domitia Longina's heart was of earlier duration. In Alma-Tadema's composition, a dewy-eyed Domitia, her fingers lightly touching those of her husband Domitian, gazes longingly over her shoulder at the covetous, decidedly venal, bearded figure of Titus.

It was late August, early in the afternoon, two months and a day after Titus' accession, when shadows closed in on the Bay of Naples. A cloud hovered above the sun-drenched seaside playground. Spreading sideways like spilt molasses, shaped like a pine tree in the eyewitness account of the younger Pliny, and distinctive in the furious depth of its colouring, it was remarkable for its sheer size: 'It rose to a great height on a sort of trunk and then split off into branches.'[25] It portended not rain but showers of pumice. So extensive was the fall of volcanic rock that, within less than twenty-four hours, the town of Pompeii lay buried three metres deep.[26] Thousands fled but many remained, sheltering from the falling rock, awaiting respite. It was not to be. The following day, to the accompaniment of apocalyptic pyrotechnics, a series of hot-ash avalanches completed Pompeii's internment. Scarlet, black and molten-gold burned the sky. Fire and cloud hugged the earth. In Cassius Dio's account, the darkness was akin to an eclipse.[27] Those who had remained died of asphyxiation. The same fatal cascades, accompanied by surges of hot gas and travelling at irresistible speed, also buried nearby Herculaneum, site of Agrippina the Elder's house arrest by Sejanus, and Oplontis, where Nero's Poppaea had kept a villa.

Quiet since Nero's reign, Vesuvius had at last erupted in spectacular fashion. Among casualties was Pliny the Elder, whom Titus' father had been accustomed to summon for advice so early in the morning that it was not yet light. The death toll surprised even the Romans. Contrary to custom, neither Pompeii nor Herculaneum was ever reoccupied. Ashen, dark and silent, they subsided into centuries of petty looting. Today Pompeii survives as a tourist destination, titivating backpackers with its insights into the scatological nature of Roman graffiti and the discomforts of the town's brothels.

The eruption of Vesuvius provided Titus with the moment when, in words and deeds, he made good that transformation in his character which Suetonius dates to his accession. His response was swift. After visiting the region, he appointed two ex-consuls to supervise a restoration programme.[28] He allocated to the rescue efforts the estates of those killed in the disaster who had died without heirs, property which under Roman law accrued to the treasury.[29] Edicts made public his anxieties as well as his efforts.

Although he could not have known it, Titus had created a template for action on which he would soon be called to draw again. It was a matter of months before fire, then plague, devastated Rome. The fire destroyed buildings across the Campus Martius, flames consuming the temples of Serapis, Isis, Neptune and Jupiter Capitolinus along with the Baths of Agrippa, the Pantheon and the Portico of Augustus' sister Octavia. Unusually, Suetonius resists characterizing this concatenation of catastrophes as portentous. Titus' own opinion clearly differed. 'I am ruined,' he allegedly claimed, before invoking assistance both human and divine and tasking himself with discovery of the perfect sacrifice to propitiate an angry firmament. He contributed to the city's slush fund decorations removed from his own palace – withholding, we must assume, that treasured golden statue of Britannicus which had surely guided him thus far. It was the latest instance of that trope of the simple-living emperor which Augustus had cultivated so painstakingly and which, more recently, had inspired Galba to ignore the delivery of palace furniture Nymphidius had dispatched from Rome to Narbo Martius, and Vespasian to spend most of his time in the Gardens of Sallust.

As with his 'donation' of Pompeian revenues, it was generosity
of a qualified variety: it demanded little of Titus beyond
inspiration and virtually nothing of the imperial treasury. As a
public-relations exercise, it earned the emperor hefty dividends.
Among them is Suetonius' celebration of his 'surpassing'
father's love for his people. With hindsight, we see that the
benefits Titus garnered from his response to the natural
disasters of his principate serve to underline the ambiguity of
another Suetonian assessment: that it was art and good fortune
as much as his nature which enabled him to win universal love
and become 'the delight and darling of the human race'

After tragedy, a party. Vespasian's laggardly deification was
probably formalized early in 80. At the same time, the four-
storey amphitheatre of marble and limestone, subsequently
known as the Colosseum, which Vespasian had begun as a
riposte to the grandeur of Nero's palace-building, was hastily
completed. Close by, also on the site of Nero's Golden House,
new baths were constructed with equal speed. In the baths, Titus
demonstrated condescension by mingling freely with Rome's
commons. In the Colosseum, he paraded his much-vaunted
generosity in an opening ceremony which lasted a hundred days.
He himself appeared in procession behind an equestrian statue
of Britannicus. It was the final symbolic gesture in the Flavian
rebuttal of Nero, linking Titus and Vespasian to Claudius and
denying Rome's intervening misfortunes by elision: Nero's hated
Golden House supplied location and building materials. On this
occasion there was no jibbing at undue moderation as there
had been at the birthday celebrations offered to Vespasian and
Domitian in the aftermath of victory over the Jews: 5,000 wild

beasts were slaughtered in a single day. Succeeding weeks saw
contests between elephants and even cranes and the dispatch
of a further 4,000 animals, some of them tame, killed by men
and women alike. Carpaphorus the hunter slew twenty bulls,
a bear and a lion. Their blood mingled with that of gladiators
and prisoners – including one Laureolus, who was crucified,
then exposed to an enraged Caledonian bear – in a baptism of
astonishing brutality.[30] Remarkable even to contemporaries as
a set piece of Roman crowd-pleasing, it inspired Martial's first
book of poems, *On Spectacles*, and the poet's assertion that all
the wonders of the ancient world would pale before Caesar's
amphitheatre. At Titus' request, the Colosseum was flooded and
a sea battle re-enacted between Corcyreans and Corinthians.
The floodwaters washed away the offal and ordure of earlier
carnage.

For Titus, it was a last hurrah. The conclusion of this
extravagant butchery was a bungled sacrifice on a day that
combined sunshine and thunder. We are reminded in the
first instance of Gaius and that bloody flamingo. Both factors
inspired unhappy presentiments in the emperor's breast. He
left the Colosseum in a state of deep depression after breaking
down in view of the crowds, 'performed no further deed of
importance', according to Cassius Dio,[31] and within months,
aged forty-one, was dead.

Jews attributed Titus' untimely demise to a mosquito.
Burrowing its way into the emperor's head, it grew to the size
of a pigeon and tormented him with seven years of unbearable
headaches which eventually overcame him.[32] Those of longer
memory, mindful of the Julio-Claudian record, blamed his
brother and successor Domitian, whom Suetonius accuses of
ceaseless plotting. The historian does not stoop to evidence.
Plutarch's explanation is more likely to have found favour with

Titus, uniting as it does father and son. He records the diagnosis of Titus' attendants: that it was the excessive coldness of the waters at Aquae Cutiliae, so harmful to Vespasian, which also dispatched his elder son. Certainly Titus' death in the Sabine country of his ancestors, as last vestiges of summer gave way to autumn, occurred in the same house, perhaps even the same room, in which Vespasian had died. Certain, too, that it was Domitian who benefited.

Titus met death protesting. He was unready, unwilling, unable to muster that flippancy which had served his father to the end. A single, unspecified fault, we know, robbed his final hours of equanimity. If his thoughts turned to Berenice, he concealed them from the ears of history. Ditto his only child Julia, celebrated on the coinage of his all-too-short reign. He referred neither to Domitian, his heir, nor to his failure to provide Rome with an alternative *princeps*, a serious fault in the eyes of history given what lay ahead. It was a modest, unpretentious end, in a simple rural homestead in the hilly vastnesses outside Rome, almost, we might assume, a piece of propagandist Flavian stage-management, reiterating the dumb show of family humility – this unpatrician, unhistrionic dynasty. In its very simplicity lies its pathos, grounds for an approach to martyrdom: the loving public servant cut off in his prime. Death came as a surprise, giving the lie to the old enemies' tradition of seven years of headaches.

Perhaps, too, it was an ungenerous passing for an emperor who had promised that no petitioner should leave his company bereft of hope. For Titus – former waywardness stifled by imperial laurels – uniquely among the first twelve Caesars had repented of a day on which he failed to confer a single favour. Unlike that of Otho, his death was no more honourable than his short reign.

DOMITIAN

(AD 51–96)

'But the third'?

Unlike Vespasian and Titus, Domitian mishandled posterity. This 'object of terror and hatred to all' – Juvenal's 'bald-headed Nero'[1] – shared with Nero Rome's ultimate posthumous ignominy: *damnatio memoriae*, the erasure of his memory. (Only underground was his name left intact, borne by the water and sewerage pipes laid during his reign, a legacy without dignity or distinction.) But despite the broken statues, the inscriptions smashed, scratched or recarved, the last Flavian was neither eradicated nor forgotten. He had built on too grand a scale. His costly, city-wide programme of construction and restoration encompassed the sacred and the profane: at least ten temples, an artificial lake for recreating naval battles, a new palace close to the Circus Maximus, a stadium whose outline survives in the Piazza Navona. Both his physical bequest to Rome and those scars he inflicted on members of the senatorial class, Rome's writers of history, ran too deep: incontinent enmity prevented the latter from consigning him to obscurity. Thanks to their animosity (which was at no point senate-wide), hostile sources occlude any balanced reading of Domitian's life. Beneath the cant an imprint of his actions survives like *pentimenti* in a painting, his designs half-lost beneath a later gloss. For this emperor who famously legislated against the planting of vines in order to increase the Empire's grain yield, the slate is not clean.

'More like Nero or Caligula or Tiberius than his father or brother... he provoked such universal detestation that he effaced the remembrance of his father's and his brother's merits,' sneered the resolutely inimical Eutropius.[2] An overstatement undoubtedly, but the Domitian of the sources, blackened by the personal and political allegiances of early chroniclers, is a man of aphotic reputation, menacing and murky. Alone he sits in palace rooms, lost in silence, catching flies and stabbing them with a keenly sharpened stylus; alone he walks in out-of-the-way places, doing nothing, seeing no one; alone he consumes immoderate lunches which make his belly heave and restrict him to a single apple at the evening banquet; alone, we assume, he broods and he plots and he plans. He likes no one, bar a clutch of unnamed women; he craves flattery but abhors the flatterer, averse to sycophancy and plain speaking alike. In the interests of the story it has to be. Given the ancients' love of pungent contrast, the shimmering goodness of the deified Titus presupposes the opposite in his successor. Willingly, it appears, Domitian embraced the expectations of the dark side.

Suetonius once planned more than twelve lives, to bring his account up to date. Like Claudius meditating a written history of the civil war during Augustus' lifetime, the imperial secretary was dissuaded from so hazardous an undertaking. Whatever the author's first intentions, Domitian makes a fitting finale to this rakes' progress. Underlying his downfall are tendencies which dogged the early principate. Absolutism, philhellenism and flirtation with divinity disturbed, and in some cases destroyed, the reigns of several of his predecessors: Domitian was nothing daunted. In themselves these troublesome aspirations evidenced unresolved tensions in this new chapter in the life of Rome. Each shaped and challenged evolving ideas of Romanness and inspired an ongoing reassessment of the significance and implications of the fall of the Republic (and in particular the curtailment of senatorial influence). Each constituted a powerful affront to the Republican mindset. In the case of Gaius, a toxic combination of all three – which that unsystematic, unhinged twenty-something did nothing to conceal – culminated in personal tragedy and the system's discredit. In Suetonius' hands, faced by the admonishments of history, Domitian is implacable. Indeed, 'he never took any pains to become acquainted with history'. In the holder of an office which throughout our story remains deeply contentious, such a stance – derived from resistance? incuriosity? arrogance? – is both baffling and culpable. For Rome, as Augustus and Vespasian had understood, was a city in thrall to visions of its past. In time, unable to reconcile past and present, Domitian shared Gaius' fate. Disillusioned Praetorians again shaped the conspiracy.

Where bad government is the taunt, there must be sexual transgression. For good measure, greed too: a panoply of unconstrained appetites. We have seen the pattern before, with Tiberius, Gaius and Nero. Domitian is no exception. Suetonius condemns him as rapacious in the extreme and 'excessively lustful', revelling in fornication – or 'bed wrestling', as the emperor himself described it; in a distant echo of Tiberius, he also enjoyed swimming with prostitutes. Compared with the affronts of his libidinous predecessors, Domitian's mostly loveless carnality appears moderate; like the milk-and-water sex lives of the older Augustus and Vespasian, it did not distract him from the business of state. For much of his life he was good-looking, too: tall, large-eyed, unassuming in his expression, quick to blush. The path of a handsome man close to the centre of power will always be strewn with temptation: his preference was for other men's wives. Previously, probably in the meagre years flanking Vespasian's departure for Africa, Domitian had offered himself to a senator called Claudius Pollio and allowed himself to be debauched by the future emperor Nerva, more than twenty years his senior.* As an adult his homosexuality seems to have confined itself to a taste for eunuchs – Dio names one Earinus – evidently a Flavian predilection: Titus enjoyed a similar frisson. More startling – and in its particularity perhaps closer to the truth – is the assertion that Domitian depilated his mistresses by hand.

He also kept faith with that persistent accusation levelled against 'bad' emperors, namely incest. The Flavii, as we have seen, enjoyed a strong family focus and corporate egotism. In the interests of genetic exclusivity and dynastic vigour, Titus urged Domitian to marry his daughter Julia. Although Domitian demurred, some time after his marriage to Domitia Longina in 71, he took Julia, then aged no more than six, into his house to live with them.

The relationship of uncle and niece altered in the aftermath of the former's divorce in 83. Perhaps initially Julia did no more than act as hostess and chatelaine for her wifeless uncle, constrained, as her portrait corpus would suggest, by that towering erection of unnaturally crisp curls whose improbable arrangement surely consumed much of her day. Soon, Dio records, gossip described them living 'as husband and wife, making little effort at concealment'.[3] They were not married,

---

* Pollio's thanks for these youthful embraces was to preserve a letter of assignation written by Domitian and afterwards to display it to prurient gazes; Nerva pursued a dignified course of silence.

however, and never would be. Instead, prompted either by widespread popular feeling in Domitia's favour or because, as Suetonius offers, he was unable to bear their separation, a grim-faced Domitian reconciled himself to the reckless ex-wife who had cuckolded him with a well-known pantomime actor called Paris. (Fearsome in his anger and black-and-white in his outlook, Domitian had killed Paris in the street, so he may have felt that the problem had been adequately dealt with. Afterwards, for good measure, he also killed an adolescent pupil of the actor, who resembled him in appearance and ability. His intention had been to kill Domitia herself. Later, Domitia's first husband, Aelius Lamia, would also die, killed for a joke at the emperor's expense. The final death in this knockabout black comedy was that of Helvidius Priscus the Younger who, quite understandably, felt moved to satirize Domitian's divorce as popular entertainment, a farce of 'Paris' and 'Oenone'.) If he expected continence from Domitia, Domitian had no intention of practising the same himself and continued his relationship with Julia. When Julia fell pregnant, Domitian insisted that she abort the baby. She too duly died. As with her father and grandfather, Domitian decided on deification: coins celebrated her ascent to heaven riding on a peacock.[4]*

Bum-boy, fornicator, eunuch-fancier and niece-lover: Domitian's 'sins' scarcely distinguished him from many of his contemporaries. That he attained the principate, however, exposed these foibles in a larger arena. Like Augustus before

---

* Last laugh in the saga of Domitian's marital discord probably went to Domitia, who survived her husband by three decades. Her revenge – possibly no more than a suggestion and appropriately served cold – waited thirteen years until she joined the conspirators in her husband's overthrow.

him, Domitian spearheaded a programme of moral legislation aimed at curbing the worst laxities of Roman sexual mores: also like Augustus, he made no efforts to toe the line himself. In Dio's account, adultery and hypocrisy combine. Among the socially prominent women who fell victim to the emperor's evangelism were those whose favours he had not scrupled to enjoy himself, while, with wonderful irony, he struck off a knight from the list of jurors 'because he had taken back his wife after divorcing her and charging her with adultery'. Legislation and a taste for senatorial wives were both factors which shaped Domitian's relationship with the ruling class: at his own instigation his private life became a matter of politics which could not be discounted. Not if we are to believe the sources, in which the most pedestrian concupiscence is exploited to Domitian's detriment. In truth, the only consistent presence in the palace bedroom was a statue of the goddess Minerva, traditionally understood as ever virgin. The emperor's devotion to this Greek-inspired goddess of poetry, wisdom and magic, 'whom he worshipped with superstitious veneration', exceeded any discernible fondness on his part for ordinary mortals, male, female, castrated, depilated, family member or otherwise; exceeded too, Dio tells us, his reverence for any other god (including, presumably, the cults of his father and his brother).

What then of sibling rivalry? Invested with 'execrable' pride by Eutropius, Domitian chafed against his bronze-medal placement in the Flavian pecking order. Briefly in 69 and early 70, following Vitellius' death and awaiting the arrival of Vespasian and Titus in Rome, he played the Caesar's part. He did so with enthusiasm.

'In a single day he assigned more than twenty positions in the city and the provinces,' Suetonius relates, 'which led Vespasian to say more than once that he was surprised that he did not appoint the emperor's successor with the rest.' It may be true. First Mucianus, then Vespasian, took it upon themselves to curb the bumptious eighteen-year-old's swagger. The poet Martial asserts that their efforts were unnecessary: 'Although alone he already held the reins of Julian power, he gave them up and in a world that had been his own remained but the third – after both Vespasian and Titus.'[5] Other sources paint a different picture in which the success of the older men's restraining orders was qualified. Tacitus has Domitian secretly petitioning his kinsman Quintus Petilius Cerialis for control of the latter's troops in Lower Germany, his plan to wage war against Vespasian or exceed Titus' record.[6] The claim is certainly an exaggeration. What did emerge from the early days of Vespasian's takeover was a forcible reminder of Domitian's youth and inexperience. It was a defeat the second son accepted without grace, forced to live in his father's house, Vespasian's purpose either to assert Domitian's place in the dynastic scheme or to curb his instincts through watchfulness. For the next decade, quickened by his fleeting taste of power, resentment lent a tang to Domitian's impatience.

The roots of the problem lay in a childhood of suburban scrimping. Add to the deficit emotional deprivation: the undated death of Vespasian's wife and Domitian's mother, Flavia Domitilla, its import impossible to quantify. Also a sense of precariousness connected to Vespasian's fall from favour after Claudius' marriage to Agrippina. Titus' birthplace we know hardly constituted a silver spoon. By the time of Domitian's birth twelve years later, despite his father's successful ascent of the *cursus honorum*, the Flavian advance had yet to reap noticeable material dividends. Still on the Quirinal, in a house on unfashionable Pomegranate Street, the family vaults remained empty of silver. Suetonius denies the existence of a single piece of plate. In *The Twelve Caesars*, the dominant characteristic of Domitian's boyhood and early youth is poverty. By senatorial standards this was probably true. The historian is not belittling Vespasian, one of his chronicle's heroes. Instead, he is preparing his readers for later revelations concerning Domitian's ungovernable covetousness and his preposterously inflated self-importance.

The latter was surely an offshoot of status anxieties and accounts for Domitian's high-handedness towards his father's freedwoman mistress Caenis, whom he refused permission to kiss him. It may also have enhanced the attractions of his errant wife, Domitia Longina. Notwithstanding her marriage to the senator Aelius Lamia, Domitian pursued Domitia with ardour and determination. As in the case of Augustus and Livia, Domitia's family distinction far outstripped that of her second husband. She was a great-great-great-granddaughter of Augustus via Julia the Younger; her father's half-sister was the empress Caesonia, ill-fated fourth wife of Gaius. Her father himself was that warrior-like general, Gnaeus Domitius Corbulo, whom Nero compelled to suicide, fearful of the extent of his military eminence and the potential threat it posed.* By the end of 81, like Livia before her, Domitia found herself invested with the title 'Augusta'. She was the first imperial wife so nominated since Poppaea.

---

* In time Domitian would fall prey to similar unease. In 84 or 85, he recalled to Rome the distinguished British commander Agricola. Agricola remained loyal. The revenge of his implacable son-in-law Tacitus continues to this day.

Titus, of course, began life with no more than his younger brother, but found himself, thanks to Narcissus' partisanship towards Vespasian, at the epicentre of the Roman world. Unlike that of Domitian, his childhood playground was the Palatine, his education a courtly affair enjoyed in company with Claudius' son Britannicus. Afterwards he shared in Vespasian's return to prominence in Judaea. By contrast Domitian remained at home, motherless, fatherless, brotherless. We ought not to be surprised at his divergent concept of family unity, nor his preference for time spent in very different company at his villa in the Alban Hills, a day's journey southeast of Rome. Too often he had been excluded from Flavian inclusiveness. If accounts indicate a loner's instinct on the part of the adult Domitian, their focus may be no more than those strategies he had developed over time to endure isolation.

In the sources Domitian's jockeying for position with Titus is a feature of Vespasian's principate from the outset. It begins in the crazy days immediately following the Flavian settlement and Titus' successes in Judaea, when Domitian planned an expedition to Gaul and Germany with the sole intent, Suetonius writes, 'that he might make himself equal to his brother in power and rank'. A decade later, worn out with waiting, he abandoned the ailing Titus to die without regret. Suetonius' version suggests that the younger brother countermanded the necessary medical assistance. Cassius Dio goes a step further, relating the rumour that, in the spirit of his previous plots against Titus (unspecified), Domitian assisted the older man's death. While chances of recovery still remained, he placed his brother in a chest. He surrounded him with snow, 'pretending that the disease required, perhaps, that a chill be administered', but knowing better, of course.[7] With his brother on ice, certain now to expire, Domitian hastened to Rome, where he received titles, power and authority in the Praetorians' camp, as well as the first of twenty-two acclamations of *'imperator'*. As with the demise of each previous *princeps*, the sources decry the possibility of a natural death. Given Domitian's future behaviour, it is important that his accession bear the stamp of illegality from the start.

Self-seeking and savvy, Rome's latest emperor expedited his brother's deification and quickly commenced work on the Arch of Titus. As with Augustus' celebration of the anniversary of Actium, Domitian meant to make capital out of the Flavians' greatest military victory. Ditto the deification of his father and brother. Once he had written a poem celebrating Titus' victory in Judaea; now he built temples to the Divine Vespasian and the Flavian family, with their own cult attendants, the Flaviales. What he never intended was to rule in Titus' shadow. No memorial games commemorated Titus' birthday during the fifteen years of Domitian's principate. Perhaps it really was the case that he considered that Titus, at his own reckoning an accomplished forger, had altered Vespasian's will and denied him joint inheritance in 79. (If so, he misread Vespasian's clear signs throughout his reign that the order of succession favoured Titus in the first instance. Certainly the brothers shared the title of *princeps iuventutis*; equally certain that it was Titus who, on six occasions to Domitian's one, shared the consulship with their father.) Dio accepts no excuses. 'This same emperor,' he declaims, 'paid no heed to the praises which men bestowed upon Titus.'[8] On the contrary, for Domitian family feeling was a question of expediency uncoloured by liking. He struggled to regard Vespasian's and Titus' legacies with equanimity and 'quite outdid himself in visiting disgrace and ruin upon the friends of his father and of his brother';[9] he also killed those remaining Flavian males who might have succeeded him: Titus

Flavius Sabinus, Flavius Clemens (whose sons were named as Domitian's heirs) and Arrecinus Clemens. Eventually Domitian would pay a heavy price for this contrariness – one, like much in Suetonius' account, presaged by portents. Disgraced and childless, he brought about the end of the dynasty within the timespan foretold in that dream of a balance once granted to Vespasian.

In place of military glory, a daredevil escapade. Titus had accompanied his father to Judaea in 67; two years later it was Domitian's turn to experience human nature red in tooth and claw. In his case, the occasion was provided by the re-eruption of civil war in Rome, that bloody contest of Vitellians and Flavians which soon transformed Domitian's world. The subjection of the Jews by Vespasian and Titus followed a dogged progression: Domitian's 'glory' emerged in an anarchic free-for-all of fire and fear in which his own role was essentially passive (appropriately, given that his was a nature described as 'incapable of exertion': he would later go to war in a litter).

The events of the night in question permit varying interpretations: a 'true' account may be beyond recall. Aside from broader Flavian propaganda determined to gloss the butchery of the dynasty's seizure of power, Domitian himself afterwards appropriated the incident (and a version of his own part in it) as the basis of a narrative of personal heroism. He exploited it, like Vespasian's long and distinguished military career and Titus' conquest of Jerusalem, as grounds of proof of his own fitness to rule.

Clearly Domitian was fortunate to escape with his life. The night Vitellian troops sacked the Capitol, burning the temple to the ground, they were in no mood to behave with kindliness towards the younger son of their enemy. In Suetonius' account, Domitian is hiding in the Capitol before the Vitellians make their entry. With him is his uncle, Sabinus, reinstated as city prefect by Otho, and a number of the troops at Sabinus' disposal. Despite Vitellian advances, Domitian successfully hides all night in the house of a temple attendant close by the temple precincts. He escapes the following morning, disguised as a follower of Isis, that Egyptian cult associated with Cleopatra, which Augustus had been at such pains to curb. His destination is a house on the further side of the Tiber belonging to the mother of a schoolfriend. Tacitus also has Domitian escaping in the linen robes of a devotee of Isis (in this case improvised for him by a dexterous freedman). His destination in Tacitus' recounting is the house of one of Vespasian's clients, where he was able to hide in safety. Either way, it was a hair-raising escapade. Sabinus' grizzly end reinforced Domitian's consciousness of the miraculous nature of his escape. Captured in the burning temple, Vespasian's elder brother was taken in chains to Vitellius and decapitated. His headless body was hurled into the Tiber.

Relief inspired braggadocio. Domitian again turned to poetry, that pastime Tacitus dismisses as a deliberate feint 'to throw a veil over his character'.[10] The subject of his poem on this occasion was his own survival. He also, as we have seen, built a shrine to Jupiter Custos on the site of the temple attendant's house. Later that shrine became a fully fledged temple, at its centre a statue of himself seated in the god's lap.[11] It was a heavy-handed gesture of gratitude and self-assertion on Rome's most sacred hill. By then, Domitian had succeeded his father and brother as *princeps*. In his own words *dominus et deus* ('master and god') of the Roman world, he found it increasingly easy to align his existence with that of the firmament. This assumption of divinity may have been politically motivated. Like Gaius' posturing with wig and caduceus, it was a means of elevating his own position above that of the senate, a riposte to senatorial dismay at his lack of experience, prestige or noble birth. First seeds of this dangerous self-aggrandizement were sown on that night of Turneresque conflagration on the Capitol.

In Suetonius' *Life*, Domitian's damnation is a matter of personal choice, the reason for its particular viciousness. Unlike earlier 'bad' emperors, he possesses few of the characteristics of a victim. Inconsistent, inclined to contradictions, Gaius had been forced to vice by mental illness; Nero, by contrast, had failed to transcend ambiguous genetics. He 'degenerated from the good qualities of his ancestors... [and] reproduced the vices of each of them, as if transmitted to him by natural inheritance'. Iniquitous and inexcusable, in neither case are their failings wholly deliberate. Suetonius' Domitian claims no such exoneration. The historical record is voluble in praise of Vespasian and Titus. Suetonius takes pains to dismiss rumours that Vespasian's grandfather Titus Flavius Petro, an associate of Pompey's, turned tail at Pharsalus, or that his great-grandfather was a labour-contractor from Reate; the honesty of earlier Flavians is matter for comment. Although Domitian shared with Gaius, Claudius and Nero inheritance of the throne through family descent, his humbler background offered no default mode of perniciousness. Instead, the bloody impulse arose alongside tyranny, after Domitian had abandoned those 'strong proofs not merely of integrity but even of liberality' which the author discerned in the first years of his reign: a preference for savage self-fulfilment above service to the state. Afraid for his life once misbehaviour made him a target for assassins, Suetonius' Domitian succumbed to cruelty; his greed increased in line with his spending, confiscations from Rome's propertied classes inspired not by malice but by need. Attempting tentative neutrality, Suetonius treats Domitian with a degree of deliberate even-handedness, balancing later venalities with earlier promise. But he omits to remind us of the long duration of Domitian's reign, itself proof that this blackguard emperor's savagery cannot have been as far-reaching as we might assume – nor the man himself as 'universally odious' as Eutropius insists.[12] Dio, Pliny and Tacitus eschew equivocation. Dio's Domitian is 'not only bold and quick to anger but also treacherous and secretive', characterized by impulsiveness and craftiness.[13] It is a combination from which no good can be expected.

All the ancient authors provide instances of Domitian's treachery, the smiling face that masked a blackened heart, a delight in wrong-footing friend and foe alike, 'the preliminary declaration of clemency that... came to be [a] certain indication of a cruel death', that pretence of amity towards the person whom he wished dead above all others. Dio's portrait is a template of wickedness scarcely differentiated from the villains of pantomime and fairytale. It is the author's ultimate revenge: to rob his subject even of individualism.

With hindsight we see that Domitian did not choose villainy unprovoked. The senate too made choices. In greeting Domitian's accession with renewed nostalgia for the vanished Republic none had experienced, a vocal minority of its members – their motivation self-interest as often as disinterest – opposed a system of which Domitian was the embodiment but not the architect. Insecure and lacking the easy bonhomie of his father and brother, a truculent emperor responded on the back foot with mulish self-assertion. Was he mindful of the deaths of Nero, Galba, Otho and Vitellius? If so, he understood the perils and precariousness of the purple. Increasingly he forswore futile attempts to win patrician favour. Perhaps his mind had been made up long ago, observing Vespasian's and Titus' careful handling of that critical and envious body of men; or informed by his reading of the memoirs of Tiberius, ominously his only literary diversion. From the moment of his accession, Domitian placed his trust in the army. He raised their pay for the first time since Augustus, a significant strain on an imperial purse soon to be depleted by the demands of an extensive building programme. In the main, the troops responded to Domitian's attentiveness with loyalty (the behaviour of legions in Upper Germany during Saturninus' revolt of 89 came as a jolt). Still, in the long term it was not enough. Domitian was murdered in Rome, out of sight of the legions he had cultivated. The hand that dealt the blow belonged to a freedman – a conspiracy with the appearance of a palace coup. Members of the Praetorian Guard and senators too were prepared for the events of that September morning. Distant legions, admiring the Flavian *gens* and indebted to Domitian, were too far away, too late.

When it came, Domitian's death was expected. The emperor himself, still just forty-five, was alert to it, attentive to the instinct for survival, only put off his guard by a slave who lied to him about the time of day and led him into the arms of his assassin. All had been foretold by Ascletarion, an astrologer with a track record for accuracy. It was a quick, agonizing struggle – again an intimate-turned-avenger; an orgy of stabbing including, as always, blows to the emperor's groin; panic and confusion within palace precincts; burial of the mangled remains by a superannuated nursemaid, Phyllis in this instance, the last who loved. Afterwards the senate greeted the news with euphoria, 'assailing the dead emperor with the most insulting and stinging kind of outcries', according to Suetonius. Reprieve unleashed volubility of a sort that only hours previously would have been treasonable. The vote of *damnatio memoriae* passed swiftly; the gleeful task of destroying Domitian's images began at once. 'It was a delight to smash those arrogant faces to pieces in the dust,' wrote Pliny the Younger, quaestor and praetor under Domitian, 'to threaten them with the sword, and savagely attack them with axes, as if blood and pain would follow every single blow.'[14] The elation of aggrieved senators was not shared by Rome's legions, which, with equal alacrity, called for the emperor's deification. Nor did the people respond with revelry; Suetonius indicates indifference. The senate's wishes prevailed. Domitian's reign had unnerved and frightened them too thoroughly to forswear vengeance. Once, in dealing with magistrates, the emperor had quoted from the *Iliad*: 'I dislike a number of rulers.' It was not idle posturing. Few would-be rulers survived. Too many senators had died.

Domitian's policy of overt disdain was at odds with that of Vespasian or Titus. It differed too from that of the majority of his predecessors. Pragmatic or guileful, they had recognized that the smooth running of the principate demanded a degree of hoodwinking. Possibly no one believed in the Augustan diarchy, that fiction of the founder which contextualized the *princeps* within an enduring Republican power structure. But the effort of lip-service on the part of the current incumbent flattered and reassured a senate house greedy for lost privileges. Like Gaius before him, Domitian discarded deceits he deplored. It was an approach revealed fitfully over time.

To start, affability and generosity. A considered liberality – as we know, the Flavian way. Integrity. Concern for the institutions of state and the welfare of the people, essential components of paternalism. 'He constantly gave grand and costly entertainments,' Suetonius writes, extravaganzas which filled to capacity the still-new Colosseum. The very building proclaimed his fitness to rule, this monument to Flavian populism and fatherly love. An emperor of bread and circuses, Domitian instituted a five-yearly festival of music, equestrianism and gymnastics and, following in the footsteps of Augustus and Claudius, celebrated spectacular Secular Games in which spectators were treated to a hundred races a day. On three occasions he gave the people donations of 300 sesterces each, as well as lavish civic banquets which replaced the earlier grain dole. 'All this naturally gave pleasure to the populace,' Dio comments. Swiftly he twists the blade:

> But it was a cause of ruin to the powerful. For as he had no funds from which to make his expenditures, he murdered many men, arraigning some of them before the senate, but bringing charges against others when they were not even present in Rome. He even went so far as to put some out of the way treacherously by means of drugs secretly administered.[15]

We have learned to treat with caution these charges of 'secret' poisoning. In the sources, there is always a shadow across the face of the sun. It is doubtful whether the people suspected the source of their entertainments; uncertain, too, when Domitian first looked to senatorial appropriations to fund his bounty.

He restored Rome's libraries destroyed by fire in 80, commissioning from the scribes at Alexandria replacements for burned books. Earnestly, with every appearance of conscientiousness and scruple, he applied himself to the *princeps'* judicial functions, targeting deceit and corruption where he found it. He took measures against Rome's underground satirists and parodists. He was vigilant in gathering taxes, notably the *fiscus Judaicus* payable by Jews, immensely valuable as a source of revenue; and conservative in his religious policy, demanding stringent punishments for Vestal Virgins who broke their vows. Dio notwithstanding, his later qualities of cruelty and avarice are not to the fore. He went so far as to overrule wills in the emperor's favour in instances where the inheritance rightly belonged to a child of the testator, and cancelled debt proceedings of long duration. So extreme was Domitian's youthful aversion to bloodshed in 69 that we read of him contemplating outlawing bulls' sacrifice. Blood and thunder were not uppermost in his thoughts in 81. Instead, he offered to Rome and her people a roundelay of civic-mindedness unglimpsed since Augustus. Suetonius enumerates his benefactions unhurriedly: we know already that it is too good to last.

If only the senate could have met him halfway. Suspecting his motives, senators reportedly belittled the achievements of his military sorties. Is this revisionism on the part of the ancient authors? Perhaps. Perhaps those nearest to him, known to Domitian and he to them since 69, greeted his reign with an accurate assessment of his true nature.

He campaigned in the first place on the German frontier, focus of military attention throughout the Flavian period. Undoubtedly he was overhasty in claiming victory. There are grounds for our sympathy. By 83 Domitian had waited so long.

Vespasian had routinely denied him opportunities to prove himself militarily; as a result he lacked the prestige not only of his immediate predecessors but of his own best generals. His first campaign, probably begun the year after his accession, was against the Chatti north of the upper Rhine. Poets of the regime including Martial celebrated a 'triumph' which cut little ice in Rome: improved frontier defences, improved lines of communication for Roman troops, improved efficiency. The Chatti themselves, however, warlike and truculent, were not comprehensively defeated. Dio described Domitian as returning to Rome 'without so much as having seen hostilities anywhere'.

He would reiterate that taunt two years later, when Decebalus of the Dacians, an accomplished militarist, led his soldiers from their homeland – modern-day Romania – across the Danube to invade Moesia. In the aftermath of the death of the governor of Moesia, Oppius Sabinus, Domitian hastened eastwards in company with Sabinus' successor, Cornelius Fuscus. Even at this juncture, with Roman hegemony seriously at risk, Dio asserts that Domitian failed to take an active role:

> Instead, he remained in one of the cities of Moesia, indulging in riotous living, as was his wont. For he was not only indolent of body and timorous of spirit, but also most profligate and lewd towards women and boys alike. He therefore sent others to conduct the war and for the most part got the worst of it.[17]

Early Roman victories under Fuscus created an artificial buoyancy. In a speedy reversal of fortune, Fuscus was killed along with most of a regiment. In Rome, Domitian took time to regroup. His successful counter-attack occurred in 89, after which Dacia became a client kingdom under Decebalus. It was not an outcome to win plaudits in Rome.*

———◦◦◦◦———

The *princeps* prepared to parley with Decebalus in 89 was older, graver and more circumspect. For the year had begun with the most serious threat to date of Domitian's reign.

Suetonius offers neither explanations nor context. He is content to record the name of the malefactor, Lucius Antonius Saturninus, and the conspiracy's locale: Upper Germany. Suetonius' interest, characteristically, is in the mystical aspect of the crisis – a magnificent eagle which enfolded in its wings a statue of the emperor in Rome, accompanying the action with exultant shrieks. This grandiose and unambiguous spectacle was vouchsafed to Domitian on the same day rebellion was roundly quashed by the governor of Lower Germany, Lappius Maximus Norbanus. Borrowing a leaf from Suetonian portent, the weather too lent assistance. German tribesmen enlisted in his cause by Saturninus were prevented from intervening by the sudden and untimely thawing of the Rhine, which left them stranded on the wrong side of the river. South of the Alps, Domitian continued full tilt towards rebel headquarters, determined to exact ferocious retribution. He had developed a novel form of torture, which combined Roman fire with the victim's genitalia.

---

* As it happened, the Dacian problem was not wholly resolved until 106, when fearsome retaliatory action under the emperor Trajan forced Decebalus' suicide and a sullen truce. It is the Dacian campaign which supplied those highly wrought vignettes that even now encircle Trajan's Column.

For Domitian, victory was not as sweet as it might have been. In Rome the Arval Brethren, that priestly college reputedly formed by Romulus, gave thanks for a happy outcome. None can have overlooked the sacrifices the unsuspecting brotherhood had previously offered: 'that the conspiracy of evil-doers may be detected.'[18]

Something in the atmosphere had changed. In Suetonius' account, it is Saturninus' revolt that unleashes the full force of Domitian's cruelty, characterized henceforth as 'savage', 'excessive', 'cunning' and 'sudden'. An emperor who mistrusted the senate had placed his confidence in the army. Parts of that army had failed him. It was a recipe for isolation. Domitian's response was an increase in that tendency to keep his own counsel which had marked his reign from the outset. And so he took a further step away from the senate, compounding his sins in their eyes. He pursued policies which bore his own stamp, among them an escalation in that witch-hunt-style moral prurience at odds with the easy loucheness of Rome's upper classes. His spotlight returned to the Temple of Vesta, where age-old standards of chasteness had deteriorated and errant Vestals had already been executed earlier in the reign. In 91 his focus was the principal Vestal herself, Cornelia. On this occasion, Domitian stood on precedent. He insisted that Cornelia receive the punishment reserved for her transgression since time immemorial. She was buried alive. Her lovers, with the exception of the Praetorian Valerius Licinianus, were beaten to death with rods.[19] Faithful to the spirit of Republican piety, Domitian's martinet stance spoke as much of his own compromised authority as of that religious conservatism which Romans once held dear. It was a chilling, distasteful incident from which none emerged unscathed.

Dio preserves an anecdote intended to illustrate Domitian's mirthless viciousness. He ordered that a room in the palace be decorated entirely in black, every surface and every object pitchy and lustreless, and filled the room with leading knights and senators. To each he gave a small stone slab shaped like a gravestone and engraved with his name, a tomb lantern and a naked attendant similarly painted black. A succession of dishes of black food was served as Domitian discoursed on appropriately tenebrous subjects, all connected with death. Then he dispatched the shaken senators for home. When, shortly afterwards, imperial messengers retraced their steps, each man expected the order of execution. In fact they received gifts: the 'gravestones', tomb lanterns and costly vessels from that Stygian banquet – plus a charming naked boy apiece, clean now and comely.[20]

Humiliation of the senate was a high-risk strategy. In Domitian's case, it was one aspect of an unwavering determination to rule with minimal senatorial interference: by humiliating the senate's members, the emperor asserted the discrepancy in their relative positions. For a decade he pursued this policy without accident. It could not continue indefinitely.

Three years after his accession, Domitian had issued coins bearing an image of Jupiter. The king of the gods, who was also the god of thunder, appeared armed with a spear and a thunderbolt. Within a year, Jupiter had yielded up his thunderbolt to a depiction of Domitian himself.[21] It marked the beginning of a process of iconographic synthesis. For the final decade of Domitian's reign, coins awarded the thunderbolt to Domitian alone. No longer illustrated, Jupiter was present only associatively. The import was clear.

It was a gesture not of vanity but of political intent. 'Be assured that nothing is more pleasing than beauty, but nothing shorter lived,' Domitian had written in a trichological treatise, *On the Care of the Hair*. Much of his own hair had since fallen out. Bald but retaining vestiges of former good looks, the emperor made an accurate estimation of the value of appearances. Undeniably his numismatic godliness was intended as a potent visual statement (proof, too, of latent megalomania). It was an expression of a need to be obeyed and a determination to dominate the apparatus of government. In 82, he had embarked on the first of seven consecutive consulships; he would hold the office again in 90, 92 and 95, bringing his total number of terms of office, including those under Vespasian, to an unprecedented seventeen.[22] In 85, like Vespasian before him, he also exercised the power of the censorship. Afterwards he declared himself censor for life. Vespasian had exploited the office to reconstitute the senate in the Flavian image; Domitian likewise, by advancing members of the equestrian class, altered its composition. Heedless of any need for conciliation, Domitian also demanded the senate's concurrence with his wishes without stooping to persuasiveness or blandishments. It was an accurate statement of the light in which he regarded it. In addition, in his role as censor, this dour, unsmiling twelfth Caesar embraced that policy of moral vigilance which overlooked his own *nostalgie de la boue* and, in its pinched officiousness, further alienated an upper class irked by his high-handedness and contemptuous of his meagre qualifications for rule. Like his grandiose building plans for Rome, it was a token Augustanism. He also revived Augustus' Julian law against adultery.

Domitian, we can assume, understood the grounds of the senate's contempt. He did not of course sanction it. Rather, by creating an imperial persona which blurred distinctions between the mortal and the immortal, he sought to pull the rug from under senators' feet. According to Republican practice,

Domitian was unsuited to high office and its related grants of power on account of family background (a deified father and brother notwithstanding) and his limited acquaintance with the magistracies of the *cursus honorum*. The Domitian who appeared on his coins as an associate of Jupiter and who, the following year, probably in 86, evolved the style of address *dominus et deus* ('master and god'), clearly did not hold sway in Rome as a result of tribunician power and *maius imperium* awarded by the senate. Nor did his eminence derive from the authority and prestige previously associated with the consulship (although, as we have seen, he took steps to monopolize any benefits the consulship continued to bestow). Instead, his power devolved from a higher authority. Unquantifiable, it was also inarguable. This vaunting trump card scarcely represented emollience towards Roman patricians. Given the recrudescence of Republicanism within the senate during Domitian's reign, it was perhaps the only alternative to reprising Augustus' affection of an age-old ladder of magistracies, the *princeps* first among equals (even if Flavian status would have permitted this). Domitian possessed neither the adeptness nor the inclination for that deceit. Instead, he shirked half-measures. Like overtly autocratic emperors before him, he confined much effective political debate to his *consilium* of friends, freedmen and hand-picked advisers, the role of the senate the equivalent of rubber-stamping. He also ordained that any statues made of him should be of gold or silver (and ordered the death of a woman whose 'crime' was to have undressed in front of his statue). In doing so, he claimed his place in a dangerous continuum which included Cleopatra and Gaius. Neither had benefited in the long term from their golden images and senatorial hostility. Nor, as we know, would Domitian.

As in his father's reign, senatorial opposition to Domitian arose on philosophical grounds. It was both abstract – a theoretical objection to the principate's vesting of far-reaching formal powers in the hands of an individual – and concrete, focusing on Domitian himself and the nature of his government. Domitian, however, was not Vespasian. Chaffed by Demetrius, harried by Helvidius Priscus, Vespasian had shown equanimity in the face of his friends' candour and patience with philosophers whose behaviour Suetonius characterizes as impudent. The response of Vespasian's son was less indulgent, as we should expect. Where Vespasian's claim to power was flawed, Domitian's was non-existent. He had not, like his father, brought to a close a period of unbridled political and civil unrest in the life of Rome; nor, thanks to the efforts of Vespasian and Titus, was the condition of the Empire such that it demanded radical approaches (a puritanical young man of gentle countenance, patchy experience and stubborn self-importance). Despite Domitian's best efforts, the deification of his predecessors did not, like the effulgence of Augustus' glory, bathe him in inviolability. Even the unique award to Domitia of the title 'Mother of the Divine Caesar', following the death of the couple's only child, a boy who was subsequently deified, fell short of the grandeur of Rome's previous dynasty.

In the doldrum years 69 to 81, Domitian had devoted himself to archery and adulterous sex. His skill at the former was such that, when hunting at his Alban villa, he regularly killed in excess of a hundred wild animals. Sometimes he deliberately shot a beast twice: the two arrows created the appearance of horns. He varied the pace by aiming instead at slaves. A slave stood at a distance and extended his right hand, with the fingers spread. Unerring, Domitian placed his arrows between the slave's fingers.

As with toxophily, so with philosophy. Like Vespasian, Domitian did not rush his aim. Careful to curry popular favour in a lavish programme of public games, he advanced against the senate gradually. It was not until 93 that he embarked on the sequence of senatorial executions which has since been likened to a reign of terror. That year he targeted a clutch of high-profile senators whose offences included ridicule of the emperor and praise of his enemies. Helvidius Priscus the Younger, son of Vespasian's old sparring partner, and Arulenus Rusticus were both former consuls; other 'philosopher' victims included Herennius Senecio, biographer of the elder Priscus, Junius Rusticus, Priscus' eulogist, the historian Hermogenes of Tarsus and a bona fide philosopher called Maternus. (The works of Arulenus Rusticus and Herennius Senecio were burned in the Forum by triumvirs especially appointed for the task.) Their downfall probably had a symbolic dimension, as Tacitus claimed, indicating Domitian's intolerance of senatorial independence, which by then was an open secret anyway:[23] 'in that fire they thought to consume the voice of the Roman people, the freedom of the senate, and the conscious emotions of all mankind.'[24] The result fell little short of panic within senatorial ranks. Other victims of Domitian's zero-tolerance policy included the governor of Britain, Sallustius Lucullus, who had loaned his name to a new design for lances; Salvius Cocceianus for observing the birthday of the emperor Otho, his paternal uncle; Mettius Pompusianus, on the strength of reports that his horoscope marked him out as a future emperor; Acilius Glabrio for impiety and Titus Flavius Clemens, father of Domitian's heirs Titus Flavius Vespasianus and Titus Flavius Domitianus, probably on a suspicion of conversion to Judaism. So flexible an interpretation of subversion on Domitian's part was indicative of that escalating fear, loathing and a kind of madness by which he evidently felt impelled to root out each ort and shard of opposition, real or imaginary. Informers did their worst, adding to the frenzied insecurity on the Palatine: Domitian's victims embraced intimates as well as strangers. 'What could be more capricious than a tyrant's ear, when the fate of his so-called friends and advisers hung on his word?' Juvenal asked with an air of deserved asperity.[25] Those whose treasonable actions or words were considered to be of a lower order escaped with confiscation of their estates. For greed alone could rival Domitian's appetite for cruelty.

While the senate quaked in fear, the emperor was tormented by paranoia. In the magnificent new palace he had built on the Palatine, he lined corridors with polished obsidian and moonstone. The glossy surface of the stone fulfilled a mirror-like purpose. It revealed to Domitian the approach of all comers. But mirrors reflect phantoms, too, shifting patterns of light and shadow, a tremulous, insubstantial imagery of nothing. It was not granted to Domitian to be all-seeing, and the effort of constant watchfulness proved exhausting. It was inevitable that eventually his vigilance would falter. That weakness proved fatal.

Impossible that the end should come unheralded by portents. In this case dreams. Minerva appeared to Domitian to tell him that she could no longer protect him; she cast aside her weapons, and riding in a chariot drawn by black horses, plunged into an abyss. It was a traumatic revelation on the part of that goddess whom the motherless emperor had chosen as his tutelary deity, amounting almost to a second bereavement. In another vision, Domitian saw a golden hump emerging from his back. We are asked to believe that he interpreted this alarming development as a sign that 'the condition of the empire would be happier and more prosperous after his time'. This latter, wholly improbable scenario differs from those auguries of impending doom with which we have seen Suetonius endow Domitian's predecessors. It is a narrative device of the historian's and clearly self-seeking, a sop to succeeding emperors, an over-neat sycophancy at the expense of Domitian's final hours. It fails to convince and not simply on account of its unlikelihood, the utter impossibility of the Domitian of the sources arriving at such a conclusion even *in extremis*. For Domitian's attacks on the occupants of the senate house imperilled neither the condition of the Empire nor its prosperity, as he surely understood. Those policies he had pursued outside the senate house constituted their own legacy for good, like the new Via Domitiana from Sinuessa to Puteoli, opened the year before Domitian's death and acclaimed by the poet Statius as the benefaction of a mature and knowledgeable ruler.[26] Palatine politics alone weakened Domitian. As the first century drew to its close, Rome's upper classes remained unprepared for that king-like absolutism which was always Domitian's aim and which, in successive generations, would stamp the principate. Unable to comprehend the possibility of its own redundancy, the senate exulted in the twelfth Caesar's downfall. But though they destroyed his statue in the Temple of Jupiter Custos, smashed the votive shields emblazoned with his image which adorned the senate house, and erased his name from the inscriptions attesting to the Sacred Games of 88, they obliterated neither the memory of Domitian nor that impulse to tyranny which they claimed as his principal flaw. In time they would discover that the will to power always increased with eminence, the simplest of the lessons of these twelve Caesars.

BIBLIOGRAPHY

SECONDARY SOURCES

Alston, Richard, *Aspects of Roman History, AD 14–117*, London: Routledge, 1998.

Balsdon, J. P. V. D., *Rome: The Story of an Empire*, London: Weidenfeld & Nicolson, 1971.
— *The Emperor Gaius (Caligula)* (Clarendon Press, Oxford, 1934)
— *Roman Women: Their History and Habits*, London: Bodley Head, 1962.

Barrett, Anthony A., *Caligula: The Corruption of Power*, London: Batsford 1989.
— *Livia. First Lady of Imperial Rome*, New Haven: Yale University Press, 2002.

Bauman, Richard A., *Women and Politics in Ancient Rome*, London: Routledge, 1992.

Bishop, John, *Nero: The Man and the Legend*, London: Robert Hale, 1964.

Bowman, Alan K., Edward Champlin and Andrew Lintott, eds, *The Cambridge Ancient History, vol. 10: The Augustan Empire, 43 BC–AD 69*, 2nd edition, Cambridge: Cambridge University Press, 1996.

Bowman, Alan K., Peter Garnsey and Dominic Rathbone, eds, *The Cambridge Ancient History, vol. 11: The High Empire, AD 70–192*, 2nd edition, Cambridge: Cambridge University Press, 2000.

Boyle, A. J. and Dominik, W. J. (eds), *Flavian Rome: Culture, Image, Text*, Leiden: Brill, 2003.

Bradford, Ernle, *Julius Caesar: The Pursuit of Power*, London: Hamish Hamilton, 1984.

D'Ambra, Eve, *Roman Women*, Cambridge: Cambridge University Press, 2007.

Dennison, Matthew, *Empress of Rome: The Life of Livia*, London: Quercus, 2010.

de Serviez, J. R., *The Roman Empresses* (1752), London: The Walpole Press, 1899.

Dixon, Suzanne, *The Roman Mother*, London: Croom Helm, 1988.

Ellis, Heather, *Optimus Princeps: Masculinity and Control in Suetonius' Lives of the Caesars*, Germany: VDM Verlag, Dr Müller, Germany, 2009.

Everitt, Anthony, *The First Emperor: Caesar Augustus and the Triumph of Rome*, London: John Murray, 2006.

Feldherr, A. (ed.), *The Cambridge Companion to the Roman Historians*, Cambridge: Cambridge University Press, 2009.

Ferrill, Arther, *Caligula: Emperor of Rome*, London: Thames & Hudson, 1991.

Flower, Harriet I., *The Art of Forgetting: Disgrace and Oblivion in Roman Political Culture*, Chapel Hill: University of North Carolina Press, 2006.
— *Ancestor Masks and Aristocratic Power in Roman Culture*, Oxford: Clarendon Press, 1996.

Freisenbruch, Annelise, *The First Ladies of Rome: The Women Behind the Caesars*, London: Jonathan Cape, 2010.

Gardner, Jane F., *Roman Myths*, London: British Museum Press, 1993.

Garland, Robert, *Julius Caesar*, Bristol: Bristol Phoenix Press, 2003.

Garnsey, Peter and Saller, Richard, *The Early Principate: Augustus to Trajan* (Clarendon Press, Oxford, 1982), Greece & Rome New Surveys in the Classics No 15

Goldsworthy, Adrian, *Caesar*, London: Weidenfeld & Nicolson, 2006.

Goodman, Martin, *The Roman World 44 BC–AD 180*, London: Routledge, 1997.

Grant, Michael, *The Twelve Caesars*, London: Weidenfeld & Nicolson, 1996.

Greenhalgh, P. A. L., *The Year of the Four Emperors*, London: Weidenfeld & Nicolson, 1975.

Griffin, Miriam, *Nero: The End of a Dynasty*, London: Batsford, 1984.
— (ed.), *A Companion to Julius Caesar*, Oxford: Blackwell Publishing, 2009.

Holland, Richard, *Augustus*, Stroud: Sutton, 2004.
— *Nero: the Man Behind the Myth*, Stroud: Sutton, 2000.

Hughes-Hallett, Lucy, *Cleopatra: Histories, Dreams and Distortions*, London: Bloomsbury, 1990.

Jones, Brian William, *The Emperor Domitian*, London: Routledge, 1992.
— *The Emperor Titus*, London: Palgrave Macmillan, 1984.
— with Milns, Robert, *Suetonius: the Flavian Emperors*, Bristol: Bristol Classical Press, 2002.

Kleiner, Diana E. E, *Cleopatra and Rome*, Cambridge, Mass.: Harvard University Press, 2005.

Kraemer, Ross S., 'Typical and Atypical Jewish Family Dynamics: The Cases of Babatha and Berenice' from *Early Christian Families in Context: an interdisciplinary dialogue*, David L. Balch and Carolyn Osiek, eds, Michigan and Cambridge: Eerdmans, 2003.

Laurence, Ray, *Roman Passions: A History of Pleasure in Imperial Rome*, London: Continuum, 2009.

Levick, Barbara, *Claudius,* London: Batsford, 1990.
— *Tiberius the Politician,* London: Thames & Hudson, 1976.
— *The Government of the Roman Empire: A Sourcebook,* London: Routledge, 2nd edition, 2000.
— *Vespasian,* London and New York: Routledge, 1999.

Liversidge, Michael and Edwards, Catherine, eds, *Imagining Rome: British Artists and Rome in the Nineteenth Century,* London: Merrell Holberton, 1996.

Manuwald, Gesine, *Roman Republican Theatre,* Cambridge: Cambridge University Press, 2011.

Matyszak, Philip, *The Sons of Caesar: Imperial Rome's First Dynasty,* London: Thames & Hudson, 2006.

Massie, Allan, *The Caesars,* London: Secker & Warburg, 1983.

Meijer, Fik, *Emperors Don't Die in Bed,* London: Routledge, 2004.

Miller, Fergus, *The Emperor in the Roman World (31 BC–AD 337)* (Duckworth, London, 1977)

Momigliano, Arnaldo (trans. W. D. Hogarth), *Claudius: The Emperor and his Achievement,* Oxford: Clarendon Press, 1934.

Mommsen, Theodor, ed. Thomas Wiedemann, *A History of Rome Under the Emperors,* London: Routledge, 1996.

Morgan, Gwyn, *69 AD: The Year of the Four Emperors,* Oxford: Oxford University Press, 2006.

Osgood, Josiah, *Claudius Caesar: Image and Power in the Early Roman Empire,* Cambridge: Cambridge University Press, 2010.
—*Caesar's Legacy: Civil War and the Emergence of the Roman Empire,* Cambridge: Cambridge University Press, 2006.

Perowne, Stewart, *The Caesars' Wives: Above Suspicion?,* London: Hodder & Stoughton, 1974.

Potter, David, *Emperors of Rome: Imperial Rome from Julius Caesar to the Last Emperor,* London: Quercus, 2007.

Richardson, Lawrence, *A New Topographical Dictionary of Ancient Rome*, Baltimore: Johns Hopkins University Press, 1992.

Rossini, Orietta, *Ara Pacis*, Rome: Electa, Rome, 2006.

Rutledge, Steven H., *Imperial Inquisitions: Prosecutors and Informants from Tiberius to Domitian*, London and New York: Routledge, 2001.

Schiff, Stacy, *Cleopatra: A Life*, London: Virgin Books, 2010.

Seager, Robin, *Tiberius*, Oxford: Wiley Blackwell, repr. 2004.

Severy, Beth, *Augustus and the Family at the Birth of the Empire*, London: Routledge, 2003.

Sommer, Michael, *The Complete Roman Emperor: Imperial Life at Court and on Campaign*, London: Thames & Hudson, 2010.

Southern, Pat, *Augustus*, London: Routledge, 1998.
— *The Roman Army: A Social and Institutional History*, Oxford: Oxford University Press, 2007.
— *Domitian: Tragic Tyrant*, London and New York: Routledge, 1997.

Shotter, David, *Tiberius Caesar*, London: Routledge, 1992.

Sutherland, C. H. V., *Coinage in Roman Imperial Policy 31 BC–AD 68*, London: Methuen, 1951.

Syme, Ronald, *The Roman Revolution*, Oxford: Oxford University Press, repr. 1968.
— *The Augustan Aristocracy*, Oxford: Clarendon Press, 1986.

Talbot, R. J. A., *The Senate of Imperial Rome*, Oxford: Oxford University Press, 1984.

Wallace-Hadrill, Andrew, *Suetonius: The Scholar and his Caesars*, London: Duckworth 1983.
— *Augustan Rome*, Bristol: Bristol Classical Press, 1993.

Wood, Susan E., *Imperial Women: A Study in Public Images 40 BC–AD 68*, Boston, Cologne and Leiden: Brill, 1999.

PERIODICALS AND JOURNALS

Braund, D. C., 'Berenice in Rome', *Historia* 33, 1984, pp. 120–23.

Brunt, P. A., 'Lex de Imperio Vespasiani', *The Journal of Roman Studies*, vol. 67, 1977, pp. 95–116.

Coleman, Kathleen M., 'Launching into history: aquatic displays in the early empire', *The Journal of Roman Studies*, vol. 83, pp. 48–74

Garton, Charles, 'Sulla and the Theatre', *Phoenix*, vol. 18, no. 2, Summer 1964, pp. 137–56

Huzar, Eleanor G., 'Mark Antony: Marriages vs Careers', *The Classical Journal*, vol. 81, no. 2, Dec. 1985–Jan. 1986, pp. 97–111.

Jones, William, 'Some Thoughts on the Propaganda of Vespasian and Domitian', *The Classical Journal*, p. 251,1973.

Jones, Brian W., 'Domitian and the Senatorial Order: A Prosopographical Study of Domitian's Relationship with the Senate AD 81–96', Philadelphia, 1979.

Krappe, Alexander Haggerty, 'Tiberius and Thrasyllus', *The American Journal of Philology*, vol. 48, no. 4, 1927, pp. 359–66.

Prettejohn, Elizabeth, 'Lawrence Alma-Tadema and the Modern City of Ancient Rome', *The Art Bulletin*, vol. 84, no. 1, Mar. 2002, pp. 115–29 .

Shotter, D. C. A., 'Tiberius and the Spirit of Augustus', *Greece & Rome*, vol. 13, no. 2, 1966, pp. 207–12.

Sigurdsson, Haraldur, Cashdollar, Stanford and Sparks, Stephen R. J., 'The Eruption of Vesuvius in A.D. 79: Reconstruction from Historical and Volcanological Evidence', *American Journal of Archaeology*, vol. 86, no. 1, Jan. 1982, pp. 39–51.

Staley, Allen, 'The Landing of Agrippina at Brundisium with the Ashes of Germanicus', *Philadelphia Museum of Art Bulletin*, vol. 61, no. 287/288, Oct. 1, 1965, pp. 10–19.

Sumi, Geoffrey S., 'Impersonating the Dead: Mimes at Roman Funerals', *The American Journal of Philology*, vol. 123, no. 4, Winter 2002, pp. 559–85.

NOTES

INTRODUCTION

1   Woolf, Virginia, 'The Art of Biography'. In *The Crowded Dance of Modern Life*, London: Penguin, 1993, p 150.

2   See Freisenbruch, Annelise, *The First Ladies of Rome: The Women Behind the Caesars*, London: Jonathan Cape, 2010, p 11.

3   Woolf, op. cit., p 151.

JULIUS CAESAR

1   Cicero, *Letters to Atticus*, 7.11.1.

2   Plutarch, *The Life of Julius Caesar*, 63.1, in Plutarch, Lives, trans. Bernadotte Perin, Loeb Classical Library, 1914, repr. 1998.

3   See Goldsworthy, Adrian, *Caesar*, London: Weidenfeld & Nicolson, 2006, p 60.

4   Plutarch, op. cit., 58.4.

5   Shakespeare, William, *Julius Caesar*, III.ii.

6   Cicero, Philippics II.161, quoted Grant, Michael, *The Twelve Caesars*, London: Weidenfeld & Nicolson, 1996, p 33.

7   See Garland, Robert, *Julius Caesar*, Bristol: Bristol Phoenix Press, 2004.

8   See Wallace-Hadrill, Andrew, *Suetonius: The Scholar and his Caesars*, London: Duckworth, 1983, p 12.

9   Velleius Paterculus, *The Roman History* II.41.1, trans. Frederick W. Shipley, Loeb Classical Library, 1924.

10   Plutarch, *The Life of Cato*, 8.8.

11   Plutarch, *The Life of Julius Caesar*, 60.1.

12   See Bradford, Ernle, *Julius Caesar: The Pursuit of Power*: London: Hamish Hamilton, 1984, p 7.

13   Plutarch, *The Life of Julius Caesar*, 2.4.

14   Pliny the Elder, *Natural History*, VII.91, quoted in Grant, op. cit., pp 31–2.

15   Tacitus, *Histories* III.38.

16   Cassius Dio, *Roman History* 37.54.3, trans. Earnest Cary, Loeb Classical Library, 1925.

17   See Massie, Allan, *The Caesars*, London: Martin Secker & Warburg, 1983, p 20.

18   Ibid.

19   Plutarch, *The Life of Julius Caesar*, 15.5.

20   See Caesar, *Gallic Wars* IV.14–15.

21   See Goldsworthy, op. cit., pp 294–5.

22   Plutarch, *The Life of Julius Caesar*, 23.6.

23   Ibid, 28.6.

24   Goldsworthy, op. cit., p 375.

25   See ibid, p 468.

26   Plutarch, *Life of Julius Caesar*, 57.1.

27   Tacitus, *Histories*, 2.91.

AUGUSTUS

1   Cassius Dio, op. cit, 56.46.1.

2   Velleius Paterculus, op. cit 2.60.2.

3   Ibid, 2.59.6.

4   Ibid, 2.66.

5   Plutarch, *Life of Antony*, 60.

6   Augustus, *Res Gestae Divi Augusti*, quoted Massie, op. cit., p 59.

7   Cassius Dio, op. cit, 53.4.

8   Augustus, op. cit, 34.

9   Propertius, *Elegies* 3.18, trans A. S. Kline.

10 See Dennison, Matthew, *Empress of Rome: The Life of Livia*, London: Quercus, 2010, p 283.

11 Cassius Dio, op. cit., 54.18.

12 Massie, op. cit., p 73.

13 Horace, *The Centennial Hymn*, trans. James Mitchie, London: Penguin, 1978, p 257.

14 Augustus, op. cit, 8.5.

15 Velleius Paterculus, op. cit., 2.100.2–3.

16 Ibid, 2.123.2.

17 Cassius Dio, op. cit., 56.30.

18 Velleius Paterculus, op. cit., 2.123.2.

TIBERIUS

1   Cassius Dio, op. cit., 57.1.2.

2   Velleius Paterculus, op. cit., 2.124.2.

3   Cassius Dio, op. cit., 57.13.8.

4   See Sutherland, C. H. V., *Coinage in Roman Imperial Policy 31BC–AD68*, London: Methuen, 1951, pp 84–5.

5   Velleius Paterculus, op. cit., 2.99.

6   Cassius Dio, op. cit., 57 13.

7   Pliny the Elder, op. cit., 28.5.23.

8   Tacitus, *Annals*, 6.50, trans. Alfred John Church and William Jackson Brodribb, 1876.

9   Cassius Dio, op. cit., 57.1.2.

10 Ibid, 57.13.5.

11 Ibid, 54.29.2.

12 Velleius Paterculus, op. cit., 2.96.1.

13 Tacitus, *Annals*, 1.53.

14　Seneca, *On Benefits*, 6.1–2; see Bauman, Richard A., *Women and Politics in Ancient* Rome, London: Routledge, 1992, p 113.

15　Tacitus, *Annals*, 4.1.

16　See Levick, Barbara, *Tiberius the Politician*, London: Thames & Hudson, 1976, p 49.

17　Tacitus, *Annals*, 6.51.

18　Ibid, 1.6.

19　Ibid, 1.7.

20　See Levick, op. cit., p 72.

21　See Barrett, Anthony A., *Livia, First Lady of Imperial Rome*, New Haven: Yale University Press, 2002, p 81.

22　Quoted Grant, op. cit., p 97.

23　Tacitus, *Annals*, 4.1.

24　Matyszak, Philip, *The Sons of Caesar: Imperial Rome's First Dynasty*, London: Thames & Hudson, 2006, p 144.

25　Tacitus, *Annals*, 4.7.

26　See Shotter, David, *Tiberius Caesar*, London: Routledge, 1992, p 47.

27　Ibid, p 59.

28　Tacitus, *Annals*, 5.3

29　Ibid, 6.51.5.

30　Cassius Dio, op. cit., 58.4.

31　Shotter, op. cit., pp 63–4.

32　See Sutherland, op. cit., p 103.

GAIUS CALIGULA

1　Augustus, *Res Gestae*, 34.1.

2　Garnsey, Peter & Saller, Richard, *The Early Principate: Augustus to Trajan*, Oxford: The Clarendon Press, 1982, *Greece & Rome New Surveys in the Classics* No. 15, pp 4–5.

3　Josephus, *Antiquities of the Jews*, 18.6.10, trans. William Whiston, 1895.

4　Cassius Dio, op. cit., 59.6.1.

5   Ibid, 59.13.6.

6   Ibid, 67.8.3.

7   Ibid, 59.11.1.

8   Josephus, op. cit., 19.2.

9   Cassius Dio, op. cit., 59.4.

10 Matyszak, op. cit., p 185.

11 Cassius Dio, op. cit., 59.2.

12 Ferrill, Arther, *Caligula: Emperor of Rome*, London: Thames & Hudson, 1991, p 101.

13 Cassius Dio, op. cit., 59.13.6.

14 Pliny the Elder, op. cit., 13.22; 37.17; 33.79.

15 Josephus, op. cit., 19.2.2.

16 Seneca, *On Benefits*, IV.31.

17 Tacitus, *Annals*, 3.1, trans. Church and Brodribb.

18 Ferrill, op. cit., p 48.

19 Sutherland, op. cit., p 108.

20 Philo, *Legatio ad Gaium*, II. 14, trans. E. M. Smallwood, quoted Grant, op. cit., p 124.

21 Cassius Dio, op. cit., 59.16.5 6.

22 Ibid, 59.16.7.

23 Philo, op. cit., quoted Matyszak, op. cit. p 189.

24 Cicero, *Phillipics* 4.13, quoted Dennison, op. cit., p 265.

25 Josephus, op. cit., 19.2.

CLAUDIUS

1   Osgood, Josiah, *Claudius Caesar: Image and Power in the Early Roman Empire*, Cambridge: Cambridge University Press, 2010, p 15.

2   Liversidge, Michael & Edwards, Catharine, eds, *Imagining Rome: British Artists and Rome in the Nineteenth Century*, London: Merrell Holberton, 1996, p 60.

3   See Grant, op. cit., p 129.

4   Osgood, op. cit., p 9.

5   Trans. Matyszak, op. cit, p 198.

6   Cassius Dio, op. cit., 60.1.1.

7   Ibid, 60.12.4.

8   See Osgood, op. cit., pp 29–30.

9   Cassius Dio, op cit., 60.15.3.

10 Ibid, 60.15.4

11 See Osgood, op. cit., p 45.

12 Pliny the Elder, op. cit., 10.83.

13 Juvenal, *Satire VI*, quoted Freisenbruch, op. cit., p128.

14 Tacitus, *Annals*, XI.1.

15 See Alston, Richard, *Aspects of Roman History, AD14–117*,
    London: Routledge, 1998, p 95.

16 Tacitus, *Histories*, 1.30.

NERO

1   Cassius Dio, op. cit., 61.10.3.

2   Sommer, Michael, *The Complete Roman Emperor: Imperial Life
    at Court and on Campaign*, London: Thames & Hudson, 2010,
    p 49.

3   Bishop, John, *Nero: The Man and the Legend*, London: Robert
    Hale, 1964, pp 21–2.

4   Cassius Dio, op cit., 63.27.2.

5   Seneca, *On the Happy Life*, 7.7, quoted Laurence, Ray, *Roman
    Passions: A History of Pleasure in Imperial Rome*, London:
    Continuum, 2009, p 9.

6   Ibid, p 14.

7   Cassius Dio, op cit., 61.3.2.

8   Tacitus, Annals, XIII.4, quoted Sutherland, op. cit., p 149.

9   Cassius Dio, op cit., 61.4.

10 Tacitus, Annals, XIII.2.

11 Ibid, XIII.5.

12 See Barrett, Anthony A., *Caligula The Corruption of Power*
    London: Batsford, 1989, pp 167–8.

13 Holland, Richard, *Nero: the Man Behind the Myth*, Stroud: Sutton, 2000, p 87.

14 Tacitus, *Annals*, 14.50.

15 Holland, op. cit., p 160.

16 Tacitus, *Annals*, 15.44.

17 Sommer, op. cit., p 74.

18 Tacitus, *Annals*, 15. 41.

19 Quoted Matyszak, op. cit., p 263.

20 Cassius Dio, op. cit., 62.24.2.

21 Quoted Grant, op. cit., p 171.

22 Cassius Dio, op. cit., 63.27.2.

GALBA

1 Tacitus, Histories, 1.18.

2 Griffin, Miriam, *Nero: The End of a Dynasty*, London: Batsford, 1984, p 27.

3 Tacitus, *Histories*, 1.6.

4 Tacitus, *Histories*, 1.13.

5 Plutarch, *Life of Galba*, 3.3.

6 Tacitus, *Histories*, 1.7.

7 Ibid, 1.49.

8 See Morgan, Gwyn, *69AD: The Year of the Four Emperors*, Oxford: Oxford University Press, 2006, p 25.

9 Ibid, p 28.

10 Greenhalgh, P. A. L., *The Year of the Four Emperors*, London: Weidenfeld & Nicolson, 1975, p 19.

11 Cassius Dio, op. cit., 64.3.2.

12 Ibid, 63.2.1.

13 Ibid, 64.16.3.

14 Tacitus, *Histories*, 1.12.

OTHO

1   Plutarch, *Life of Otho*, 4.4.

2   Ibid, 15.4

3   Ibid.

4   Tacitus, *Histories*, 1.50.

5   Plutarch, *Life of Otho*, 4.3.

6   Tacitus, *Histories*, 1.36.

7   Morgan, op. cit., p 97.

8   See ibid, p 94; Vinius: Tacitus, *Histories*, 1.37.

9   Tacitus, *Histories*, 1.30.

10   Plutarch, *Life of Galba*, 20.2.

11   Tacitus, *Histories*, 1.45.

12   Ibid, 1.21.

13   Ibid, 1.43.

14   Morgan, op. cit., p 97.

15   Cassius Dio, op. cit., 63.7.3.

16   Plutarch, *Life of Otho*, 3.

17   See Greenhalgh, op. cit., p 56.

18   Tacitus, *Histories*, 1.71.

19   Ibid, 1.83.

20   Plutarch, *Life of Otho*, 1.

21   Juvenal, *Satire II*.

22   Plutarch, *Life of Otho*, 4.3

23   Ibid, 4.4

24   Ibid, 5.5

25   Ibid, 9.2

26   Martial, *Epigrams* 6, quoted Grant, op. cit., p 195.

27   Plutarch, *Life of Otho*, 16.2.

VITELLIUS

1   Tacitus, *Histories*, 2.95.

2   Ibid, 2.94.

3   Cassius Dio, op. cit., 65.3.

4   Ibid, 65.2.

5   Tacitus, *Histories*, 2.67.

6   Ibid, 2.66.

7   Cassius Dio, op. cit., 65.10.

8   Ibid, 65.3.

9   Tacitus, *Histories*, 1.52.

10 Ibid, 1.53.

11 Ibid, 2.62.

12 Ibid, 2.55.

13 See Grant, op. cit., p 203.

14 Quoted Morgan, op. cit., p 215.

15 Cassius Dio, op. cit., 65.16.

16 Tacitus, *Histories*, 3.68.

VESPASIAN

1   Cassius Dio, op. cit., 65.14.3–4.

2   Levick, Barbara, *Vespasian*, London and New York: Routledge, 1999, p 126.

3   Laurence, op. cit., pp 44–5.

4   Cassius Dio, op. cit., 65.8.3.

5   Tacitus, *Histories*, 1.10.

6   Cassius Dio, op. cit., 66.2.

7   Southern, Pat, *Domitian: Tragic Tyrant*, London: Routledge, 1997, p 4.

8   Freisenbruch, op. cit., p 168.

9   Levick, Barbara, op. cit. p 15.

10 Tacitus, *Histories*, 2. (For a brief discussion of Vespasian's style of generalship, see Greenhalgh, op. cit., p 125.)

11 Josephus, *The Wars of the Jews*, 1.4 trans. H. St J. Thackeray.

12 Levick, op. cit., p 31.

13 Augustus, op. cit., 22.16.

14 Greenhalgh, op. cit., p 133.

15 Alston, op. cit., p 169.

16 Grant, op. cit., p 221.

17 K. Hopkins: see Levick, op. cit., p 95.

18 Cassius Dio, op. cit., 66.2.5.

19 Greenhalgh, op. cit., p 247.

20 Levick, op. cit., p 76.

21 Shakespeare, William, *Julius Caesar*, II.ii.

22 Cassius Dio, op. cit., 66.17.2.

23 Levick, op. cit., p 197.

24 Sumi, Geoffrey S., 'Impersonating the Dead: Mimes at Roman Funerals', *The American Journal of Philology*, vol. 123, no. 4 (Winter, 2002), p 559

25 Flower, Harriet I., *The Art of Forgetting: Disgrace and Oblivion in Roman Political Culture* (University of North Carolina Press, Chapel Hill, 2006), p 106.

TITUS

1 Cassius Dio, op. cit., 66.18.1.

2 Ibid, 66.18.3; Ausonius, see Grant, op. cit., pp 238–9.

3 Richardson, Lawrence, *A New Topographical Dictionary of Ancient Rome*, Baltimore: John Hopkins University Press, 1992, pp 350–1.

4 For an alternative interpretation, see Levick, op. cit., p 21.

5 Jones, Brian William, *The Emperor Titus*, London: Palgrave Macmillan, 1984, p 22.

6 Horace, *Odes* 4.4, quoted Dennison, op. cit., p 47.

7 Quoted Freisenbruch, op. cit, p 158.

8 Tacitus, *Histories*, 2.1; see Jones, op. cit., p 45.

9 Jones, op. cit., p 46.

10   Josephus, *The Wars of the Jews*, 6.254ff.

11   See Tacitus, *Histories*, fragment 2: Titus 'holding the destruction of this temple to be a prime necessity in order to wipe out more completely the religion of the Jews'.

12   Josephus, *The Wars of the Jews*, 7.3.1.37ff, quoted Grant, op. cit, p 229.

13   Laurence, op. cit., p 135.

14   Salisbury, Joyce E., *Women in the Ancient World*, California: ABC-CLIO, 2001, p 29.

15   Freisenbruch, op. cit., p 163.

16   Tacitus, *Histories* 2.2; see Freisenbruch, op. cit., p 164.

17   See Alston, op. cit., p 168.

18   Jones, op. cit., p 78.

19   Grant, op. cit., p 230.

20   Josephus, *The Wars of the Jews*, 7.4.1.

21   Alston, op. cit., p 168.

22   Jones, op. cit., p 116.

23   Tacitus, *Histories*, 2.1.

24   Cassius Dio, op. cit., 65.15.3.

25   Pliny the Younger, *Letters* 6.16, trans. Betty Radice, London: Penguin, 1969.

26   Sigurdsson, Haraldur, Cashdollar, Stanford and Sparks, Stephen R. J., 'The Eruption of Vesuvius in A.D. 79: Reconstruction from Historical and Volcanological Evidence', *American Journal of Archaeology*, vol. 86, no. 1, Jan., 1982, p 39.

27   Cassius Dio, op. cit., 66.22.4.

28   Ibid, 66.24.3.

29   Jones, op. cit, p142.

30   See Laurence, op cit., p 133.

31   Cassius Dio, op. cit., 66.26.1.

32   Meijer, Fik, *Emperors Don't Die in Bed*, London: Routledge, 2004, p 46.

DOMITIAN

1 Juvenal, *Satire IV*

2 Eutropius, *Abridgement of Roman History*, 7.23, trans. Rev. John Selby Watson, 1886.

3 Cassius Dio, op. cit., 67.3.2.

4 Freisenbruch, op. cit., pp 182–3.

5 Grant, op cit., p 241.

6 Tacitus, *Histories*, 4.86.

7 Cassius Dio, op. cit., 66.26.2.

8 Ibid, 67.2.4.

9 Ibid, 67.2

10 Tacitus, *Histories*, 4.86

11 See Southern, Pat, *Domitian Tragic Tyrant*, London and New York: Routledge, 1997, p 18; Morgan, op. cit., p247.

12 Eutropius, op. cit., 7.23.

13 Cassius Dio, op. cit., 67.1.

14 Pliny the Younger, *Panegyricus* 52.4–5, quoted Freisenbruch, op. cit., p 184.

15 Cassius Dio, op. cit., 67.3.5.

16 Ibid, 67.4.

17 Ibid, 67.6.3.

18 Massie, op. cit., p 222.

19 Southern, op. cit. (*Domitian*), p 110.

20 Cassius Dio, op. cit., 67.9.

21 Janzen, E., 1994, 'The Jesus of the Apocalypse Wears the Emperor's Clothes', *SBL 1994 Seminar Papers*. Atlanta: Scholars, p 648, footnote 55.

22 Southern, op. cit., p 35.

23 See Alston, op. cit, p 183.

24 Tacitus, *Agricola* 2, trans. Edward Brooks Jr. 1897.

25 Juvenal, *Satire* IV.

26 Flower, op. cit., p 256; *Statius, The Silvae*, 4.3.

GLOSSARY

Aedile – One of the senatorial magistracies which together made up the 'cursus honorum' or sequence of offices followed by Roman politicians. Responsible for public and private buildings, roads, aqueducts and sewers, public lands, public spectacles and police, as well as the distribution of corn, markets, weights and measures.

Atrium – The hall, close to the entrance of the Roman house; among the most important rooms of the house.

Auctoritas – A Roman senator's prestige and influence – greatly increased by military achievements.

Consul – The most senior magistracy of the 'cursus honorum'. Two consuls were appointed annually, with powers roughly akin to a shared prime ministership.

Cursus honorum – The 'course of honours' was a sequence of offices followed by career politicians of the Republic and early Empire.

A minimum-age qualification attached to each administrative appointment, with regulations governing the interval between appointments and repeat office holding.

Damnatio memoriae – Official condemnation after death of those felt to bring discredit and dishonour on the Roman state; the intention was to eradicate all traces of the offender and his or her existence from Roman life and included, for example, the destruction of states and erasure of inscriptions.

Dictator – Under the Republic, a six month appointment granting supreme military and civil power to an individual during a period of extreme crisis.

Imagines maiorum – Roman portraits of their ancestors. Sources suggest that these took the form of realistic wax masks. Displayed in cupboards called *armaria* in the atrium, they were worn or carried by actors in funeral processions.

Imperium – A concept of power which implied sovereignty or command and the official right, among others, of inflicting punishment. It exceeded simple authority.

Interrex – A provisional office of principal magistrate, rare in the late Republic. Among traditional duties of the 'interrex' was overseeing the election of new consuls

Magister Equitum – The 'Master of the Horse' was the second-in-command to the Republican dictator, chosen by the dictator, the two offices expiring simultaneously; traditional duties included command of the cavalry; invested with imperium, but of a lesser variety to that of the dictator himself.

Novus homo (*'new man'*) – A man not born into Rome's ruling class, who became the first member of his family to serve in the Senate.

Ovation – A public celebration in which a general rode through the city on horseback (a lesser form of the triumph).

Paterfamilias – The male head of the family who, possessing *patria potestas* ('the power of the father') held far-reaching legal powers over descendants through the male line or adoption. In practice, by the late Republic, these powers had been significantly eroded.

Patron/client – The patron/client relationship was one respectively of protection and dependency and existed between individuals – a wealthy Roman and his freedman, for example – and between influential individuals and communities, for example, a Roman senator and a community outside Rome who, as the senator's clients, could expect him to advance the community's needs in Rome. The patron offered support (both financial and legal) to his client; the client responded with support in public elections and attendance at the morning *salutatio* (an informal business forum held in the patron's atrium, at which clients formally greeted their patron and received in return a monetary handout or *sportula*).

Pontifex maximu*s* – The chief priest of the Roman state cult, a lifelong appointment.

Praetor – A magistracy of the 'cursus honorum', senior to the position of Aedile, with responsibility for administering justice.

Proscripti – Those whose names were publicly 'proscribed': their lives were forfeit and their property confiscated or sold. Proscription was developed in 82BC by Sulla as a means of disposing of his enemies, and reintroduced by the second Triumvirate in 43BC.

Quaestor – A junior magistracy of the 'cursus honorum', with mostly financial duties.

Tribune of the plebs – An elected office open to plebeians, the only form of plebeian representation in the Senate.

Triumph – The public celebration, in the Senate's gift, awarded to a successful general. The general processed in a chariot along Rome's Sacra Via in company with the captives of his victory and the spoils of conquest.

INDEX